THE HONEST ADVISOR INVESTING

LEARN WHAT THE EXPERTS AREN'T
TELLING YOU AND INVEST WITH
MORE CONFIDENCE THAN EVER

Christopher D. Munchhof

Editing by Kristina Raynor

Hardcover ISBN: 979-8-9909574-8-0
Paperback ISBN: 979-8-9909574-1-1
eBook ISBN: 979-8-9909574-0-4

MONK HOUSE PUBLISHING, LLC
EST. 2018

www.monkhousepublishing.com

CONTENTS

PART II
WHAT YOU'RE WORKING WITH

PART III
STRATEGY

INTRODUCTION

What is it like to be a goose? For the goose, when Winter approaches, he can only fly South. But what if South doesn't look particularly inviting one year? What if East or West are better directions to fly? Tough luck for the goose. He can only fly South. The goose will do this every year, no matter how bad flying South looks. His instincts compel his actions, but how much different is the goose's instinct compared to ours? The goose has a built-in compass and knows he needs to fly South, yet he doesn't necessarily know where he's headed. Ultimately, it's the goose's friends and family that show him the specific route and destination. Of course, his friends and family learned the route from *their* friends and families, and that process just keeps passing down through generations. No one asks if there is a better way to get there or whether they're even going to the best place possible. Some geese head to Nebraska, and some vacation in Florida. Nothing's wrong with Nebraska, but I'd think they'd be willing to give Florida a shot if they only knew about it. Once the goose is shown a route and destination, he'll repeat the same flight year after year. If our life goes in a particular direction year after year, why does it seem just as impossible for us to change directions as it is for the goose?

When it comes to investing, each of us, like the goose, have an ingrained belief system we've subconsciously developed over our lifetime through hundreds or thousands of scarcely noticeable inputs. Hearing about the stock market crashing while watching the news, advice from a wealthy uncle, knowing a co-worker who made thousands of dollars on a quick investment, or witnessing a family member get bilked out of their retirement by a con artist are all examples of experiences that can shape your mindset. A lifetime of these inputs has molded your investment beliefs into what they are today, and those beliefs are guiding you like the goose, but are you flying in the best direction? And will you like the destination when you get there? Chances are that the investment advice you've gotten up until now is wrong.

61% of adults say investing is "scary or intimidating." Being afraid to invest or lacking the confidence and knowledge to invest successfully severely limits your ability to live the best life possible. Investing can turn seemingly impossible dreams into possibilities. Invest so you can take that dream vacation. Invest so you can send your kids to college. Invest so you can finally walk away from that job while flipping your nasty boss the bird (you'll need investments to do this because you can forget about getting a good reference).

I started my financial planning career when I learned that members of my family had given up large portions of their life savings after being sold high-fee, high-commission investment products. Over the past decade, I've had thousands of interactions with clients, and each time a discussion about investing came around, every single client had fears. The fears varied in scope and intensity; some had fears buried a little deeper under the skin, but ultimately, everyone has expressed trepidation about investing. Often, they weren't even sure what they were afraid of. Was it losing money? Getting scammed? Not getting the best returns? Or was it looking stupid? Mostly, they wanted to hear it straight. Fears not only stop people from investing, but they also prevent those who do invest from getting the best returns they deserve by shying away from better investment performance in exchange for a perception of safety. The truth is that investors have been getting the wrong advice from professionals, institutions, and their friends and family for more than fifty years. Through my clients, I've learned the topics and concerns that come up over and over again and how to address them with honest answers so the person in front of me can move forward and invest with confidence. Now, I'm excited to be passing what I've learned on to you.

This book is arranged to systematically address the questions and concerns about investing that impact people the most. My goal is to strip away your current conceptions of investing and give you a fresh start. To accomplish this, the book is organized into three different parts. First, Part One will discuss the investment environment and how it may have shaped your present mindset, how to avoid common scams, and a thorough discussion about financial advisors. Part Two provides an education on the technical aspects of various investment options, from traditional choices like stocks and bonds to alternative investments like cryptocurrencies and crowdfunding. Finally, Part Three helps to develop your investing mindset and discusses the specifics of investment strategy. Combined, all three parts work together to help you form a broad investing philosophy that you can put to work immediately.

As a financial advisor, I've gone through hundreds of books as well as thousands of articles and courses on investing. I've never felt any of them adequately covered everything that investors like you wanted to know. Some were too vague, while others were too technical, and they always seemed to hold back on some of the ugly truths that investors deserve to know. Most importantly, they all boiled down to investment advice based on long-standing investment theories that prevent you from getting the best returns. Over the past five years, I've striven to write the best book on investing available. After reading this book, I'm confident you'll have a more well-rounded education in investing and the confidence to invest more wisely than the next thousand people you cross paths with. Don't let that last line intimidate you if you're new to investing. While the book is loaded with valuable information, it's written so anyone can understand it using real-life stories to both entertain and explain the concepts. Even if you're already an experienced investor, you'll become a better one from the ideas and examples in this book.

How long have you wanted to become a better investor? Up until now, have you been investing without really knowing why you're flapping your wings in the direction you are? Are you a goose, or will you change your course when you learn there's a better destination out there? Turn to chapter one to start your journey.

PART I

THE INVESTING LANDSCAPE

CHAPTER ONE

The Wizard

"For I consider brains far superior to money in every way."
- L. Frank Baum, The Wonderful Wizard of Oz

ON A COOL DAY IN FEBRUARY decorated soldier and recent retiree, 65-year-old Major William Foxton left his home and walked to a nearby park in Southampton, England.

Mr. Foxton served as part of the French Foreign Legion before enlisting with the British Army in 1968. He eventually became a sergeant while serving with the Royal Green Jackets, an infantry regiment of the British Army. In 1976, he lost an arm to a grenade explosion while in combat, but with the help of a prosthetic limb, he would continue a successful career. He was known as an exceptional man who had once crawled across a minefield to rescue a child. Among other decorations, in 1999, Mr. Foxton was named Officer of the Most Excellent Order of the British Empire, an honor reserved for exemplary British subjects.

On this day, however, February 10th, 2009, Major Foxton sat on a park bench, raised a nine-millimeter pistol to his head, and pulled the trigger.

Burt and Joanne Meerow were several years into a comfortable retirement after Burt sold his successful consumer testing business. The New Jersey couple enjoyed an upper-middle-class lifestyle with frequent visits to their Florida golf-club condominium and ski trips at their shared Vermont vacation home.

In December 2008, experiencing pain in her hip, Joanne attended an end-of-year doctor's appointment in an attempt to mitigate her discomfort. Burt was accompanying his wife in the doctor's office as she sat with her jeans pulled down to her knees waiting for a shot of cortisone in her hip. He answered a call on his cell phone. After listening to the caller on the other end for just a few moments, Burt started crying out in panic. As soon as Burt shared the news, Joanne hurriedly drove her distressed husband back to their New Jersey home. Once there, Joanne was finally able to process the news for herself, ran to the bathroom, and began to vomit.

Rene-Thierry Magon de la Villehuchet had enjoyed an impeccable career in finance and was known as an honorable man by those close to him. He had already experienced a variety of successes in the industry before co-founding Access International Advisors in 1994. Access International Advisors specialized in connecting extremely wealthy European investors with top-notch fund managers. On December 12th, 2008, Access sent a note to its clients reminding them that Access practiced extensive due diligence on the funds in which it invested clients' money and also hired private investigators to perform "extensive background checks" on the individual fund managers.

Shortly after that letter was sent out and just a few days before Christmas, Mr. de la Villehuchet casually asked his young assistant to buy a box cutter and leave it on his desk. He later borrowed the assistant's key, informing the assistant he would be working late and would need the key to lock up for the night. De la Villehuchet also told his wife he would have a late evening and suggested she not wait for him. Sometime after the cleaning crew left for the night, de la Villehuchet swallowed some sleeping pills, took the box cutter from his desk and began cutting his arm from his wrist up to the bicep. He put his feet up on his desk and arranged a wastebasket beneath his arm to minimize the mess. He was found dead the next morning.

What could have caused such an extreme and violent response in these otherwise upstanding individuals? Their investments. More specifically, learning they'd lost everything in an instant.

By the end of 2008, the global stock markets had been in turmoil for months and the markets would continue to crash through the early months of 2009. Once the dust settled, the stock markets had lost nearly 50% of their value in one year, leaving most investors shell-shocked. Still, people like Major Foxton, Burt and Joanne Meerow, and Rene-Thierry de la Villehuchet were among over 10,000 individuals who had fared much worse. These people were part of an unfortunate group that lost nearly everything in one of the most significant investment scams in history.

HOW THEY WERE DRAWN IN

People tend to be drawn to someone who can create magic, someone who can defy the odds, someone who can beat the system. That's what so many people felt they were getting by investing with Bernard L. Madoff. Bernie Madoff was an undeniably brilliant man who understood how to make money in ways that most other investment managers didn't. Sure, he could be charming and charismatic, but more pertinent was the quiet confidence about him, which helped him reassure investors that they were in good hands.

There was no reason to doubt him. His reputation preceded him, and the history was there to back it up. His firm, Bernard L. Madoff Investment Securities, was a pioneer of technology in the investment field. He led the way to fully adopting the use of computers for buying and selling stocks which gave him a distinct advantage over other companies. Computers allowed the Madoff firm to buy and sell stock much faster and cheaper than other firms. Madoff would profit by finding deals on stocks and trading them faster than anyone else. In the early 1980s, the number of trades being completed by the Madoff firm was the equivalent of nearly 10% of all the trades on the entire New York Stock Exchange, a staggering number for a single firm.

The technology developed by Madoff was eventually used to establish the National Association of Securities Dealers Automated Quotations Stock Market, more commonly known as the NASDAQ Stock Market. For three years, Bernie Madoff served as the chairman of NASDAQ, now the second-largest stock exchange in the world. Madoff was also an active participant in the National Association of Securities Dealers, an association that helps regulate the financial industry.

In addition to Madoff's prominent role as an industry insider, by the time the 1990s rolled around Bernie Madoff had provided his clients with nearly thirty years of steady returns. Clients who invested with Madoff may have seen their investments face a down month here or there, but over the course of a year, they could almost always expect to see a 10%-20% gain on their investment, regardless of what was happening in the stock markets. This was an almost irresistible draw. Ordinarily, to earn those types of returns, an investor would have to be willing to tolerate huge ups and downs in their investments over years of investing.

What was canny about Madoff's sales technique was that he never seemed to want new clients. It was as if he placed a red velvet rope in front of his exclusive club and wasn't going to let anyone in. Some clients remarked that getting to invest with Bernie was like winning the lottery. You just had to get in and you'd be set.

Of course, this exclusivity intensified his demand, but at the same time, it created an environment where clients were willing to ignore the details of *how* their money was being invested. The techniques that Madoff used to generate these steady returns were deemed too complicated for outsiders to understand and if investors wanted to keep their steady returns, they generally had to submit to not understanding where those returns were coming from. Even if his investors were concerned about his methods, he regularly refused to meet face-to-face with them. In a way, this added to the mystique of investing with Bernie Madoff. He was like the Wizard of Oz working behind the curtain, creating magic. Many large Madoff investors were worried that if they did press Madoff for too much information, they'd be kicked out of the club. They made the decision like so many others to go along with Madoff's secretive nature and kept cashing in the steady returns.

Another appealing aspect of Bernard L. Madoff Investment Securities was that they were a close-knit family business. Madoff's two sons, Mark and Andrew, played prominent roles at the firm. Mark took great pride in being known as the son of Wall Street wizard Bernie Madoff. Bernie's younger brother Peter Madoff was also a huge presence at the firm as its chief compliance officer. Peter's two children, Shana and Roger, worked with the firm as well as other nieces, nephews, and extended family members.

Eventually, some doubts began cropping up amongst industry insiders. Other professional investors looking in from the outside were having a hard time understanding how it was possible for Madoff to produce the constant returns he seemed to keep generating. Some called the returns impossible. Complaints were ultimately filed with the Securities and Exchange Commission. The Securities and Exchange Commission, more commonly called the SEC, is an agency of the United States federal government charged with enforcing various investment laws. Madoff drew so much attention from the SEC, that they examined and investigated his firm over half a dozen times. As far as the SEC could tell, however, there was no wrongdoing taking place at Bernard L. Madoff Investment Securities. Naturally, Madoff was able to parlay the clean bill of health from the feds to bolster investors' confidence in his firm.

Madoff's success and exclusivity inadvertently created an opportunity for others. Some of those who had made their way into Bernie Madoff's good graces channeled their entrepreneurial spirits. They established a means for outsiders to invest with him by pooling together money from groups of small investors Madoff would ordinarily ignore and funneling that money into the Madoff firm. Of course, the individuals doing the leg work of rounding up these small investors would collect fees of their own. At first, there were only a handful of these arrangements, but over a couple of decades the number would grow into the hundreds.

By 2006, Bernie Madoff had investors on nearly every continent, but whether or not they knew they were investing with Madoff was another story. These arrangements, which first started informally, were eventually developed as formal hedge funds. Each fund would take a share of investors' money before passing it on to Madoff to be invested. These funds became unofficially known as Madoff "feeder funds." These feeder funds grew so vastly that eventually, most Madoff investors weren't even aware they were investing with him.

The proliferation of Madoff feeder funds ultimately led them to become wholly convoluted. In one example, Anchor Holdings LLC marketed a hedge fund that split investors' money into a diversified mix of six international hedge funds. All six of those funds fed directly into Bernie Madoff's firm. Individuals who invested with Anchor Holdings believed they were prudent by spreading their investment risk over several different funds; they were, in fact, handing all of their money to a single man.

WHEN IT UNRAVELED

On December 11, 2008, Bernard L. Madoff was arrested for securities fraud. In the months leading up to his arrest, the crashing stock market was igniting investor fears, causing many of them to withdraw large amounts from their investment accounts with

Madoff. For any ordinary investment firm, these withdrawals would hurt the company's short-term profits, but otherwise, wouldn't cause lasting issues. Bernard L. Madoff Investment Securities was no ordinary firm. When clients started withdrawing large amounts of the over $65 billion they had invested with Bernie, it was a major problem for the Madoff firm because the money clients thought they had was simply not there.

It seems impossible that after so many examinations by regulators, banks, and other sophisticated investors, no one ever caught on to one of the biggest frauds in history. In the end, it was his children who turned him in. They were unaware of their father's decades-long fraud, and it was not until they began questioning him about large, oddly timed bonuses that he confessed.

The Madoff firm had two separate arms: a legitimate, successful trading firm and a secretive, massive Ponzi scheme. Bernie Madoff ran the Ponzi scheme in separate offices from the trading firm and kept that business very private from most of the company's employees. When markets were crashing in 2008, Bernie's Ponzi scheme was hemorrhaging money. He even began to borrow significant amounts of cash from the firm's legitimate trading business to keep up his fraud. When Madoff proposed large end-of-year bonuses while his business was hurting for cash, it sent up red flags for his two sons.

Eventually, Bernie confessed to running a massive scam where he wasn't investing his clients' money but simply taking in money from new clients and using it to pay other investors. It was a classic Ponzi scheme on the largest scale ever. Bernie explained to his sons that he wanted to get as much cash as possible transferred out of the scam to friends and family before all of it was gone, and he would spend the next week or so doing that before turning himself in. It was all over. His sons, Mark and Andrew, still in shock, went to the authorities right away, denying their father the extra time he wanted.

The SEC had been in his offices and peered over his records several times. Major banks and feeder funds had sent investment experts to meet with Madoff and diligently examine his practice time and time again. How did these top experts miss the basic fact that Madoff wasn't even investing his clients' money?

The Madoff firm's records were exquisite. An investigator could pick any client from the firm's books, review his or her investment returns for a quarter, and see the records of the precise trades that occurred to generate that client's returns. Madoff would even occasionally allow his major investors to view his firm's private online depository account which would confirm that all the stocks the firm owned were safely held by a third party.

His records were elaborate in every detail, extensive, and, most importantly, fake. While most employees of his firm had no idea about the fraud, he did have several accomplices loyal enough to help him perpetuate it for decades. These employees helped keep the bogus records in order so anyone who examined them would have no doubts that their money was safe and that the firm was operating legitimately.

Before the client statements were created, an investment return was determined for each client, for example, "Client A" will receive a 10% return for the quarter. The diligent employees would then use the recent stock market history to enter fake trades for the client's statement based on real-life stock market prices. As the scam grew, they developed a customized software program to minimize the effort it took to generate the falsified statements. Anyone could look at these statements and see which stocks Madoff supposedly bought or sold for them, when he did it, and for what price. One could then look up the real-world stock price history to compare the dates and prices on the statements. Everything would match and investors would believe their earnings were legitimate.

The fraudulent arm of the Madoff firm went to great lengths to maintain the false records, like keeping a supply of old letterhead stationery for the times they wanted to create a phony, backdated record from years ago and needed it to look its age.

Even the supposedly real-time look into his firm's online depository account was an elaborate fake. Instead of allowing access to his actual online depository account, the Madoff firm had created a replica website that was identical to the one used by professional traders at the time. This fake site made it appear to anyone who reviewed it that all the stocks reported on his clients' statements were right there in Madoff's account, safe and sound. The real site would have told another story. One of Madoff's largest investors would later testify that the fake website was used to successfully convince him that his investments were secure with Madoff.

There are a number of reasons why the SEC couldn't quite connect the dots and stop this massive fraud earlier. They suspected something was happening at Bernard L. Madoff Investment Securities that wasn't legal simply because the returns seemed too good to be true, but they weren't sure what. They investigated him thoroughly for something called "front-running." This is an illegal method that large traders can use to boost their profits. Because they process so many trades, they can see large orders coming before they are processed. Large orders can quickly raise or lower the price of a stock. Stockbrokers who process these trades have the ability to identify stocks that may go up or down in price based on large pending trades before they happen. Once the pending price movement is identified, the firm decides if it should buy or sell any shares and then executes its own trades before executing the large trades that will affect the stock's price. Needless to say, the SEC never found evidence that Bernie Madoff was generating his client's returns by front-running.

SEC investigators were in over their heads with Madoff. Later reports found that Madoff worked to impress and even intimidate SEC investigators. In one examination he told them that he was on the list to become chairman of the SEC. With considerable success, Madoff attempted to dictate which documents examiners could and could not see. Madoff was undoubtedly more knowledgeable than nearly any SEC investigator could be in those days, and he was more than willing to exploit that fact. The SEC was suffering terrible personnel turnover after long-standing budget shortfalls, so finding experienced examiners was difficult, if not impossible.

A top Madoff employee later testified that during one audit, examiners requested documents from a specific date which he knew there were no records for. He instructed one of the firm's computer programmers to go "into the archives" to retrieve the non-existent records. Later that day he came across the programmer in an office tossing a stack of papers back and forth with another employee. They had just printed new falsified records for the auditor. They had already put the papers in a refrigerator to cool them off because they were still warm from being printed. By tossing the papers around, they would make the freshly printed records look worn as if they had been used for some time. Even if an investigator had the experience to catch any gaps in the elaborate falsification machine behind the Madoff records, the insufficient SEC budget would leave the agency too short-staffed for the follow-up needed to catch him.

There was another reason why no one caught Bernie Madoff sooner, and it was simply due to a lack of imagination. Investigators and his more sophisticated investors could imagine Madoff was cheating a little here and there in order to produce the high, consistent returns that he did, but the idea that Madoff was not making any investments at all was one that simply did not come to mind, and so no one sought to investigate the potential for a Ponzi scheme.

REVERBERATIONS

The aforementioned Major William Foxton, Burt and Joanne Meerow, and Rene-Thierry Magon de la Villehuchet were all victims who were directly impacted by the massive Madoff Fraud.

Major Foxton began investing in two hedge funds in the 1980s, the Herald USA Fund and Harold Luxembourg Fund. It was in these two funds that he invested his entire life savings, which is believed to have been worth around $3 million. Major Foxton had no idea that he was a Madoff investor until it was too late, and he discovered that he had lost everything. Days before taking his own life on a park bench, he sent an email to his son:

> *"Dear Will, I will be brief. I had some in fact all my money in two funds Herald USA Fund and Herald Luxembourg Fund invested in Austria. I have now found out that the office is closed and the money was invested in Hedge funds of Madoff of the Ponzi scheme. I have lost everything. I am now considering whether or not to get myself declared bankrupt. Feeling pretty low and depressed. That's about it for the moment."*

Major Foxton was an honorable man and was pained by the thought of being a financial burden on anyone. He left two suicide notes which helped confirm that the financial problems caused by the Madoff scandal were the reason he took his own life.

Burt and Joanne Meerow heard about Bernie Madoff through a friend at their country club. He had clients around the world and produced consistently high returns. Burt had recently retired, and the couple ended up investing 80% of their savings with Madoff through the money-management unit at a major insurance company. Burt and Joanne considered themselves lucky not to be among those Madoff victims who lost the means to care for their health or provide for loved ones. While they were grateful for what they had left, they were forced to immediately and aggressively downsize. They were undoubtedly robbed of the security and lifestyle they had worked so hard to earn.

Rene-Thierry Magon de la Villehuchet the financier who was found dead in his office the morning after committing suicide, was also described as an honorable man and extraordinarily generous. De la Villehuchet's offices were just three blocks from the Bernard L. Madoff Investment Securities office in New York. De la Villehuchet began investing his clients' money with Madoff just a few years before Madoff's arrest. By the time the Madoff scam collapsed, De la Villehuchet had over $1 billion in client assets invested with Madoff along with tens of millions of his personal wealth.

Early on, de la Villehuchet had hoped to recover some of his clients' funds, but he soon believed it was hopeless. Friend and fellow investment fund founder Leon Cooperman sensed he was down and tried to console him, "Listen, people make mistakes. You're not at fault and you have to pick yourself up from this," he recalled telling his friend. Cooperman went on to describe the situation, "This guy is aristocracy, one of his ancestors was the admiral for Napoleon in the Napoleonic wars. I think this thing brought great disgrace and embarrassment, and he didn't have the capacity to deal with it. In the end, he was sensitive to the disgrace and being involved with this thief."

Eventually, de la Villehuchet's wife was sued in an attempt to recover money for other victims of the massive Madoff fraud.

While the direct impact Bernie Madoff had on his victims is clear, the magnitude of his massive Ponzi scheme had an even larger impact across the world. Bernie Madoff gave investment fraud a spotlight in the mainstream media like no one before him ever had. If the amounts lost in the nearly $65 billion fraud weren't enough to get Main Street's attention, celebrity Madoff victims like Steven Spielberg, John Malkovich, Kevin Bacon, Sandy Koufax, Zsa Zsa Gabor, former New York governor Eliot Spitzer, and Nobel Peace Prize winner Elie Wiesel would undoubtedly catch the common investor's eye.

The damage beyond Madoff's Ponzi scheme victims extended immediately and dramatically to his close family. While no evidence was ever found throughout numerous investigations by the SEC and FBI that his wife or children had any knowledge of his crimes prior to his confession, his family was publicly tried and found unanimously guilty by association.

Dearest friends and extended family refused to speak or associate with them. Bernie's wife, Ruth, while given sufficient money to live out her life, was forced to sell off what was essentially her every possession. Her home, jewelry, coats, furniture, everything, right down to a pile of her used socks. What was undoubtedly more painful than losing her home or family heirlooms was the loss of her close connection with her two sons, Mark and Andrew.

Mark and Andrew immediately decided to disown their father. For Ruth, however, after 50 years in a loving marriage, cutting her husband off cold wasn't so easy. She was incensed with Bernie after the betrayal and humiliation he had caused her, but for so many years, being with Bernie was all she knew. The simple fact that she was still willing to visit him in prison a few times a year was enough for her children to cut off contact and stop her from seeing her grandchildren.

Bernie's eldest son, Mark Madoff, probably took the betrayal hardest. So much of his identity was tied to being the son of "The Wizard of Wall Street" prior to the scandal that the weight of now being the son of "The Wizard of Lies" was crushing him.

By the two-year anniversary of Bernard Madoff's arrest, Mark had established a reasonably successful daily real estate letter. He made sure that his name, the Madoff name, was nowhere to be found in the letters. Mark would wake each day at 4 AM and scour the Internet for industry news before compiling and sending the newsletter at around 9 AM. Precisely two years after his father's arrest, he was again awake at 4 AM, but the morning email went to his lawyer, not his subscribers: "Nobody wants to believe the truth. Please take care of my family." He was home with his twenty-two-month-old son and the family dog while his wife was on a Disney World vacation with their daughter. "I love you," he messaged her, "Please send someone."

When Mark's wife read the message several hours later, she

urged her stepfather to rush to their apartment. He found Mark dead, hanging from a black dog leash secured to a metal beam across their living room ceiling. A snapped vacuum cleaner cord was found attached to that same beam; the other half was found tied in a noose on a nearby table. Mark's son and the family dog were found safe in another room.

Mark was determined to take his life. Just over a year earlier he had attempted suicide by taking sleeping pills, but he survived and sought help. After Mark's tragic death, Ruth Madoff, who had attempted suicide herself two years earlier, finally cut off all contact with her imprisoned husband. Less than four years later, Madoff's youngest son, Andrew, passed away in a New York hospital after losing his battle with lymphoma.

Of all the pain and suffering Bernard L. Madoff must have feared his crimes might one day cause, I don't believe he ever considered that his scam would lead to the decimation of his family.

While presiding over Bernard Madoff's sentencing, the Honorable Denny Chin considered arguments from Madoff's defense that victims were seeking mob justice against his white-collar crimes. Judge Chin noted the defense's request for a 15 to 20-year sentence, and given Madoff's age, any sentence over 20 years was effectively a life sentence. "But the symbolism is important," Judge Chin said before handing down a sentence. He understood that the crimes were even larger than the monetary damage suffered by his direct victims. Judge Chin continued, "The victims put their trust in Mr. Madoff. That trust was broken in a way that has left many—victims as well as others—doubting our financial institutions, our financial system, our government's ability to regulate and protect, and sadly, even themselves."

Judge Chin made a few more comments and paused shortly. "Mr. Madoff, please stand. It is the judgment of this Court that the defendant, Bernard L. Madoff, shall be and hereby is sentenced to a term of imprisonment of 150 years." Bernie Madoff died in prison in April of 2021. He was 82 years old.

Now that over a decade has passed since the collapse of the world's largest Ponzi scheme, the Madoff case has found itself the subject of numerous academic studies. Recently, such a study out of Cornell University was published examining the extended impact on the investment advisor landscape.

The study described investors as "trust shocked" as investor trust rapidly evaporated after the Madoff scandal. The trust shock spread far beyond those who were directly impacted by the Madoff fraud. A loss of trust in the financial system had spread by word of mouth throughout the elderly Jewish community. As a Jew, Madoff leveraged his connections throughout the Jewish community to expand his business in the early years. This resulted in a disproportionate number of his victims being Jewish. As it goes in so many religious communities, friends and families shared their horror stories of falling victim to Bernie Madoff, and those stories were passed on to neighbors, co-workers, and anyone else who may have been in their personal network. It was found that investors who merely felt socially connected to Madoff victims, even if they did not know any personally, suffered a loss of trust in the financial system.

The Cornell study also revealed a trust shock based on an investor's geographic location. Individuals who lived in close geographic proximity to one or more Madoff victims were more likely to experience a loss of trust. While most individual victims did not make national headlines, they were commonly featured in local news stories. People in these areas were more likely to be aware of the fraud and feel a more direct connection, especially if they happened to recognize one of the victims.

Additionally, people who had more exposure to stories about the Madoff fraud reported a loss of trust in the criminal justice system, and the SEC's failure to catch Madoff early on exacerbated a loss of trust in the financial system. Furthermore, any time federal securities enforcement successfully catches a firm engaging in fraud, investing fears climb and households in the fraudulent firm's entire state cut back their investments.

THE COST OF LOST TRUST

Here's why all of this matters to you. Investors who suffered a shock to trust as a result of learning about the Madoff fraud pulled $363 billion out of their accounts with financial advisors. Clients pulled out their money even if those advisors had nothing to do with Bernie Madoff. Significant amounts of those funds were moved into conservative, safe assets such as bank deposits. In fact, the withdrawals were so substantial that investment firms located in geographic areas affected by the fraud were 40% more likely to go out of business.

Research found that even as long as four years after Madoff's Ponzi scheme collapsed, trust-shocked investors continued to be apprehensive about investing in stocks. The timing here is significant because investing in stocks for the four years following the Madoff fraud would have resulted in an 86% return for investors. If investors who pulled out their $363 billion from advisors had that money invested in stocks over those four years, it would have grown to $675 billion! In the 10 years following the Madoff fraud, stock investments returned 288%. Meanwhile, over that same time, safe and secure bank deposits provided returns of less than 1% to investors each year.

The monetary harm caused by the Madoff fraud went far beyond his personal victims. His scam reverberated through the entire financial system and penetrated the core of investment culture. Bernie Madoff single-handedly altered beliefs about investing for millions of people around the world, shrouding their decision-making in fear. This fear resulted in lost potential returns worth hundreds of billions of dollars to everyday investors. The fears that permeated from Bernie Madoff's fraud have become part of your investment philosophy, even if you've never heard of him until now. His frauds changed the investment philosophies of people close to you, people who have written investing articles you may have read, and the institutions you invest with. In turn, those who were influenced have influenced you. Now, it's these very influences that continue to cost you the best investment returns possible.

Ernest Hemingway said, "The best way to find out if you can trust anybody is to trust them." Fortunately, when it comes to building your faith in investing, you can rely on more than blind trust. In the rest of this section, we'll be working on building trust within the investment industry, in part by talking about some of the things wrong with it.

-CHAPTER SUMMARY-

- Bernie Madoff's victims were drawn into his scam because of his promises for higher-than-normal investment returns.

- Investors were willing to ignore the fact that they did not understand how the returns were generated.

- Victims gave Madoff full control of their invested funds.

- The implications of the fraud spread far beyond his victims, causing losses to investors who never had direct dealings with his firm.

- Today, investors are still negatively influenced by the Bernie Madoff fraud.

CHAPTER TWO

Watching for Dirty Birdies

"Anyone who believes what a cat tells him deserves all he gets."
-Neil Gaiman

L ET'S GO BACK TO THE MIDDLE of 1821. Gregor Mac-
Gregor had just returned home to England after spending
nearly a decade as a Military General, fighting against the Span-
ish alongside revolutionaries in South America. He proclaimed
to the English citizens that he was recently named Cazique, or
prince, of Poyais, a burgeoning Central American territory.
MacGregor said he had returned to London in order to attend the
coronation of King George the IV on behalf of the Poyasian
people.

MacGregor also announced that he was seeking investors and
immigrants to develop and leverage the new land's resources to
their fullest. He shared that Poyais had an established democratic
government, civil services, and a military. Soon he was joined in
London by the Princess of Poyais and the royal couple received
countless social invitations which they frequently indulged.

All the while, MacGregor was hard at work attracting investors
and settlers to the new land. He shared extensive details about
Poyais with anyone who would listen. He offered up elaborate
illustrations of military uniforms for each branch of the Poyais

military and details about its banking system and constitution. He gave interviews to national newspapers, paid advertisers for leaflets, and had songs composed about Poyais to be sung in the busy streets.

In 1822 a 355-page handbook for the settlers of Poyais went into print. Written by Thomas Strangeways, Captain of the 1st Native Poyer Regiment, the handbook prepared new settlers for what to expect when they arrived. According to Strangeways, Poyais was a land with a moderate climate, quite suitable for European settlers. The soil was "everywhere fertile in a very uncommon degree." Various timber grew plentifully, including valuable mahogany as well as seemingly every type of wood needed for the construction of various necessities from housing to ships. Also abundant were fruit-producing plants including citrus and avocado trees. Horses, cattle, and oxen could be found in "great numbers" in this country. Only one mineral had been discovered in Poyais so far, gold, and by running the sands of the rivers through sieves the natives had produced globules of it.

One could commute between the Royal Palace, the Parliament, the Cathedral, or the Opera House in the capital city of Poyais along its splendid paved, tree-lined boulevards.

Soon London offices were in business selling land certificates for plots throughout Poyais at the price of roughly one day's wages per acre. Due to the new land's popularity, MacGregor was able to double the selling price without seeing a slowdown in purchases. At the same time, MacGregor was busy setting up a program through the London Stock Exchange to allow investors to lend money to the Poyasian government in exchange for 6% interest on their investment. This program helped MacGregor raise £200,000, the equivalent of £25 million today.

Gregor MacGregor had done very well for himself, and the first settlers were about to start their journey to the new land. Among the immigrants were doctors, a banker, civil servants, and those whose families paid their way to join the Poyais military. Many of the travelers brought with them their life savings in coins. While MacGregor was personally seeing off the settlers, he was courteous enough to offer them the chance to exchange their gold coins for the official paper currency of Poyais. Over 200 people made the journey to the new land on two separate ships. The trip took nearly two months. When the first ship arrived at its destination, the travelers had dressed themselves in their best and the ship fired its cannons to announce their arrival at the Poyasian port. No one came to greet them. In fact, the settlers soon discovered that the promises of Poyais were all an elaborate scam. The land was little more than a desolate jungle. Where they expected a developing civilization, settlers only found two abandoned huts. While the settlers arrived with sufficient supplies for starting off in an established colony, they were ill-equipped for building a new settlement from the ground up. Less than fifty of the nearly 250 people who originally made the journey survived.

Gregor MacGregor has since been nicknamed "The Father of Securities Fraud." While he may not have been the first to bilk investors, he certainly orchestrated the largest-scale scam of his time.

MacGregor did own the land he called Poyais, but each detail he sold investors on was part of an elaborate fabrication. He was the author of the 355-page settlers handbook, not Captain Strangeways. He printed the official paper dollars of Poyais. He fabricated the territory name, its flag, military uniforms, government system, and of course, his own title, Cazique.

WHY IT MATTERS TO YOU

Fraud isn't new, and unfortunately history teaches us that it's never going away. Bernie Madoff wasn't the first and he certainly wasn't the last. Part of building up trust is understanding the facts whether they're good or bad. When it comes to investing, you're going to have to be your last line of defense. So, before we dive directly into how to invest, we need to spend some time discussing key areas to stay away from. By having a fuller understanding of common investment fraud, you'll be free to focus on legitimate investing and won't be distracted by scams. This is important because being scammed is one of the top fears that stops people from investing. In this chapter you'll learn about the most common types of investment fraud, how rules and regulations offer limited protection, and some steps you can take to minimize your risk.

AFFINITY FRAUD

Affinity frauds target members of identifiable groups, such as the elderly, or religious or ethnic communities. Madoff's Ponzi scheme was also considered an affinity fraud due to the way he targeted the Jewish community. Gregor MacGregor also utilized affinity fraud to recruit settlers for Poyais. While MacGregor worked his fraud in England, he was originally a Scotsman and used his heritage to help convince other Scots to make the deadly journey. The fraudsters involved in affinity scams often are – or pretend to be – members of the group. They may enlist respected leaders from the group to spread the word about the scheme, convincing them it's legitimate and worthwhile. Many times, those leaders become unwitting victims of the fraud they helped to promote.

A traditional church provides an excellent example of how affinity fraud can consume a group. Imagine the fraudster connects with the minister extolling the church's values and how his investment is aligned with what the church believes. He sells the minister on the idea of his scam. If the minister is convinced that the plan will be beneficial for those involved, he's likely to invite members of his congregation to participate. If those people are happy with the investment plan, they'll encourage others in the group to join. Soon, almost everyone in the church will be invested in the scam.

These scams exploit the trust and friendship that exists in

groups of people. Because of the tight-knit structure of many groups, outsiders may never know about the affinity scam. Victims may try to work things out within the group rather than notify authorities or pursue legal remedies. Affinity scams often involve "Ponzi" or pyramid schemes where new investor money is used to pay earlier investors, making it appear as if the investment is successful and legitimate.

PONZI SCHEME

A Ponzi scheme is an investment fraud that pays existing investors with funds collected from new investors. Ponzi scheme organizers often promise to invest your money and generate high returns with little or no risk, but in many Ponzi schemes, the perpetrators don't invest the money at all. Instead, they use deposits from new investors to pay the investment returns for earlier participants.

With little or no legitimate earnings, Ponzi schemes require a constant flow of new money to survive. When it becomes hard to recruit new investors, or when large numbers of existing investors cash out, these schemes tend to collapse.

Ponzi schemes are named after Charles Ponzi, who duped investors in the 1920s. Ponzi claimed to be able to generate huge profits by taking advantage of the price variations of a special postage coupon available at the time. The coupon could be purchased in one country and redeemed in another. Ponzi sought to buy the coupons where they had a lower rate and redeem them in a country where they were worth more. He'd pass on the profits to his investors. He paid his initial investors a rate of 60% interest. The positive experience of early investors convinced others to invest, and within six months of starting, Ponzi had drawn in the equivalent of what would be hundreds of millions of dollars today. The scheme collapsed only eight months after it began when financial journalists started investigating. Once it was reported that Ponzi needed 160 million postage coupons to generate the promised profits for his investors and only 27,000 existed in the world, the scam was done for.

Ponzi scheme "red flags"

Many Ponzi schemes share common characteristics. Look for these warning signs:

High returns with little or no risk: Every investment carries some degree of risk, and investments yielding higher returns typically involve more risk. Be highly suspicious of any "guaranteed" investment opportunity.

Overly consistent returns: Investments tend to go up and down over time. Be skeptical about an investment that regularly generates positive returns regardless of overall market conditions.

Unregistered investments: Ponzi schemes typically involve investments that are not registered with the SEC or with state regulators, like postage coupons for example. Registration is important because it provides investors with access to information about the company's management, products, services, and finances.

Unlicensed sellers: Federal and state securities laws require investment professionals and firms to be licensed or registered. Most Ponzi schemes involve unlicensed individuals or unregistered firms.

Secretive, complex strategies: Avoid investments if you don't understand them or can't get complete information about them.

Issues with paperwork: Account statement errors may be a sign that funds are not being invested as promised.

Difficulty receiving payments: Be suspicious if you don't receive a payment or have difficulty cashing out. Ponzi scheme promoters sometimes try to prevent participants from cashing out by offering even higher returns for staying put.

PYRAMID SCHEMES

In the classic "pyramid" scheme, participants attempt to make money solely by recruiting new participants, usually where:

- The promoter promises a high return in a short period of time.

- No genuine product or service is actually sold; and

- The primary emphasis is on recruiting new participants.

All pyramid schemes eventually collapse, and most investors lose their money. Fraudsters frequently promote pyramid schemes through social media, Internet advertising, company websites, group presentations, conference calls, YouTube videos, and other means. Pyramid scheme promoters may go to great lengths to make the program look like a business, such as a legitimate multi-level marketing (MLM) program, but Pyramid Scheme operators use money paid by new recruits to pay off earlier-stage investors (usually recruits themselves). At some point, the schemes get too big, the promoter cannot raise enough money from new investors to pay earlier investors, and people lose their money.

Here are some of the hallmarks of a pyramid scheme:

Emphasis on recruiting: If a program focuses solely on recruiting others to join the program for a fee, it is likely a pyramid scheme. Be skeptical if you will receive more compensation for recruiting others than for product sales.

No genuine product or service is sold: Exercise caution if what is being sold as part of the business is hard to value, like so-called "tech" services or products such as mass-licensed e-books or online advertising on little-used websites. Some fraudsters choose fancy-sounding "products" to make it harder to prove the company is a bogus pyramid scheme.

Promises of high returns in a short time period: Be skeptical of promises of fast cash – it could mean that commissions are being paid out of money from new recruits rather than revenue generated by product sales.

Easy money or passive income: There is no such thing as a free lunch. If you are offered compensation in exchange for doing little work such as making payments, recruiting others, or placing online advertisements on obscure websites, you may be part of an illegal pyramid scheme.

No demonstrated revenue from retail sales: Ask to see documents, such as financial statements audited by a certified public accountant (CPA), showing that the company generates revenue from selling its products or services to people outside the program. As a general rule, legitimate MLM companies derive revenue primarily from selling products, not from recruiting members.

Complex commission structure: Be concerned unless commissions are based on products or services that you or your recruits sell to people outside the program. If you do not understand how you will be compensated, be cautious.

In 2020, at the heart of the COVID-19 pandemic, Marlon and LaShonda Moore created an opportunity designed to help Black communities achieve "generational wealth." The program was called, "Blessings in No Time." Prior to launching their business, the pair had crafted an image as a God-loving, power couple and they were even featured on an Oprah Winfrey Network reality show. The couple devised a system that would provide participants with as much as an 800% return on their investment in as little time as one week. After paying into the system, members were then encouraged to level up by recruiting new members. Once participants reached a certain level they would receive financial "blessings" from the company. The Moore's described the program as a new type of investing called "linkfunding." To help boost confidence in the program, LaShonda told members that high-ranking officials at the IRS, Pentagon, and FBI were all participants. Unfortunately, in order to pay the promised returns, Blessings in No Time was dependent on the continuous and exponential growth of its membership. It took over a year for the Pyramid Scheme to get shut down after participants had already contributed tens of millions of dollars. Blessings in No Time was an example of a pyramid scheme that used affinity fraud involving both the African American community and individuals of faith.

Pyramid Scheme Breakdown

This image depicts a pyramid scheme that requires each member to recruit six additonal members and the number of participants needed at each level to sustain the scheme.

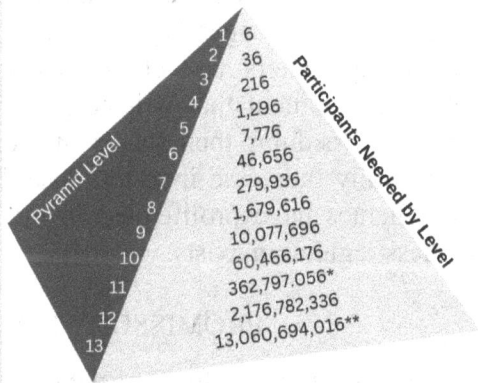

Pyramid Level	Participants Needed by Level
1	6
2	36
3	216
4	1,296
5	7,776
6	46,656
7	279,936
8	1,679,616
9	10,077,696
10	60,466,176
11	362,797.056*
12	2,176,782,336
13	13,060,694,016**

*Surpasses entire U.S. Population
**Surpasses global population

Figure 2.1

What makes pyramid schemes so impossible to maintain is the sheer magnitude of growth required. Imagine a scheme where one participant must find six other participants, who, in turn, must find six new recruits each. After only eleven layers of the "downline," you would need more participants than the entire population of the United States to maintain the scheme. See Figure 2.1.

When fraudsters attempt to make money solely by recruiting new participants into a program, that is a pyramid scheme, and there is only one possible mathematical result – collapse.

PUMP AND DUMP SCHEMES

"Pump-and-dump" schemes consist of two parts. In the first, promoters try to boost the price of a stock with false or misleading statements about the company. Generally, they attempt to build a buzz and generate excitement for the stock which helps the stock price rise. Once the stock price has been pumped up, fraudsters move on to the second part, where they seek to profit by selling their own holdings of the stock, "dumping" shares into the market.

Today, these schemes often occur on the Internet where it's common to see messages urging readers to buy a stock quickly. Often, the promoters will claim to have "inside" information about a development that will be positive for the stock. After these fraudsters dump their shares and stop hyping the stock, the price typically falls, and investors lose their money. Pump-and-dump schemes have proliferated in the cryptocurrency market where less regulation exists.

PROMISSORY NOTES

Promissory notes are a form of debt that companies sometimes use to raise money. They typically involve investors loaning money to a company in exchange for a fixed amount of periodic income. Promissory notes can provide a higher-than-average interest rate. Although promissory notes can be appropriate investments for many individuals, some fraudsters use fake or high-risk promissory notes to defraud investors, especially the elderly. Perpetrators often promise investors higher rates than possible, that the investment is guaranteed when it is not, or the notes could be entirely fake.

The North American Securities Administration Association (NASAA) noted that in 2021, state regulators initiated far more action against promissory notes than any other financial product. Cases against promissory note transactions were more than double Ponzi and pyramid schemes combined. Promissory notes can be attractive for individuals looking for a steady income stream from their investments. Typically, promissory notes are sold to institutions or sophisticated investors, so in most cases, a promissory note that is marketed to the general public should be a red flag.

Chris Burns was an investment advisor based in Atlanta, Georgia. He allegedly began selling promissory notes to his clients in 2017. According to a lawsuit filed by the SEC, Burns advised his clients of an investment opportunity as part of a peer-to-peer lending program. He informed his clients that the program served businesses that wanted to borrow money. Burns told investors that the businesses to whom they lent money would make monthly payments which included a return of principal plus interest. Burns provided investors with promissory notes stating the term length of the investment and the rate of interest the investor would receive. The term length ranged anywhere from a few weeks to several years and the interest rates went as high as 20%. Burns told investors that the notes were secured by collateral held in a Charles Schwab account and he signed a personal guarantee to pay investors 100% of their initial investment in the case of a loss.

The entire story was a sham. Burns raised $10 million from his customers through 2020. The money was never lent to other businesses but was instead used to fund Burn's lifestyle expenses (a lake house, cars, and a boat to name a few), pay the operating expenses of his firm, and buy airtime for his local radio show so he could reach even more victims. Burns disappeared on September 24, 2020 (a day before he was required to hand over documents in an SEC investigation) with all but $75 from his clients' investments transferred to his personal accounts or withdrawn as cash. As of this writing, he remains one of the FBI's most wanted fugitives. He left behind his wife, three kids, and a dog.

MICROCAP FRAUD

If you're considering investing in a company based on an unsolicited stock promotion or tip, be cautious. The promotion may be from a paid promoter or company insider who stands to profit at your expense from selling shares after creating a buying frenzy and pumping up the stock price as part of a pump-and-dump scheme.

What are microcap stocks and why are they more susceptible to stock price manipulation?
Publicly available information about microcap stocks (low-priced stocks issued by the smallest of companies), including penny stocks (the very lowest-priced stocks), often is scarce. This makes it easier for fraudsters to spread false information. In addition, it is often easier for fraudsters to manipulate the price of microcap stocks because it's been historically harder to find willing buyers for microcap stock compared to the stock of larger companies. If you've seen the movie *The Wolf of Wall Street*[1] starring Leonardo DiCaprio you may remember Jordan Belfort

---

[1] Unbeknownst to the artistic creators and actors involved in the movie during production, *The Wolf of Wall Street*, a film about fraud in finance, was funded through one of the biggest frauds in history when Jho Low masterminded a theft of $4.5 billion dollars from a Malaysian sovereign wealth fund. $100 million of the embezzled funds were alleged to be used for the production of the movie.

(The Wolf) buying large quantities of an obscure stock from other stock brokers at inflated prices in order to raise the perceived demand for that stock. He would turn around and have his high-pressure salesmen sell those inflated shares to unwitting individual investors. With the price of the stock artificially raised, he'd quickly sell off a large number of shares he personally owned for a massive profit. This type of manipulation is much easier to do with small, obscure microcap stocks.

What are some warning signs of microcap fraud?

- You may observe an unsolicited stock recommendation or heavy stock promotion. Be wary if the company's stock seems to be more heavily promoted than its products or services.

- The company has no real business operations. Penny stocks that are aggressively promoted may be stocks of dormant shell companies.

- You witness an unexplained increase in stock price or trading volume. Some microcap stocks are quoted on "over-the-counter" markets meaning outside of a major stock exchange like the New York Stock Exchange (NYSE).

- The SEC has suspended trading of the stock. Visit the SEC website to search if a particular stock has been suspended from trading.

- There have been frequent changes in the company name or type of business. Frequent changes in a company name or business plan may suggest no real business operations.

Where can I get information about a microcap company?
Read recent reports that the company has filed with the SEC. Note that fraudsters often attempt to take advantage of the news as a hook for investment schemes touting "the latest growth industry." For example, they may promote companies that claim to be developing products or services relating to marijuana, cryptocurrencies, or artificial intelligence which are areas that are relatively new investment options.

What If I received the stock promotion through a legitimate source?
Fraudsters may promote a stock in seemingly independent and unbiased sources including social media, investment newsletters, online advertisements, email, Internet chat rooms, direct mail, newspapers, magazines, and radio.

What if the promoter discloses receiving compensation to promote the stock?
Even if a promoter makes specific disclosures about being compensated for promoting a stock, be aware that fraudsters may make such disclosures to create the false appearance that the promotion is legitimate. Additionally, the disclosures may not reveal that the underlying source of the compensation is a company insider or affiliate.

PRECIOUS METALS AND COINS

Many investors like investing in precious metals and coins. We're going to discuss investing in both of those a little later in the book. For right now, let's talk about how these investments are often part of fraudulent scams.

Coin Scams
Often rare coins forged out of precious metals are seen as good investments. There's a potential the value can rise over time,

however, these types of investments are more challenging to regulate than investments like stocks or bank accounts. This helps open the door to unscrupulous salespeople. Typically, the scam is executed by overstating the rarity or quality of the coin. For example, the salesman may state that the coins are extremely rare, and they had just obtained a new lot through a recent estate sale. They'll often promise to resell the coins on your behalf to another investor for a profit so you don't feel like you're taking any risk. Once they have your money, however, the coins they ship may be of poor quality or not arrive at all.

Bullion Scam
One of the most popular ways to buy gold or silver is with the purchase of bars. The challenge with these types of purchases is securely storing the valuable bricks. Scammers have a solution. After you purchase gold or silver bars from them, you can have them stored in a vault at the seller's facility. How convenient! In 2015, precious metal dealer Bullion Direct filed for bankruptcy with its customers believing the company was holding as much as $25 million worth of their hard investments. In reality, their vaults only held a tiny fraction of that total. For the most part, the company was never buying or storing the metals their customers were paying for.

Mining Scams
Occasionally, fraudsters will offer discount prices on valuable metals like gold and silver by suggesting they have a direct link to a productive mine that cuts out the middlemen, allowing you to benefit. More commonly, mining scams primarily involve investments in precious metal mining companies. A salesman may contact you offering to sell you shares in a mining company. They'll have a compelling reason for why you should buy before the share price skyrockets. Common lines are that the company has developed a new mining technology that allows it to extract more of the precious material, that the company has started a

new mine that is in close proximity to another mine which was very successful, or over-estimated claims about how much gold has already been found at a new mine during exploratory ventures.

In the late 1990s, Canadian mining company Bre-x spent years making overzealous claims about the potential of their new Indonesian mine. The company repeatedly told investors that they were confident that the mine would prove to be one of the largest gold discoveries the world had ever seen, and the stock price climbed from around $2 a share to well over $200. Company insiders sold off their shares in droves. When an independent analyst drew samples from the same site, they found very little gold at all. Later it was found that the company had taken gold from existing jewelry and added it to test samples which had been used to prove how dense the gold deposits were at the mining site. The stock price crashed, and the company went bankrupt, costing investors billions.

ADVANCE FEE FRAUD

Advance fee frauds ask investors to pay a fee upfront – in advance of receiving any proceeds, money, or stock– in order for the deal to go through. The advance payment may be described as a fee, tax, commission, or incidental expense that will be repaid later. Some advance fee schemes target investors who already purchased underperforming securities and offer to sell those securities if an "advance fee" is paid.

Other advance fee frauds try to fool investors with official-sounding websites and e-mail addresses. These addresses may contain ".gov" somewhere in the address to fake legitimacy but end in ".us" or ".org." U.S. government agency websites or e-mail addresses end in ".gov," ".mil," or "fed.us." Be wary of a website or correspondence claiming to be from a U.S. government agency whose e-mail address does not end with one of the appropriate domain extensions (.gov, .mil, or. fed.us).

PRIME BANK INVESTMENTS

If someone approaches you about investing in a so-called "Prime Bank" program, "Prime World Bank" financial instrument, or similar high-yield security, you should know that these investments do not exist. They are all scams

Prime Bank programs often claim investors' funds will be used to buy and trade "Prime Bank" instruments. Promoters make the schemes seem legitimate, using complex, sophisticated, and official-sounding terms. The investment may be described as debentures, standby letters of credit, bank guarantees, an offshore trading program, a high-yield investment program, or some variation.

To reassure investors, promoters may claim that the instrument is issued, traded, or guaranteed by a well-known organization such as the World Bank, the International Monetary Fund (IMF), a central bank, such as the U.S. Federal Reserve, or the International Chamber of Commerce (ICC). Gregor MacGregor's debt sale was similar to prime bank fraud as he stated that investors' loans were guaranteed by "all the revenues of the Government of Poyais."

Secrecy is another tip-off. Prime Bank scheme promoters frequently claim that investment opportunities of this type are by invitation only and limited to select wealthy customers. They cite secrecy if potential investors ask for references, and sometimes ask investors to sign non-disclosure agreements.

Some promoters are audacious enough to advertise in national newspapers. They may avoid using the term "Prime Bank note" and tell prospective investors that their programs do not involve Prime Bank instruments. Regardless of what they're called, the basic pitch remains the same, and investors should remain vigilant against offers to invest in high-yield, risk-free international finance programs.

HIGH-YIELD INVESTMENT PROGRAMS

The Internet is awash in so-called "high-yield investment programs" or "HYIPs." These are unregistered investments typically run by unlicensed individuals – and they are often frauds. The hallmark of a HYIP scam is the promise of incredible returns at little or no risk to the investor. A HYIP website might promise annual (or even monthly, weekly, or daily!) returns of 30 or 40 percent – or more. Some of these scams may use the term "prime bank" program. If you are approached online to invest in one of these, you should exercise extreme caution - it is likely a fraud.

REGULATORY PROTECTIONS

Regulators have made a valiant effort to protect you from fraud and bad actors. Regulations seem to be expanding on a continuous basis. Certainly, Bernie Madoff's massive fraud was an eye-opener for lawmakers. While strong protections existed in 2008, Madoff somehow wriggled through the cracks. In the decade following the Madoff scandal, sweeping regulatory reform like the Dodd–Frank Wall Street Reform and Consumer Protection Act in 2010, has closed many of the gaps in protection throughout the financial services industry.

Most regulatory responsibilities in the investment industry fall to the Securities and Exchange Commission (SEC). The SEC covers a lot of ground, but as far as the regulation of investments is concerned, the SEC's two jobs are making sure that investors are as informed about investments as possible and that investment professionals are playing by the rules.

While the SEC has produced excellent educational resources for the investing public through pamphlets and on their website, the majority of the work they do to keep investors informed focuses on disclosure. The SEC requires financial services companies and professionals to clearly disclose fees, the types of risk that are involved with your investments, potential conflicts of interest, and a ton of other information. Unfortunately, the amount of information investment advisors need to disclose to you as a potential client is now so voluminous that these disclosure packets span dozens of pages. For example, when I help establish an Individual Retirement Account for a client at my firm, I'm required to provide over seventy pages of disclosure documents. I don't know if anyone ever reads all that. Are disclosures like these really helping investor confidence or competence? Or are these long disclosures just an extra cause of confusion and concern?

To ensure investment professionals are playing by the rules, the SEC requires scores of documentation. Not only does an investment advisor need to follow every regulation, but she must also be able to sufficiently prove with written records that she has done so. All investment advisors are subject to random, short-notice examinations and if an advisor can't prove they've followed every regulation, they'll likely be subject to fines, suspensions, or prison. Auditors expect advisors to prove that their investment recommendations are appropriate for their clients, that they are billing the correct amounts based on the client contracts, that client notices are being sent in a timely manner, that appropriate marketing practices are followed, and much more. SEC audits are very thorough. For perspective, during my firm's last audit, the examiner poured through thousands of transactions and uncovered a $0.75 discrepancy between our general ledger and profit and loss statement. It turned out that one transaction simply hadn't been processed in our accounting software yet and it corrected itself by the next day. Regardless, the examiner caught it and instructed us to cease operations until it was corrected. With today's regulations, it would take a much more elaborate document falsification scheme than what Madoff was orchestrating to sneak past a modern examiner's eyes.

Three years after the Titanic sank, Congress passed legislation - as they often do following highly publicized disasters - requiring all sea vessels to carry enough lifeboats for at least 75% of the vessel's passengers. The bill was signed into law by President Woodrow Wilson. In order to comply with the new law, the Great Lakes steamer *Eastland* was fitted with eleven lifeboats, up from its original six. It also carried thirty-seven life rafts and enough life jackets for all 2,570 passengers and crew.

On a July morning in 1915, just a few months after the law was signed, some 2,573 passengers and crew loaded onto the *Eastland* preparing for a special excursion for employees of the Western Electric Company and their families. Unfortunately, the added weight of the safety equipment caused the ship to capsize while still tied to the dock.

"When the boat toppled on its side those on the upper deck were hurled off like so many ants being brushed from a table," wrote Harlan Babcock, a Chicago Herald reporter. "In an instant, the surface of the river was black with struggling, crying, frightened, drowning humanity. Wee infants floated about like corks."

Less than a year prior, 785 passengers were killed when the Lusitania was torpedoed and sunk. The Titanic disaster resulted in the deaths of 829 passengers (plus 694 crew members). The *Eastland* tragedy surpassed both when it took the lives of 844 passengers in an area where the water was just twenty feet deep.

The *Eastland* disaster is an example of how regulations can have unintentionally negative consequences for the very people they are meant to protect. There is no question that due to the SEC's work, it is harder today for an unscrupulous advisor to break the rules and take advantage of clients than it ever has been, but it is also becoming more difficult for ordinary people to get the investment advice they want due to the regulatory challenges investment professionals face.

In his book *Capitalism and Freedom*, Milton Friedman explains that the biggest advocates for increasing industry regulations are typically major industry players, not consumers. I witnessed this firsthand early in my career while I worked for H&R Block, the country's largest tax preparation firm. At the time, the IRS was pushing to dramatically increase the requirements to become a professional tax preparer. Even though the new standards would be very expensive for H&R Block to comply with, the company was among the new policy's biggest advocates.

Why would H&R Block press for a policy that would cost them so much money? They argued that it was the right thing to do for consumers, but what they really knew was that they had the infrastructure to train people on a massive scale that smaller tax preparation companies simply wouldn't be able to keep up with. The more difficult the regulations were to comply with, the greater the number of small tax firms H&R Block could push out of business. Large companies can absorb the cost of expanded regulations, while smaller companies may be forced to close or merge with another company in order to survive. In the end, the result is fewer choices for consumers, less competition, and higher prices.

Outside of major industry players, politicians are the next biggest advocates for regulation. After all, politicians need to constantly propose and pass new laws to convince us they're doing something. Here are two instances where Congress passed laws resulting in terrific protection for consumers.

The Federal Deposit Insurance Corporation (FDIC) was created by Congress in 1933. The FDIC provides insurance for bank customers against losing their deposits when a bank fails. Currently, the insurance amount covers up to $250,000 in bank deposits, which include checking accounts, savings accounts, and CDs, but it does not include investments like stock and mutual funds or annuities and other insurance contracts. Contents of safe deposit boxes are also excluded from FDIC protection.

First off, you'll want to verify that the bank you are using is a member of the FDIC. Most major banks are, but you can look up your bank on the FDIC website to be sure. You'll want to note that the $250,000 coverage amount is per depositor, not necessarily per account. For example, if you have $100,000 in a savings account, $150,000 in CDs, and $50,000 in a checking account for a total of $300,000 at one bank, you'd be insured for only $250,000 while leaving $50,000 without coverage. You may not think bank failures are something you need to worry about, but consider that nearly 500 banks have failed in the last ten years alone. Would you want to risk leaving any money unprotected?

There are two easy ways to protect deposits over the $250,000 limit. The first is to move some of your money to another bank. At a separate bank, you'll receive an additional $250,000 in coverage. As a note, it's important to be certain that the second bank is its own entity and not a subsidiary of a bank you already have deposits with. The second way to boost your deposit insurance is to utilize joint accounts. Establishing a joint account in most banks qualifies you as two separate depositors, even if you already have individual accounts at that bank. Each signer on the joint account receives $250,000 in coverage on their deposits so the joint account can be covered up to $500,000. Each of you would still be eligible for $250,000 in coverage on individual account deposits at the same bank. This would effectively allow a couple to cover up to $1 million with FDIC insurance at a single bank.

In 1970, congress acted to create **The Securities Investor Protection Corporation (SIPC)**. SIPC works in a manner similar to FDIC protection, but, instead of offering you protection on your bank deposits, SIPC protects assets you have at a brokerage firm if the firm is a SIPC member. SIPC will protect up to $500,000 of your securities if they go missing from a failing brokerage firm. This protection covers lost stocks, bonds, mutual funds, various other investments, and up to $250,000 in cash. It's important to understand that SIPC coverage does not protect you from the value of your investments falling. As an example, say you use $5,000 to buy 100 shares of a stock for $50 per share, then the price of that stock falls to $25 per share. You would have lost $2,500 and SIPC does not offer any protection for that loss. However, if the brokerage that held your shares collapsed and lost your 100 shares, SIPC would replace the current value of those lost shares whether that value is more or less than what you originally paid for them.

In the years following Bernie Madoff's arrest, SIPC hired Irving Picard as Trustee for the Madoff victims. Through the SIPC, Picard has recovered over $14 billion on behalf of Madoff victims to date. He continues to work on recovering additional lost funds more than a decade after the fraud was discovered. Most of the recovered $14 billion has been distributed to victims.

PROTECTING YOURSELF

Regulators have done the best they can to protect you, but at the end of the day, protecting your money comes down to you. Fraudsters are counting on you not to investigate before you invest. Fend them off by doing your own digging. It's not enough to ask for more information or for references, fraudsters have no incentive to set you straight. Take the time to do your own independent research. Let's close out this chapter with some tips to protect yourself and red flags to look out for.

Protect yourself with layers

If working with a financial advisor, make sure you don't hand your money directly to the advisor. When you write a check for funds to be invested, it should never be made out to your advisor. Instead, use a separate, reputable company to hold your investment assets and only give your advisor the authorization to make changes to how that money is invested. Don't allow an advisor to transfer money out of your account or write checks on your behalf. The institution that holds your assets, known as a custodian, will send you independent statements so that you can verify what's in your account and the transaction history. If your advisor goes out of business, gets arrested, or dies, your assets won't go down with him because they are safely held at a stable custodian and readily accessible by you.

Research before you invest
Unsolicited emails, message board postings, and company news releases should never be used as the sole basis for your investment decisions. Understand a company's business and its products or services before investing. Look for the company's financial statements on the SEC's EDGAR filing system online.

Know the salesperson
Spend some time checking out the person touting the investment before you invest – even if you already know the person socially. Always find out whether the securities salespeople who contact you are licensed to sell securities in your state and whether they or their firms have had run-ins with regulators or other investors. You can check out the disciplinary history of brokers and advisors for free using the SEC's and FINRA's online databases. Your state securities regulator may have additional information. You'll learn a lot more about advisors and how to check them out in Chapter Four.

Be wary of unsolicited offers
Be especially careful if you receive an unsolicited pitch to invest in a company or see it praised online but can't find current financial information about it from independent sources. It could be a "pump and dump" scheme. Be wary if someone recommends foreign or "off-shore" investments. If something goes wrong, it's harder to find out what happened and to locate money sent abroad.

Know what to look for
Make yourself knowledgeable about different types of fraud and red flags that may signal investment fraud. Learning the examples in this book has put you ahead of 99% of the population, but there are always new angles being developed to scam you out of your money. Keep learning.

Red flags for fraud and common persuasion tactics.
How do successful, financially intelligent people fall prey to investment fraud? Researchers have found that investment fraudsters hit their targets with an array of persuasion techniques that are tailored to the victim's psychological profile. Here are red flags to look for:

If it sounds too good to be true, it is
I know that's a cliché, but it's always a good reminder. Watch for "phantom riches." Compare the returns that you're being promised with current returns on well-known stock indexes. Any investment opportunity that claims you'll receive substantially more on your investment could be highly risky – and that means you might lose money. Be careful of claims that an investment will make "incredible gains," is a "breakout stock pick," or has "huge upside and almost no risk!" Claims like these are hallmarks of extreme risk or outright fraud.

"Guaranteed returns" aren't
Every investment carries some degree of risk, which is reflected in the rate of return you can expect to receive. If your money is perfectly safe, you'll most likely get a low return. High returns entail high risks, possibly including a total loss on the investments. Most fraudsters spend a lot of time trying to convince investors that extremely high returns are "guaranteed" or "can't miss." They try to plant an image in your head of what your life will be like when you are rich. Don't believe it.

Beware the "halo" effect
Investors can be blinded by a "halo" effect when a con artist comes across as likable or trustworthy. When we view the messenger in a positive light, we're less likely to question the message. Credibility can be faked. Check out their actual qualifications.

"Everyone is buying it"

Watch out for pitches that stress how, "everyone is investing in this, so you should too." Think about whether you are interested in the product. If a sales presentation focuses on how many others have bought the product, this could be a red flag.

Pressure to send money RIGHT NOW

Scam artists often tell their victims that this is a once-in-a-lifetime offer, and it will be gone tomorrow, but resist the pressure to invest quickly. Take the time you need to investigate before sending money.

Reciprocity

Fraudsters often try to lure investors through free investment seminars, figuring if they do a small favor for you, such as supplying a free lunch, you will do a big favor for them by investing in their product. There is never a reason to make a quick decision on an investment. If you attend a free lunch, take the material home and research both the investment and the individual selling it before you invest. Always make sure the product is right for you, that you understand what you are buying, and are aware of all the associated fees.

I've also included a list of questions to ask about particular investments or salespeople before you invest at the back of this book.

Unfortunately, there are so many types of frauds occurring today, ranging from identity fraud to charity fraud, that I couldn't cover everything here. However, learning the red flags to look out for will generally help you to quickly identify fraud before it's too late.

While becoming a victim of outright fraud is a frequent fear for investors, the chances of it happening to you are unlikely if you stay alert. Aside from fear of fraud, more people are concerned about being cajoled into investment products that they don't necessarily want. People fear winding up face-to-face with a high-pressure salesman and being forced into a decision they don't want to make. The next chapter covers in detail the sales techniques used to manipulate unsuspecting investors which is exactly why financial advisors don't want you to read it.

-CHAPTER SUMMARY-

- Falling victim to fraud remains one the biggest fears facing investors.

- Investing while fear persists reduces potential invest-ment returns.

- Fraud scams are numerous and varied. One of the best ways to avoid fraud is through patience.

- Requests for urgent action are the top hallmark of a fraudulent proposition.

- Investment disclosure documents may provide more information than everyday investors are willing to weed through.

- Regulations will provide you with some protections, but you are your best first and last defense

CHAPTER THREE

A Particular Set of Skills

*"There are worse things in life than death. Have you ever spent
an evening with an insurance salesman?"*
– Woody Allen

B Y 8AM, HUNDREDS OF PEOPLE filled the Anaheim
Convention Center's event hall. There was a buzz of excitement and anticipation as financial services professionals
poured in, each of them eager to enhance their careers with a set
of improved skills they hoped to acquire over several days of
intense training. Successful financial advisors complete some of
the most rigorous courses in any field. For hours on end, we intently focused on the teacher's every word as we feverishly
scribbled as much as we could onto our notepads. Each skill we
learned and mastered at this conference would increase our personal income. The more skills we mastered, the more money we
could make. At the end of the conference, we'd to be tested with
the highest-scoring individual earning the prize of an original oil
painting. I have no recollection of who the artist was honestly,
but I remember I wanted it.

After a full day of lectures, all I wanted to do was spend the
rest of my time studying. I drove my partner insane asking to be
quizzed incessantly and carried my study materials to breakfast,
lunch, and dinner. After days of staring at charts, graphs, and
various other illustrations, I felt prepared though less confident I

would have the top score. There were no multiple-choice questions on this test; either you knew the answer word for word or it cost you points.

Once the scores were tabulated and returned to the students, the instructor had all of us rise to our feet. He complimented us for even showing up and going through this enhanced learning process. Anyone serious in their field must continuously seek to improve their skills, and we were doing just that. Our instructor, who was an experienced multi-millionaire, announced he would begin to call out scores, and if a student's score was below the score called, they should take a seat.

With about 400 people standing, our instructor asked everyone who scored below 75 to be seated. Two dozen people took their seats. He called out, "80," and thirty-five more people sat. "85." Nearly fifty people dropped off. "90." One-third of those left standing were now seated.

At this point, I looked around the room and saw a hundred people still on their feet. Impressive numbers considering the material we had just covered and the difficulty of the test. I was proud to still be standing, scoring better than most of the students, but would I be the one to win the painting? I scored 104. There were a few bonus points I picked up, so I knew I had done well despite missing a couple of questions.

From here on, our instructor graduated the scores he called out by one number at a time. "91...92...93." Each score called out prompted another handful to take their seat. By the time he got to 100, less than 20 people were standing, and I started thinking I had a chance. "101...102...103." Still six others on their feet. Damn. The best I could do was tie. When 104 was called I had hoped everyone would sit with me, but I was the lone casualty. I don't recall what the top score was, but I came to the conclusion that the winner must have been a cheater. The painting was going home with someone else.

What motivates so many people to pay hundreds and thousands of dollars just for the pleasure of a weekend spent studying? The skills we were learning had nothing to do with investments. We didn't discuss new trends in investing, the latest financial products, or diversification. We were there to become incredible salespeople. We were studying like maniacs to learn how to convince customers who were ready to tell us "No" to say "Yes" instead.

In this industry, there is no skill that determines one's success more so than their ability to close a sale. It is so important that major financial service companies spend as much time training their employees in sales techniques as they do on product and investment knowledge. So, for those of us at the seminar, the promise of increasing our income by improving our ability to finalize sales every time we sat down with a potential customer was rather alluring.

Learning how much effort financial professionals put into honing their sales skills certainly won't help you trust the system much, but you must understand that this is the reality of the industry. The top salespeople in the financial services industry have a sophisticated set of selling skills, and when you meet with one of these sales experts, you won't even detect they're utilizing a sales technique with you. They'll simply sit down with you, have a seemingly casual discussion, and end the interaction accepting the check you were happy to write. Get the idea of the pushy car salesman out of your head. Yes, there are some "pushy" salespeople in the finance industry, but they don't usually stay in business very long.

In this chapter, I'm going to share with you some of the most common sales techniques used by financial salespeople today. Throughout the process of putting this book together, I debated whether to include this section or not. I asked not only was it appropriate in a book about investing, but could this section provide value to you. You're reading it now, so it's obvious that it made the cut. The information is valuable for a few reasons.

One, if someone is excessively using selling techniques on you, it may be an indicator of fraud, or at the least, a sign that you are being sold a product that doesn't necessarily serve you well. Second, even if you presently have no intentions of working with a financial advisor, most people experience rare events in their life that cause them to seek out professional advice, so understanding the sales techniques will be useful in that scenario. Third, salespeople are generally seen as individuals interested in helping themselves without providing a lot of benefit to the customer, but I'll talk about why that may not be entirely true.

Unfortunately, there are enough sales methods and tricks to fill a book - a lengthy one at that. I'm going to keep this section brief and cover a few of the most common tactics. Understanding some of these basic techniques will help you recognize when you're being sold to and help you keep your guard up when coming face-to-face with a great salesperson. By being aware of sales techniques, you can make the decisions based on what's right for you rather than being swayed by an unexpectedly persuasive pitch. What's exciting is that these techniques are frequently used by real estate agents, car salesmen, and virtually anyone who wants to get you to buy from them, and you'll be able to use the information in this chapter in other areas of your life.

KNOCKING YOUR GUARD DOWN

The salesperson's first step is to quickly build a relationship and knock down the walls that you put up when you first walked into his office. People are so used to being preyed upon by pushy salespeople, they have already adapted to preemptively put-up internal barricades and even form husband and wife pacts: "Honey, let's agree that whatever happens when we meet the advisor today, we are not buying *anything*!" Professional salespeople are prepared for this and methodically work to set you at ease and unbind loving couples from their pacts.

To get off to a good start, the professional salesperson will greet you kindly with a generous smile, a firm handshake, and a practiced amount of eye contact. Almost immediately he will drum up conversation about anything except finance. If he's any good at his job, he'll get you talking about yourself as much as possible. Great salespeople know that there is no topic a person is more interested in than themselves. A Harvard study showed that talking about ourselves is linked to pleasure and improves our self-perception. Most interesting, however, the study shows that talking about ourselves improves our impression of the person we're talking to! I'd guess that's why so many people fall in love with their therapists.

When I'm meeting with new clients, I'll usually start off with a seemingly generic question. "How long have you lived in the area?" That initiates a whole platform of questions I get to ask like, what part of town they live in, where they lived before, how they decided to move here, what schools their kids go to, if they have extended family in the area, do they commute for work, etc. It's not that I'm not genuinely interested in all of that, but I know the conversation is absolutely vital to getting their guard down. The goal for the salesperson is to get you talking about yourself as much as possible. He'll make sure to personally relate, when possible, but he wants to be the one listening, not talking.

In Dale Carnegie's *How to Win Friends and Influence People*, Carnegie puts it this way, "A person's toothache means more to that person than a famine in China which kills a million people. A boil on one's neck interests one more than forty earthquakes in Africa." When the salesperson shows the client that he is eager to listen about the topic nearest and dearest to that client's heart, it may be the first time in years anyone has really done so, and this spontaneously creates a positive connection between seller and client. After getting some time to talk about himself, the client will have almost entirely let the guard down, and he may sign a contract without even seeing a presentation.

ASKING QUESTIONS

If a salesperson sits back and lets you ask all the questions, it puts her in a reactionary position. When the salesperson is asking the questions, she can guide you in the direction she chooses. Many of the questions will be the expected exploratory questions used to determine appropriate products for you or to narrow in on what you might be willing to buy. Other questions have a little more intention to them.

Expert sales trainer and top-selling author Tom Hopkins teaches the phrase, "If *I* say it, they tend to doubt me. If *they* say it, it's true." The idea behind this phrase is that less successful salespeople attempt to *tell* their potential clients why their product's features are important and valuable. Unfortunately, people tend to distrust salesmen to begin with, so they instinctively dismiss any positive points a salesman shares with them. As consumers, we know he's going to tell us anything he can to get us interested, but, if I can get my client to state the value of a feature on their own, they will believe it.

For example, if I tell a client, "You should invest in stable and secure companies," she may doubt me or question the motive behind my statement. But, if I ask her whether she thinks it's a wise idea to invest in stable and secure companies she will say, "Yes, of course that's a good idea." Because *she* was the one to tell me it was a good idea; it would be almost impossible for me to convince her it wasn't.

Another question I commonly ask to lead my clients is, "In your opinion, do you think it's smarter to invest for the long-term rather than the short-term? Why?" Now I have the client selling me on the idea of investing long-term. Both of those questions guide my clients to believe what I want them, to even though I never actually tell them what I think. All I need to do is let the customer know we're going to make a plan to invest just the way they told me to.

As a way to enhance the effectiveness of asking questions, a professional salesperson has designed and rehearsed questions that are easy for you to say yes to. Adding phrases like "don't you agree", "wouldn't you", "isn't it", "aren't they," makes it virtually impossible for you to say no. "You want to live your golden years in comfort and security *don't you?*" No one can say no to that question. "If there was a way for you to meet your financial goals and dreams, you'd want to know all about it, *wouldn't you?*" Of course you would. If throughout your discussions, the salesperson has guided you to say yes to enough of his directed questions, it's simply a natural progression for you to say yes when he asks you to move forward with a new investment, buy a product, or approve the contract. You've already agreed to almost everything he's said, so what reasons could you possibly give to justify saying no when he asks you to sign on the line?

TAKING ADVANTAGE OF EMOTIONS

While we all like to think we are logical calculating creatures when it comes to investments or any major purchase for that matter, the truth is the absolute opposite. The biggest factor in our decision-making process is how that decision will make us feel. There are very few logical reasons to buy a new BMW, yet millions are sold every year. Why? Because owning a BMW helps a person feel important, feel successful, feel superior. Even though a BMW is far less reliable than a Toyota, people make the decision to pay double or triple the price of that reliable Toyota for the emotional gratification of driving the BMW.

Don't worry, salespeople know this, and they are ready for you. While a salesperson will cover the logical reasons you need to make a decision, they will focus on how the decision will affect you emotionally. If we continue with our car analogy, you may have noticed how eager car dealerships are to get you inside the car and behind the wheel. The test drive has nothing to do with you "testing" the car. Once you are behind the wheel, you subconsciously begin to imagine yourself owning the car. The emotions behind this are enhanced if your children come along for the ride. While on the test drive, the salesperson may ask which way you drive to work. This will help you imagine yourself driving your new car to work and showing off to your co-workers. If it's a particularly flashy car, the salesperson may suggest you drive near the local mall or other crowded areas to help you experience the feeling of being seen in a high-end car. After a successful test drive (and already owning the car in your mind), you may find it nearly impossible to return to that old jalopy you drove up in.

To help my clients' emotions take over, I deploy more intentional questions. While I can't offer a test drive, what's easy to do is ask questions. "What are some of the things you'd like to do if money wasn't an issue?", "How would it make you **feel** to know you were a millionaire?" , "Wouldn't it **feel** great to know your loved ones will be taken care of financially if anything happens to you?"

After answering simple questions like these, my clients are eager to start their financial plans. Nearly all decisions a person makes are based on how each of those decisions will make him feel. We tend to decide emotionally, then look for logical reasons to reinforce our emotional decisions. Be mindful of salespeople who stir your emotions; they are doing so with a purpose.

TRICKS

There are a few techniques in sales that I would classify as tricks. Here are a few examples:

Three Choices

Whenever possible, financial professionals want to offer three price ranges for a product. A low-priced, mid-priced, and high-priced choice. The professional will list the price he wants you to pay in the middle because he knows that's the most likely choice you'll make. This is due to something called extremeness aversion, and it preys on a person's inclination to avoid purchasing items in either the upper extreme or lower extreme. No one wants to overpay or be known as a cheapskate, so when three pricing options are available, people tend to pick the middle option. You've probably noticed that fast food restaurants offer three drink sizes. Even if the large is the least popular choice, simply having it available prompts customers who were considering the small to upgrade to medium instead.

Reducing Perception of Price

If there is ever an inkling that a customer may have a problem with the price, the salesperson will work to break it down to the smallest amount possible, making the customer feel foolish for claiming they can't afford it. Most commonly, the breakdown will be expressed in dollars or cents per day. For example, if a client claims an investment is $60 over her monthly budget I'd work into the conversation a phrase like, "You wouldn't say just $2 a day is too much to ensure the financial security of your family, would you?"

Either/Or Choice

This is simply a tricky way to get you to move one step closer to finalizing a purchase. The financial professional will ask you a question that offers you two choices, but whichever you choose, you're committing to buying. Before you've even stated you'd like to move forward, the salesperson will ask a question like this, "Would you like to add to your investments on a monthly basis or would you rather do so weekly?" Either way you answer this question, you've told the salesperson you want to start adding to your investments. It is easier for you to simply choose one of the options than it would be to object completely and say something like, "No, I'm not ready to move forward yet." This trick takes advantage of a person's natural tendency to take the path of least resistance.

The Door in the Face Technique

This is a simple method used by a salesperson to shock you into agreeing to a purchase. First, the professional will propose something fairly outrageous to which you immediately refuse to agree. He then proposes a much more reasonable suggestion, and you are happy to accept the scaled-back proposition. For example, the professional says, "I recommend you invest every penny you own in this amazing annuity!" To which you reply, "I need to think about it." The professional then counters with, "I'm glad you want to think about putting all your money into this annuity. Take all the time you need. While you're thinking about putting *all* of your money in, why don't we just start with about a quarter of all your money and go from there?" You say, "Oh, sure. That sounds much better!" Enjoy your new annuity!

Benjamin Franklin Method

Benjamin Franklin is considered one of America's wisest men. If something was the right thing to do, Ben wanted to be sure to do it. If it was the wrong thing, he wanted to be sure to avoid it. Whenever Benjamin Franklin had a difficult decision to make, he would take a sheet of paper, draw a line down the center, and label one side yes and the other no. Ben listed out the pros for making the decision under yes and any reason against making the decision under no. Once done, Ben would tally up each side and his decision was made. When using this method, the salesperson might explain that it was the method Benjamin Franklin used or she might not. The important distinction will be that the salesperson will be feeding you ideas she already knows you like for the yes column, but not offering any suggestions for the no column. When you're finished totaling your columns you might be surprised to see the yes column with two or three times as many reasons as the no column. With that staring you in the face, you'd have to defy the wisdom of Benjamin Franklin to walk away without buying.

Exclusivity/Scarcity

This is a common technique used across all industries. For some reason, we love having things that other people don't and hate missing out. Often, all a salesperson needs to do is say, "This is the last one we have," and they've made the sale. When it comes to financial advisors, it will be used to convince clients to act now. "There might not be a better time to invest than right now." "You might want to buy now before these low rates are gone." "I can only take on so many more clients before I need to turn people away." These phrases are all sales techniques.

Referrals Pulled from Thin Air

In his book on the psychology of persuasion, *Influence*, Dr. Robert Cialdini writes that "We view a behavior as more correct in a given situation to the degree that we see others performing it." This is why review sites like Yelp have become so popular in recent years. What's interesting is that people tend to trust reviews and opinions of strangers at least as much as they trust reviews from friends and family. Before making a decision, people want to see social proof that someone else has made that same decision and was happy with the outcome. A good salesperson knows that clients don't even need to know another person's name to accept their actions as social proof before deciding. The salesperson simply needs to tell the story of a previous client who was in a similar situation, how the salesperson's product resolved their problem, and how happy that previous client is now. Wondrously, the new client will feel more comfortable making the decision to buy even though they'll never meet or talk to the salesperson's prior client.

WHAT IF THIS IS A GOOD THING?

What I hope you have now is a basic understanding of this concept: your casual conversation with a financial professional may have many underlying layers of subtle manipulation steering you in the direction the salesperson wants you to go. Don't be afraid to leave the meeting without making any final decisions. An honest advisor would be happy to let you take the time you need to think about your decision. Now that you have a general understanding of some of the sales techniques finance professionals may use on you, do you consider it to be a negative factor or would you consider their sales skills a plus for you, the customer?

A few years back I sat down with a client to help her with her budget, and we discussed her overall financial situation. One of my favorite customers, she'd walk into a room with an infectious smile, no matter the challenges she faced. It was a characteristic that was easy to admire. She was struggling financially as a single mother after a recent divorce and just wondering how to make ends meet. Through the course of our discussion, it came out that she had no life insurance. I suggested she obtain at least a minimal amount in case something was to happen to her. I showed her pricing of just $30 per month, but given that she had mentioned to me she was having a hard time just keeping gas in her car, I made the decision to not use any sales techniques with her and not push any further.

Ordinarily, I would have needed to apply four of the sales techniques I covered earlier to ensure she would purchase the insurance. First, and most importantly, I would appeal to her emotions by asking, "How would you feel if something unexpected happened to you, and it was up to your friends and family to pay for your final expenses at the worst possible time?" Second, I would point out that the cost of the insurance was less than one dollar a day. Even your brokest friend would have a hard time arguing they couldn't afford just one dollar. Third, I would ask a question that was easy for her to say yes to, "You'd be happy knowing everything was taken care of financially if something happened to you, wouldn't you?" Last, I would ask, "Would you like to have your payment start on the 1st of the month or the 15th?" Using just those four techniques would be enough to convince 90% of people to go ahead and purchase. There is no skill more important for a financial professional than the ability to get other people to say, "yes."

Now my question for you is, should I have used all of my sales skills to persuade this customer, one who could barely afford gas, to purchase a life insurance policy? Would that be considered manipulative? $30 a month can add up quickly in hard times. I knew the policy was appropriate for her, and I'd earn a small commission if I sold it to her, but I also was aware that the monthly payment would be an additional burden on her.

She left without buying life insurance, and I would never see her again. Just a few weeks later, she lost control of her car, causing it to violently flip multiple times. That lovely lady died at the scene. Her friends and family resorted to an online fundraiser to scrape together enough money to pay for her funeral costs. Yes, I should have pushed her to get the insurance. Her family at this point would likely agree. One could argue that it was her decision to make, but it's human nature to put off any kind of financial planning decisions until a "better time." That's why, as a financial planner, I have a responsibility beyond giving appropriate advice, and it's to convince people to make the right decisions and implement them quickly.

Salespeople have a poor reputation, and in many cases, justifiably so, but it's also important to understand that selling skills for financial professionals are vitally important to making sure that our customers get on the right track and have the proper financial plan in place. Have you ever put off setting up an IRA, preparing a will, or buying life insurance even when you knew you needed to do it? A good salesperson would have made sure you got it done, and when it comes to investing, waiting can cost you serious money. The story I told is not the only incident where I let a customer slip away without being able to get the necessary aspects of their financial plan in place. In the past, I've been unable to convince a potential client to change their investment plan, only to cross paths with them again years down the road. They never made any changes and had missed out on life-changing investment gains. Dalbar research found that stock market investors in 2021 earned returns that were 10% lower than stock market returns in general. Perhaps if those individuals had been "sold" a better investment plan, their returns would be much higher.

We do need to make the distinction between the right and wrong recommendations. There is no question that some financial professionals use powerful sales techniques to sell products that benefit the salesperson more than the client. These are not the honest advisors you want. When advanced selling skills are used to sell you the wrong investments, the better the salesperson, the more harm they can do. But when the plan they are selling is high quality, you'd better hope they close the deal with you and convince you to act.

There are several different types of financial advisors, but the techniques we have covered here apply to them all. When the time comes for you to seek guidance from a financial advisor, remember to be aware of the tricks and sales methods they'll be using. There is no reason for you to make a decision on the spot. An important aspect of working with a financial advisor is understanding exactly what type of advisor they are, the type of advice they can and cannot give, and the surprisingly complicated ways they earn money by convincing you to take their advice. By understanding the differences in advisors, you can feel confident about working with one who specializes in the advice you need

-CHAPTER SUMMARY-

- Financial services companies spend as much time training their agents on sales techniques as they do training them for technical skills.

- Expert salespeople utilize questions to control your conversation and influence your opinion on the decision.

- Financial salespeople will deliberately evoke your emotions to help convince you to buy.

- Sales tricks are commonly used to manipulate your decision.

- Working with a good salesperson can benefit you if it helps you implement important financial decisions you would otherwise put off.

CHAPTER FOUR

The Professionals

*"Good advice is always certain to be ignored,
but that's no reason not to give it."*
– Agatha Christie

IF YOU'RE LIKE ME, at one point in your life you've owned
a car that was a few years older and had a few more miles on
the odometer than you would've liked. You may have had an
experience where you hit the gas, and out of nowhere, the car
sputtered as the check engine light flickered on. For you maybe
it was something else like the temperature gauge suddenly
climbing into the red, a new suspicious noise coming from under
the hood, or an ominous puddle on your driveway. The last thing
you'd want to do at that point is pay for major repairs. After all,
if you had money to spare, you wouldn't be driving that old car
to begin with, right? But what did you decide to do? If you're
like most people, after a period of denial, finger-crossing, and
hope that whatever the problem was would go away on its own,
you'd end up taking the car to a mechanic. Why though? You're
an intelligent person, you could study the problem, read a book
on cars, research online, talk to friends, and figure out how to fix
the car on your own saving a lot of money.

Changing a set of brakes is fairly simple. Most people can
handle the job in about an hour, and it usually doesn't require
special tools beyond a set of wrenches. So why do most people

fork over hundreds of dollars to have someone else do the job for them?

The process of changing your brakes may be a simple one, but it's also one of the most critical tasks in your life. Imagine making the tiny mistake of forgetting to tighten a bolt. You'd be putting your family's lives at risk. This is why we trust the job of replacing our brakes to professionals. The task is routine for them, something they might do a half-dozen times daily. Most likely, they have a system that ensures the job is done right, and certainly, no bolts will be left undone. Meanwhile, as the mechanic performs the task, he'll probably catch a few other things you didn't even know to look for like your brake fluid running low or a torn CV boot. We pay that extra money for the peace of mind that the job is done right, not necessarily because of the difficulty of the job. In many cases, this is the benefit of working with a financial advisor.

In an episode of one of my favorite shows, *Seinfeld*, Jerry laments a problem he's facing while working with a new mechanic after he had a falling out with his old, trusted mechanic. Jerry explains to his best friend, George, that he's worried the new mechanic might be trying to screw him. George emphatically responds, "Well of course they're trying to screw you! That's what they do. They can make up anything! Nobody knows!" Then George explains if the mechanic said you needed a new "Johnson Rod," you'd just have to take his word for it, 'Oh a Johnson Rod? Well, I guess you better put one of those on!'" I believe this is what we all fear when seeking help from experts. None of us want to be taken advantage of and sold a "Johnson Rod" because of our ignorance.

You could personally handle just about everything a financial advisor can do for you. The caveat is that you must commit to studying the investing process, learn investing strategies, understand tax laws, and more. And you need to do a thorough job of it. I already know you're the type of person who's made a commitment to understanding investing because you've chosen to read this book. It's something you need to take seriously. Missing one concept can cost you thousands or hundreds of thousands of dollars. Not to mention, studies show that investors who work with professional advisors earn a higher rate of return on average.

Think about it this way, if you consider yourself partially competent with your investing, it means you must consider yourself incompetent at the same time. There are so many concepts and pitfalls that it's relatively simple to take a misstep because of what you haven't even realized you don't know. I can't tell you how many times I've seen people lose thousands of dollars to taxes by making "backdoor" ROTH contributions after reading *almost* everything about it online and missing one important snag. Unless you've made the decision to get highly competent with your finances, you'll eventually need to find someone competent to help. After you've finished reading this book, you'll know more about investing than 99.9% of the entire world. Not bad, but a professional advisor will know even more. FINRA, the agency that develops exam requirements for investment advisors, now offers a free seventy-five-question practice version of its Securities Industry Essentials exam online. If you decide to compare your knowledge to the beginning requirements of industry experts, it's worth a go.

This chapter will clear up everything you need to know about financial advisors, from understanding how they work to how they get paid, and how to choose the right one for you.

PROFESSIONAL DESIGNATIONS

According to the Financial Industry Regulatory Authority (FINRA), there are close to two hundred designations for financial professionals. Professional designations allow people to list fancy letters after their names on business cards and advertisements. There are designations for virtually any professional specialization in finance, from the most well-known designation,

CPA (Certified Public Accountant), to the obscure RFG (Registered Financial Gerontologist).

What are they? Each of these designations has the principal purpose of helping the professional market himself to potential clients or employers by advertising that he or she has completed specialized studies in a particular concentration. Each designation is obtained through various certifying agencies which have developed their own particular standards for each designation they issue. Almost all issuing agencies are independent of government entities and are frequently non-profit organizations. The two most notable exceptions are the CPA and Enrolled Agent (EA) designations, both subject to government oversight.

Most professional designations do not give the designation holder the legal right to practice in any given field, that is, they are not licenses. However, they do demonstrate that the designation holder has gone above and beyond in his or her studies on a particular subject. Let's talk about some of the most common designations and what they mean to you.

CPA- Certified Public Accountant
The CPA designation is one of the most widely known and understood. The requirements to earn the CPA certification vary from state to state. For an individual to earn the right to display the designation in California, she must first obtain a bachelor's degree with a specific amount of coursework in accounting and business studies. Secondly, she must meet a minimum requirement of 500 hours of work experience in a field related to accounting. Third, she must pass the CPA examination. The CPA exam has four sections and lasts up to a combined 16 hours. An individual can expect to pay several thousand dollars for the initial CPA registration plus ongoing renewal fees and continuing education costs. The Certified Public Accountant designation is among the most respected and challenging to obtain.

Typically, a CPA can help you with those tricky tax situations. However, one misconception about CPAs is that they primarily focus on income taxes. A typical CPA spends most of his time working with businesses, helping them make sure their record-keeping and financial statements are in order and advising them on potential business operating decisions. To put it in perspective, the CPA exam has four main sections, and the topic of personal income taxes only makes up about 30% of one of those sections. Starting in 2024, recent updates to the CPA exam allow candidates to select a specialization, and one of the available options is a specialization in tax compliance and planning. If you want a CPA to prepare your personal income taxes, make sure it's something that particular CPA specializes in. If you run a business, a CPA can be extremely valuable to you.

CFP - Certified Financial Planner
Amongst professional designations in financial services, the Certified Financial Planner designation is one of the most sought-after. The CFP designation is the only designation that resembles the credibility and recognizability of the Certified Public Accountant designation. The CFP Board oversees the CFP certification. The CFP Board is a non-profit organization founded in 1985 to promote competent and ethical financial planning services.

Requirements for obtaining a CFP certificate are similar to those of a CPA although slightly less stringent. The CFP board requires anyone who hopes to earn the CFP designation to hold a Bachelor's degree from an accredited college. The degree can be in any field of study, from economics to political science and everything in between. The CFP Board requires specific additional coursework covering the many aspects of financial planning. The CFP Board suggests this coursework should take most candidates one to two years to complete and covers insurance, investment, income tax, retirement, and estate planning.

In addition to the education requirements, a CFP candidate must have 6,000 hours of financial planning-related work or 4,000 hours under the supervision of an experienced CFP. However, the required experience can be something as simple as gathering client data and not necessarily developing or providing financial planning advice.

The third requirement for acquiring the right to use the CFP designation is to take and pass the CFP exam. The CFP exam is not quite as intimidating as the CPA exam, but it is still extraordinarily challenging. The test consists of a pair of 3-hour sessions with a 40-minute break between the two. Only 63% of those who attempt the exam pass.

When it comes to financial planning, the CFP certification is considered the gold standard. A CFP is well-equipped to help you set up a comprehensive financial plan or solve a challenge you have in a targeted area of your finances.

ChFC - Chartered Financial Consultant

A Chartered Financial Consultant is an expert at financial planning. The Chartered Financial Consultant designation is not nearly as well known as the CFP, perhaps because it's just not as easy to say, but the knowledge and skill necessary to obtain either designation is about equal. The ChFC certification process requires more extensive coursework than a CFP certification. A ChFC must pass an exam after each course, rather than a single comprehensive exam like the CFP. A Chartered Financial Consultant must complete continuing education programs every two years and have at least three years of experience before earning the designation. As far as most consumers should be concerned, a CFP and ChFC are equally qualified.

EA - Enrolled Agent

An Enrolled Agent is a tax specialist who has earned the privilege of representing taxpayers before the Internal Revenue Service by either passing three separate four-hour comprehensive IRS exams or through experience as an IRS employee. Enrolled agent status is the highest credential the IRS awards. Individuals who obtain this elite status must adhere to ethical standards.

While there is no formal education requirement before becoming an Enrolled Agent, they must complete 72 hours of continuing education courses every three years. Enrolled agents specialize in preparing tax returns, offering tax advice, and representing clients with the IRS if they are audited or have other tax issues.

CLU - Chartered Life Underwriter

The Chartered Life Underwriter specializes in life insurance and estate planning. To earn this designation, the individual must complete eight courses through the American College as well as pass eight 100-question, two-hour exams. The CLU is the oldest designation, established in 1927, and is considered the most respected designation in the insurance field.

CFA – Chartered Financial Analyst

This designation is issued by the CFA Institute and, according to them, is the most respected and recognized investment management designation in the world. Individuals who have earned this designation are experts in analyzing and choosing investments. The CFA courses are some of the hardest courses required amongst any of the designations listed here. A CFA's specialization is primarily on the technical aspects of investments and very little on topics like personal taxes and insurance. If you're looking for someone to give you advice on your investments but not necessarily provide a comprehensive financial plan, a CFA is a top choice.

RIA - Registered Investment Adviser

You may see RIA listed on business cards or on a company's website, but an RIA is not a professional designation. The Registered Investment Adviser name is a little confusing because it does not refer to an individual. An RIA can only be a business, not a person. The fact that a company advertises itself as an RIA means that they are registered with the Securities and Exchange

Commission or their state's regulatory authority to charge a fee for providing investment advice. Many of the professionals who carry some of the designations covered in this section will work for a Registered Investment Adviser. I'll cover RIA's in more detail in the next section.

PFS - Personal Financial Specialist
The PFS designation can only be given to an individual who is a CPA. The Personal Financial Specialist education and exam requirements cover topics like investing, estate planning, insurance, and more. CPAs who are generally well-versed in business operations, as well as tax laws and tax advice, will pursue the PFS designation if they want their clients to know they are knowledgeable in general financial planning as well.

In addition to the most common designations above, many focus on clients with specific needs. For example, the three most credible designations for retirement experts are:

RMA - Retirement Management Analyst, CRC - Certified Retirement Counselor, RICP - Retirement Income Certified Professional
Each of these designations are frequently considered "add-on" designations. Meaning they are often earned by a professional who already has additional certifications, such as a Certified Financial Planner who wants to focus on clients in or nearing retirement. The focus of professionals with these designations is to make sure clients have the retirement income they need (or want) from year to year, while also maximizing potential investment growth. In addition to investment advice, these professionals are useful for developing strategies involving such subjects as Social Security, pensions, and annuities.

Other areas where specialized financial designations are available include divorce, college savings, estate planning, real estate investing, and more. It's important not to assume that because an individual lists a few letters after their name on a business card or advertisement, that they have a specialized level of knowledge or are more qualified to help you. Some designations don't require much more from an advisor than to pay a fee for the right to use that credential in marketing materials. Therefore, it's important to investigate not only what the designation stands for, but also what requirements a financial professional must fulfill to obtain the credential.

Fortunately, the Financial Industry Regulatory Authority (FINRA) has developed a useful tool to help weed out any inferior or even fake designations. They have listed all accredited designations on their website with a brief summary of the prerequisites, education requirements, examination type, and what, if any, continuing education is required to obtain and keep the designation.

You can access the tool on their site here:
http://www.finra.org/investors/professional-designations

When it comes to a financial professional's designations, make sure you understand what they mean and how that professional's credentials relate to what you want to accomplish. An advisor will definitely use his or her credentials to justify charging you more. A professional can have one, many, or none of these designations and their level of service and expertise will vary regardless of which credentials they carry.

HOW THEY GET PAID

Now that you have an understanding of what various professional titles mean, let's talk about the three major types of advisors you're most likely to encounter when seeking investment advice. While professional designations help you get a clearer picture of the educational background and an advisor's area of specialization, it's even more important to understand what type of advisor the person is. Knowing what type of advisor you're working with will help you understand exactly what type of advice they are authorized to give, how they are being paid, and makes it easy for you to identify their conflicts of interest when serving you.

Life Insurance Agent

This book is about investing, so why is a life insurance agent the first type of financial advisor you need to know about? Life insurance can be very complicated, and I believe a lot of the complication is intentional to confuse consumers. Many life insurance agents market themselves as financial planners, retirement experts, or wealth managers, but without additional licenses, life insurance agents cannot legally give you advice on the one thing you need most in any financial plan: investments.

So how can they possibly market themselves as financial planners? Agents can get around this restriction by presenting you with a life insurance policy with investment-like components or suggesting an annuity. There are two main categories of life insurance, low-cost term policies that cover you for a specific period of time (which I recommend) and high-priced cash-value policies that have a savings or investing component. It will take an entire book to cover life insurance sufficiently, but for the vast majority of people, cash-value life insurance policies do nothing for you and everything for the person selling them.

If cash-value life insurance policies are such bad investments, why do people continue to buy them? Recall the sales techniques we talked about in the previous chapter and know that when it comes to using them, life insurance agents are the best of the best. There is a common saying that life insurance is sold, not bought. I've found that to be very accurate. Life insurance agents are typically paid solely by commission, so if they aren't good at selling, they'll starve. When selling these policies, agents typically focus on the fact that a cash-value life insurance policy can potentially give you access to funds without incurring taxes by borrowing money from the policy instead of withdrawing it. The agents tend to ignore that the many costs and restrictions in the underlying policy will severely handicap your investment returns.

The agent's commission is based on a percentage of the premium their customer pays to buy the policy, so the more expensive the policy, the more the agent makes. Not only is the agent compelled to sell the more expensive cash-value policy simply because his commission will be based on a larger premium, but, in general, a life insurance company provides even further incentive to agents who sell cash-value policies instead of term policies. An agent who sells the more economical term life policy will earn an average commission of about 70% of the policy's first year's premium.

For example, if the policy he sells is $50 per month, the agent's commission will be based on a $600 first-year premium. $600 x 70% = $420 in commission. However, insurance companies typically pay agents who sell the more expensive cash-value policies anywhere from 80%-110% of the first year's premiums. So not only will the agent's commission be based on a higher amount of premium dollars for a more expensive policy, he will also earn a higher commission percentage for selling the more expensive policy.

Cash-value policies are the insurance companies' most profitable life insurance policies. How likely is it that the same product could generate the most profit for the insurance company providing it, the highest commission to the agent selling it, and still be the best for the person buying it?

In the vacuum of only being able to sell life insurance policies and not investments, it makes sense in the life insurance agent's eyes that the cash-value policy is the best option for the consumer. Insurance companies train their agents to sincerely believe that high-cost cash-value life insurance is the very best product for virtually every type of consumer.

The barrier to entry for becoming a life insurance agent is relatively low. To become a life insurance agent, an individual must take a pre-licensing course of around 25-60 hours, depending on their state, pass a background check, and they must pass a life insurance exam. That's generally all it takes to legally start a life insurance advisor career. This is why many financial services professionals start their careers selling life insurance, myself included. However, for the agents, it's also an "easy come, easy go" story as four out of five agents will quit within their first two years. Without learning the sales skills we covered earlier in the book, most new agents' careers end before they even get going.

So, is there a time when it makes sense to work with a life insurance agent? Yes, but when it comes to your investing strategy, you should avoid these types of advisors. They are simply not equipped to offer you investment advice and cannot serve you in that capacity. Reserve meeting with a life insurance agent for when you seek life insurance protection for you and your family, not investment advice.

Full-Service Broker-Dealer

The next category of advisor involves two different titles. However, the two are very similar, and many firms operate as both, so it makes sense to combine them here. One is a broker, and the other is a dealer. You will frequently hear them referred to as broker-dealers. The term broker-dealer may be used to describe an individual person or an entire firm. Frequently, the advisor you work with will be an agent of a broker-dealer firm and, in that case, the agent would be known as a Registered Representative.

The differences between how a broker and a dealer operate are slight. A broker will execute trades of stocks, bonds, and mutual funds in a customer's account. A full-service broker can charge a flat fee as high as $150 to execute a trade for a customer. More frequently, however, a broker will be paid a commission for selling you a mutual fund. This specific commission is known as a load or sales charge and is commonly as much as 5% of your investment amount.

Imagine investing $100,000 dollars. With a 5% sales charge, only $95,000 would actually be invested while the remaining $5,000 would be paid to the broker as a commission. That seems like a high price to pay, doesn't it? Generally, as you increase the dollar amount of your investment, the sales charge rate goes down. For example, an individual who purchases $1,000 of a particular mutual fund may pay a 5% sales charge, while someone who purchases $50,000 may pay 4%. This fee-per-transaction model creates an unwanted incentive for brokers to make unnecessary trades in a customer's account.

If they are paid every time you buy or sell an investment the broker is motivated to suggest that you switch investments more frequently. When brokers make frequent unnecessary trades in an individual's account for the purpose of generating commissions, the activity is referred to as "churning," and it's illegal. Because of this conflict of interest, and the growing stigma of the commission-based advisor, some brokers have begun to provide investment advice and execute trades for an annual fee based on a percentage of assets under management. This fee is often 1%-1.5% annually, but this arrangement is less common among brokers.

When operating as a dealer, the broker-dealer buys and sells investments for its own account. The dealer can then sell those investments to individual investors for a marked-up price, and the difference will be the dealer's profit. A simple way to remember the difference between a broker and a dealer is to imagine a real estate broker and a car dealer. The real estate broker finds some property that's a good fit for you and then arranges a deal with a seller so that you can buy it. The broker is then compensated with a commission once the purchase is complete. The car dealer owns the vehicles at the dealership and sells them to you for more than his purchase price to make a profit. Either way, they can only earn money if you purchase from them. So any advice one of these two advisors offers will almost always suggest that you change your investments, regardless of what you may already own.

It's somewhat more difficult to become a broker-dealer than a life insurance agent. In order to become a broker-dealer, an individual typically needs to be sponsored by a financial services company. In most states, the individual will be required to pass two exams that cover a wide range of investment topics. She may take the FINRA Series 7 exam, which will allow her to sell individual stocks for a commission, or she may take the Series 6, which gives the individual the authorization to sell mutual funds and earn commissions. In addition, to become a broker, most states require an individual to pass the Series 63 exam, which covers the specifics of financial industry rules, regulations, and ethics. The exams are significantly more difficult than the life insurance exam, and along with passing a background check, they are the only requirements that need to be met for someone to start selling you investments.

Working with a broker-dealer is a better option for investors than working with someone who is strictly a life insurance agent. A broker-dealer is at the very least, equipped to provide you with the investments you'll need to achieve your goals and dreams. In many cases, however, most people will find the commissions to be too high, especially when purchasing mutual funds with a high sales charge.

Many experts say *never* buy a mutual fund with a sales charge, but there's at least one scenario where it may make sense to do so. Investors who are starting with very little could benefit from working with a broker. In an instance where an individual can only afford $25 a month to invest, it would be very difficult to find an investment advisor who will work with them. However, many full-service brokers are willing to take on small accounts and provide investment advice.

With that being said, is working with a broker-dealer the best choice for most investors looking for professional help? Probably not. Until recently, an investor starting with smaller amounts would find it cost prohibitive to invest on their own as most discount brokers (Ameritrade, E-trade, etc.) would charge $6 on average each time you wanted to purchase an investment. Imagine trying to invest $25 a month and having $6 of that go towards fees. In a scenario like that, working with a broker made a lot of sense. However, due to recent competition and advancing technology, most discount brokers have eliminated their fees to buy an investment. In most scenarios, it would be difficult to get completely unbiased advice from a broker-dealer because you know they absolutely must sell you something to get paid. It may make sense for you to keep your money in an old 401(k), but I doubt you could ever find a broker who would tell you that. As long as your money is in the 401(k), he can't make any money.

Discount Brokers

I briefly mentioned discount brokers earlier. They are a subset of the Broker-Dealer family but don't quite merit their own section. A discount broker does the same job of orchestrating the buying or selling of various investments that a full-service broker does, but the discount broker does so without advising you on which investments to pick. Most of these types of brokers work primarily online. Fidelity, Charles Schwab, and Vanguard are examples of popular online discount brokerages. When using a discount brokerage, you must decide which investments you want to make on your own. You then typically enter instructions to buy or sell investments on their websites, and the brokerage executes those instructions on your behalf. Most transactions will result in a fee of $10 or less, but some may be much higher or even free depending on the particular investment. Many discount brokerages also offer a full-service brokerage plan and will often work to convince you to upgrade to a more expensive service.

Registered Investment Adviser

As we previously discussed, a Registered Investment Adviser (RIA) is not a person but a firm registered with either the Securities Exchange Commission or their state's regulators to offer investment advice and for a fee. The individual who works for a Registered Investment Adviser (RIA) is an Investment Adviser Representative (IAR). You'll almost never see the letters IAR or title of Investment Adviser Representative on a business card.

To become an IAR, the individual must pass a single exam, the Series 65, or hold a specific professional designation such as a Certified Financial Planner (CFP). The Series 65 exam covers content similar to the Series 6, 7, and 63 exams required for brokers. The exam is challenging, but no other requirements must be met to offer investment advice other than following strict regulations and record-keeping requirements.

An Investment Adviser Representative is held to the highest standard of fiduciary duty for his clients. This means that the advisor is required to make decisions solely based on what is best for the client. While that's something that you might expect to go without saying, it's unfortunately not the case universally.

Surprisingly, this standard of care has been lacking in other forms of advisors (i.e. brokers or life insurance agents). Previously, other advisors would simply have to follow a standard of suitability for their clients. Meaning the advisor would have to make sure the type of investment was, at the least, appropriate for the client but could still suggest investments that are unnecessarily expensive to generate larger commissions. An Investment Adviser Representative is held to a fiduciary standard and is legally obligated to suggest the best investment type for the client while also considering costs and other factors. Financial planning expert Michael Kitces described the differences in these two different standards in terms of buying a new suit. If adhering to the lesser standard of suitability, the individual selling you the suit would have to make sure it fits. If adhering to the higher fiduciary standard, the salesperson would not only have to make sure the suit fits but also make sure it looks good on you.

An Investment Adviser Representative does not earn commission unless dual-licensed as a broker or life insurance agent. You pay an IAR for advice, not to sell you something. Most commonly, an IAR will charge an hourly fee for their advice or charge a fee based on the amount of assets under management (the dollar value of your account with the IAR). More recently, some IARs have started charging a monthly subscription fee for ongoing advice, but this is still fairly uncommon. When an IAR charges a fee based on assets under management, the fee will typically range from 0.50% to 3% annually. Like the breakpoints in mutual fund commission rates, an IAR will discount rates for larger account sizes.

When an Investment Adviser Representative charges clients a fee based on a percentage of assets under management, the advisor still has an inherent conflict of interest. Although he will not earn a commission based on his various investment recommendations, he must convince you to move your assets under his management. This can mean that an IAR may still persuade a client to switch investments even if there is no benefit to the client, simply so the client's assets can be placed under the advisor's management and provide him with ongoing fees.

A common occurrence of this practice is when a client comes to an IAR wondering if she should move money out of an old 401(K). In most cases, an IAR charging you based on assets under management will have difficulty collecting their fees if they don't persuade you to move those assets out of that old 401(K). Now, sometimes it is the best advice to roll over an old 401(k) from an employer you no longer work for, but in some cases, particularly if your old employer was a very large company, it makes sense to just keep the assets there. So, how can you get unbiased advice from anyone?

Investment Adviser Representatives who charge you either a fixed fee or hourly fee for advice are the only option to truly get unbiased advice. There is a disclaimer, however. If an hourly fee or fixed fee IAR is also licensed as an insurance agent or broker, that conflict of interest still exists, and you cannot be completely confident that their advice is unbiased. Fortunately, an Investment Adviser Representative is legally required to disclose whether they are licensed insurance agents or brokers and specifically spell out conflicts of interest to you prior to signing any contracts. Be aware that this disclosure may come buried in a stack of paperwork that you are likely to gloss over. IAR's who never earn commissions will typically market themselves as "fee-only" advisors.

There are very few conflicts of interest while working with a fee-only advisor. The advisor works with you to go over your financial situation, reviews your assets, liabilities, income, insurance coverage and then provides you with a game plan. You then write him a check for the services. Since the advisor gets paid whether you take his advice or not, you can be confident that he has no ulterior motivation behind the advice he has given.

Ok, one more small disclaimer on that. In some cases, advisors will earn referral fees from agents, lawyers or brokers they recommend. Again, if they do receive referral fees from various professionals, this would need to be disclosed to you (clearly and specifically in a large stack of papers you are likely to gloss over).

Overall, a fee-only advisor gives you the best opportunity to obtain unbiased advice and also provides the most transparency when it comes to how much you are paying. The only significant downside to working with a fee-only advisor is that you need to pay the money out of pocket instead of having it deducted from your investment accounts. This can be difficult for people working on a budget, as even though good advice will be well worth the cost, fee-only advice can range from a few hundred dollars for a complete review to thousands.

HOW TO PICK THE RIGHT ONE FOR YOU

One of the great things about people is that we can usually figure out quickly when we're in over our heads and need help. How much time can you spend working a plunger before you call a plumber? When your car breaks down, and you pop the hood, how long do you need to stare at the engine before you know you need to see the mechanic?

Many people are willing to make a decision regarding when they need to contact a financial advisor in the same way; waiting for something to go wrong and then finding someone to help them fix it. Of course, there's nothing wrong with seeking help when you have a problem, but when it comes to your personal finances, you're usually better served by assuming you'll face some financial challenges at some point and working on a plan to handle those challenges *before* they arise.

In lieu of becoming a Certified Financial Planner yourself, it's a safe assumption that whether you take a proactive approach to your finances or wait until you're facing an immediate challenge, you will eventually need to find a financial advisor for help. Let's discuss tips on how to find the right advisor for you.

Interview More Than One Candidate

When you have a pressing problem to solve, it can be tempting to hire the first candidate you meet, especially if you've been referred to that person by someone you respect. At a minimum, you should meet with two candidates, but interviewing three or more candidates would be ideal.

The most common method people use to find a financial advisor is getting a reference from a friend or relative. However, this method alone comes with inherent peer pressure to hire the referred advisor. You wouldn't want your friends or family to feel like you don't trust their judgment when you reject their trusted advisor, would you? For that reason, make sure at least one advisor you interview is referred to you by a source you don't know personally, such as an industry association or even an online search.

If you interview only one advisor, you'll probably feel like he or she seems competent and well-equipped to solve your problems. However, a second candidate may not only be competent but also relate to you better and be more attentive to your personal needs. People spend more time looking at options when they pick out a new appliance than they do when selecting a financial advisor. Take the time to look at some options, and at the very least, you'll be able to affirm your first choice is the best fit for you.

When choosing advisors to interview, schedule your interviews so that any advisors who require a consultation fee are interviewed last. Paying a fee for an initial meeting puts pressure on you to hire that advisor for the long term.

Before You Meet an Advisor
Take some time before setting up a meeting with a potential advisor to get to know their business. Either contact the advisor or her assistant or do some research on the firm's website before setting up a face-to-face interview. If you have significant concerns about setting up a retirement plan for your small business, but the firm specializes in trusts and estate planning, it might be a waste of both the advisor's time and yours to set up a face-to-face meeting.

Don't Forget a Background Check
It's easy to get swept off your feet by a friendly personality, great reviews, and a fancy office, but those factors shouldn't get your advisor candidates off the hook from your due diligence on their backgrounds.

The online tool at BrokerCheck.org is the first place to start. There, you can enter your candidates' details and find extensive reports on an individual and a firm's history in the industry. Any formal complaints and violations can be found there. Also, take the time to verify the candidates' credentials as discussed earlier in this chapter, verify that any licenses they claim to have are active, and contact any references the advisors provide.

Review Their Contracts and Understand How They Get Paid
Have the patience to take the advisor's contract home to read and understand it before signing. Make sure that whatever an advisor tells you during your meeting, that those promises are spelled out in the contract. If something in the contract doesn't make sense to you, make a note to ask the potential advisor to clarify what it means.

Pay close attention to what kind of control over your investments an advisor will have. Many unknowingly give an advisor unlimited control of their assets, including the ability to move money in and out of their account without consultation. Be wary of an advisor who asks for too much control.

Signing over any control of your investments to an advisor is unnecessary. The advisor can simply give you recommendations, and you can execute them on your own. However, many people find it convenient to allow an advisor to execute investment recommendations on their behalf. You can authorize your advisor to use either **discretionary authority** or **non-discretionary authority**. With either, your investments are safely held by a third-party custodian, and your advisor is allowed special access only to change how your funds are invested. If an advisor is authorized to use discretionary authority, he can change your investments without consulting you first. This can be useful when there is a sudden change in the market, or a limited-time opportunity for a profitable investment, and the advisor needs to act quickly but lacks the time to get your approval. An advisor with non-discretionary authority can make changes to your investments on your behalf, but only after getting your approval for the specific changes. Giving an advisor non-discretionary authority is a great way to balance convenience and safety. Unless you really want to be hands-on and be the person who physically provides the trading instructions to your broker, a non-discretionary advisor is a good fit.

The contract will lay out exactly how the advisor will be paid. Most people should avoid an advisor who is compensated solely through commissions due to various conflicts of interest. When working with a fee-based advisor, you'll need to understand if she is billing you at an hourly rate, as a percentage of your assets, a monthly retainer fee, or some other method. Additionally, you'll want to know the specifics of how those fees will be paid. Will they be automatically deducted from your investments, billed to a credit card, or will you receive an invoice? If billed automatically, always review how much your fees are each quarter.

Discuss Your Expectations

All advisors work differently. Some will want to meet with you each quarter to review your progress; others may prefer to do so annually. With the advances in technology, many advisors forgo face-to-face meetings altogether. Ensure you discuss how often an advisor will follow up with you and how that follow-up will happen. Also, discuss what happens if you have questions in between meetings. Some advisors will bill you for a simple phone call while many will gladly take your questions at no additional charge.

Also, be explicit in your initial meeting with what you hope to accomplish and what you expect the advisor to do. If there are specific areas of concern you want solutions for, talk about them. If all you want is a quick review of your investments, let him know. It's a good idea to request a sample financial plan from an advisor to see what kind of analysis and advice a candidate can offer.

Once You've Made Your Choice

After you've gotten to know your candidates and found one that has the right combination of background, competence, and ability to relate to you and your needs, it's time to start working together. Be sure that your expectations are continuously being met by your advisor, and if they aren't, either reach out to your advisor to let them know what else you need from them or start looking for someone new.

Here are some warning signs to look out for when working with an advisor:

- **They ask you to sign paperwork you don't understand**
  This is an easy way for an advisor to have you sign over control of your money to him without you realizing it.

- **You don't receive statements from your custodian or your statements are not on time**
  You should receive statements at least quarterly from the company that holds your investments. It could be a sign that your money isn't there if you don't. An advisor can create and send fake statements (the way Bernie Madoff did). If the only statements you receive come directly from your advisor, it's time to contact your custodian directly. Delayed statements can also indicate that something unusual is happening with your account.

- **"Computer errors"**
  If something shows up on your statement that shouldn't be there, an unscrupulous advisor might try to explain it away as a computer glitch. Don't settle for that kind of excuse. Get to the bottom of what really caused the error, and ensure it's corrected to your satisfaction.

- **Significant and unexpected declines in your investment value**
  If you're invested in the stock market, you can expect some ups and downs, but part of a financial advisor's job is to walk you through those difficult times. If you open your quarterly statement and are shocked to see your account balances have substantially declined, it's a sign that your advisor is a poor communicator at least. If your

advisor is too busy to keep you informed about your investments, what else are they too busy to do?

- **You have trouble getting help from your advisor**
  If you initially expected to work with one advisor at a firm, but after you've signed on, you're constantly being handed over to an assistant, this is a sign that you're just not that important to the advisor and the situation will likely worsen over time.

- **Your advisor does not return calls or emails promptly**
  You deserve a high level of service. If you're not happy with an advisor's attention and follow-up, you might need to move on. Slow responses can indicate she's trying to serve too many clients or that you're simply not the type of client she prefers to work with. Either way, you probably want to move on.

Choosing to work with an advisor is ultimately your choice. More informational resources about money are freely available to us today than ever before. Take advantage of those resources, but remember that if your goal is to accumulate and manage a significant amount of wealth, you need to decide how much of your time you're willing to spend solving those inevitable challenges bound to pop up.

Beyond getting you the best returns on your investments, beyond saving you money on your taxes, beyond helping you pay off debt faster, one of the most valuable elements an advisor can give to you is more time. Time is something you can never get back. Think of how much money you save by washing your own car. Between hauling out the supplies, getting the car washed and dried, and then getting everything put away, is it worth all the time you lose to save a few dollars? You could spend a lot of time learning how to be a great chef, cook yourself incredible meals, and save a ton of money by eating luxuriously at home, but how much of your life do you really want to give up learning how to cook, and how much time do you really want to spend cooking? I certainly understand that doing things yourself can also be rewarding. It's hard to put a price tag on your time. If a plumber charges you $200 for an hour's work but saves you fifteen hours of trying to figure it out on your own, is that a good value? I guess it depends on what you'd rather be doing. You are the only one who can put a dollar value on an hour of your time.

-CHAPTER SUMMARY-

- Professional advisors will identify opportunities that you may never catch on your own. They know what you don't realize you don't know.

- All professional designations are not created equally. Some credentials are difficult to obtain and are relevant to your needs, others are not.

- The manner in which advisors are compensated will create conflicts of interest that may be impossible to overcome.

- An advisor who offers services in exchange for a flat fee or hourly fee will give you the best opportunity for unbiased advice.

- Perhaps the biggest benefits of working with a professional investment advisor are the greater peace of mind and the return of your time.

- Don't give an advisor the benefit of the doubt. Do your diligence and never give them full control of your money.

PART II

WHAT YOU'RE WORKING WITH

CHAPTER FIVE

Traditional Investments

"Personally, I am always ready to learn,
although I do not always like being taught."
– Winston Churchill

UNDERSTANDING THE ENVIRONMENT that encompasses investing, learning how others have fallen for fraud schemes so you can protect yourself, and who to ask for help when you need it was all part of the first step to eliminating fears surrounding investing. In this next section we're going to get technical. When you're investing, you'll find your money being summoned to hundreds of different directions so it's up to you to decide the best ones to choose. Through this chapter, you'll learn important details about the most common traditional investment options and develop an understanding of how to evaluate each. This chapter is heavy on information, so don't feel the need to race through it. Take the time you need to review the subjects until you understand them. We'll be referring back to this section throughout the rest of the book.

STARTING WITH THE BASICS

Let's start with the basics. Yeah, maybe this seems a little too basic, but I've always found it most beneficial to start from the beginning. You may be surprised to hear that the youngest work-force generation is setting aside more money and starting to save at a younger age than the two previous generations before them. What's also surprising is that the younger generation reports that 25% of their retirement savings is invested in savings accounts or something with similar risk and return.

A savings account is quite simple. You set aside money into a designated account and as a reward, the bank pays you an agreed amount of interest throughout the year. Some checking accounts will also pay a nominal amount of interest, but it's generally much less than an account specified as savings. A savings account will usually limit the number of withdrawals you can make in a specified period, but other than that, there are few restrictions on accessing your money.

Savings accounts are extremely safe, low-risk places to keep your money and also allow easy access to your funds should you need them. Everyone needs to have a savings account for unexpected expenses.

Most banks or credit unions will offer you a higher interest rate on your savings account if you have a minimum amount saved there (for example, at least $5,000). Also, many online-only banks will offer you a higher rate of return compared to traditional brick and mortar banks due to their lower overhead costs and newer reputation. Each organization will set its own rates and offer incentives to save based on the specific institution's goals.

Because savings accounts are so secure and offer such easy access to your money, the rate of return you receive is very low. Only recently have savings account interest rates climbed to 4-5% after paying well below 1% for nearly a decade. The interest rates banks are willing to pay for savers vary based on many economic and political factors.

In the early 2000's it was easy to find a savings account that would pay you 5% interest. Not bad! Even better for savers were the 1980s when savings account interest rates were 10% or higher. That's tough to beat. Those high-interest rates weren't all good news, however. Generally, higher interest rates can dampen the economy because it becomes more expensive for people and businesses to borrow money, which in turn slows overall spending. Mortgage rates in the 1980s climbed as high as 17% versus 5% or 6% today. So, back then, the ability to earn a high rate of return on your savings was largely canceled out by the higher amounts of interest you'd be paying on any debt you had.

A savings account should be part of everyone's financial plan due to the security and accessibility of your money, but the rate of return earned from a savings account is still very low. Money invested in a savings account with a 4% rate of return would take over eighteen years to double. For this reason, you'd only want to use a savings account for money you might need to use in the next six to twelve months. You should look for investments with a higher rate of return than what's offered through savings accounts for money you know you won't need for a year or longer.

Money Market Account

A money market account is another type of savings account, with some minor differences. In most cases a money market account will offer a slightly higher interest rate compared to an ordinary savings account. Many money market accounts will provide you with a debit card or checks for occasional use which is not common with typical savings accounts. However, money market accounts have traditionally limited their owners to only a few transactions per month. Additionally, most money market accounts will require higher minimum deposits when compared to a common savings account.

Certificates of Deposit

A Certificate of Deposit (CD) is a lot like a savings account as far as safety and stability but with a slightly higher rate of return. The downside is that CDs require you to lock in your money with the bank for a set term.

Certificate of Deposit interest rates vary substantially over time. Historically they have provided an interest rate that is from around 0.5%-2% higher than a savings account.

To earn higher interest rates with a CD, you need to commit your money to the bank for a set amount of time. Some common CD terms are 6 months, 12 months, 18 months, or several years. The bank will offer a higher rate of return the longer you commit to keeping your money in the CD. Banks are willing to pay you more interest when you agree to keep your money locked-in for a set amount of time because knowing you won't be withdrawing the money at any given moment allows them to use that money for longer-term investments like lending it to other customers.

In the majority of cases, you can access your money from a CD before the term is up, but you will have to pay an early withdrawal penalty which can leave you with less than you initially deposited.

If you plan to invest money in CDs for a period of years, it may seem like a no-brainer to pick the longest term CD available because it will pay the highest rate, but that's not always the best decision. Say you lock into a five-year CD that pays 3% at a time when one-year CDs were only paying 2.5%. You'll be coming out ahead at first, but if interest rates begin to rise, you could wind up locked into an unnecessarily low rate. Additionally, you'd be at a higher risk of needing to access your money unexpectedly with a five-year term instead of a shorter commitment.

There's no definite way to know if rates are going to rise or not, but take a little time to study what experts are saying about the current interest rate environment before making a long-term commitment to a CD. If it looks like rates are falling, use longer terms, but while rates are increasing, shorter-term CDs are a better bet.

A good strategy for investing in CDs is to use a method called laddering. With this technique, you'd spread your money over several CDs with a variety of terms. For example, you have $5,000 to invest in CDs. You put $1,000 into each a 1-year, 2-year, 3-year, 4-year, and 5-year CD. Once the term on the 1-year CD expires, you can reinvest that money into a new 5-year CD. After the 2-year CD term expires, do the same and invest in another 5-year CD. Continue doing this until you have five 5-year CD's. This will put you in a position to earn the highest CD rates available but still have a different 5-year CD maturing every year giving you flexible access to funds.

Special CDs

Many banks offer CDs with special benefits. Here are a few common variations:

- **Liquid CD** - This type of CD account gives the depositor the ability to withdraw their money with either no penalty or a reduced penalty. In exchange for this extra flexibility, however, the interest rate you earn on your savings will be less than a standard CD rate.

- **Bump Up CD** - This is a special CD that helps protect you from rising interest rates. If interest rates increase during the term of a CD, a bump-up CD or step-up CD allows the CD owner to "bump up" their original interest rate to the current higher rate. Most bump-up CDs only allow a one-time increase in the interest rate.

- **Callable CD Account**- A callable CD will typically offer the investor a slightly higher interest rate than a standard CD, somewhere from 0.5%- 1% extra. However, a callable CD gives the bank the option to cancel or "call" your CD after a certain amount of time. Banks offer a higher rate of return for callable CDs because they know that if interest rates drop, they won't be stuck paying you a higher rate. For example, you invest in a 5% callable CD, and if after a year, interest rates for CDs have fallen to 4%, the bank can cancel your CD, and you'd have to reinvest the funds at the new lower interest rates.

- **Zero-coupon CD Account** - These types of CDs are fairly uncommon and many banks don't even advertise them. Typically, they pay a higher rate of return compared to regular CDs but usually require a much longer term (some as long as 20 years) and a larger deposit amount. Zero-coupon CDs don't distribute interest payments to you each year like other CDs. Instead, you know ahead of time what the zero-coupon CD will be worth at the end of the term and purchase it for a discount. For example, you'd buy a CD that will be worth $75,000 in seven years for $50,000 today. An interesting downside to a zero-coupon CD is that you must pay taxes on the interest earned within the CD annually, even though you don't receive the funds until the CD matures.

BUYING COMPANIES

Generally, when people talk about investing, they're talking about investing in stocks. You probably already have some understanding of how stocks work, but let's discuss the details.

When a company needs money to expand its operations, one of the most common ways it can raise funds is by selling stock to the public. When you buy a stock, you're effectively buying a small piece of the company. Buying a stock makes you one of the owners of the company, albeit a small one. When the company profits, you typically receive a portion of those profits. When the company performs poorly, your investment will do poorly.

In investing terms, the words "stock" and "share" are mostly interchangeable. In both cases, the term describes an ownership stake in a company. The real difference is in the way the two terms are typically used. The term "stock" is typically used in a broad reference, while "share" is used when discussing an investment in a specific company. For example, one might use the phrases, "I've invested a lot of money in different stocks," or, "I own shares of Netflix." It is also common to use a phrase like, "shares of Apple stock," which, while redundant, is acceptable and typical.

Owning stock in a company will usually give you the right to vote on some of the company's actions. The most common issue shareholders can vote on is who will serve on the company's board of directors. Some companies allow one vote for every share of stock an investor owns. This arrangement gives investors who own a significant number of shares more influence over the board of directors and, therefore, more input on the company's direction.

One concept I see a lot of people have confusion over is that in terms of their stock, a company only receives money when they initially sell the stock to the public, not based on how high the price of the shares climb. For example, if a company offers one million shares to the public and sells them for $10 each, that company takes in $10 million dollars (minus some fees to the firm that manages the initial sale). If the shares quickly rise to $20 each, it has no impact on the initial $10 million that the company received. Conversely, if the share price suddenly drops to $5 each, the company won't lose any money. After the initial sale of stock to the public, the variations in prices day-to-day reflect the price an individual share would sell for between two investors on the open market.

When a company makes shares of stock available to the public, it is called an initial public offering, or IPO. A company remains interested in the price of its stock even after the initial public offering for a few reasons. First, the board of directors has a duty to provide value to their shareholders, and a significant portion of providing value means share prices need to keep going up. If shareholders aren't happy with the value they're receiving for their investment, they can vote out the board of directors. Second, many companies retain some of their own shares or, once profitable enough, buy some of their shares back from the open market. When a company holds its own shares, the company will obviously be very concerned with the price of its stock. Additionally, many company executives receive compensation in the form of company stock. These executives will also have an interest in how much each share is worth.

How Owning Stocks Can Earn You Money

As mentioned previously, owning stock in a particular company makes you a partial owner of that company. So when that company is successful, you share in that success. The most well-known way you can earn money with a stock investment is when the price of a stock you own increases, also known as capital appreciation. For example, you invest $1,000 to purchase 100 shares of Walmart stock for $10 each, and, over time, the share price increases to $20. Now your investment would be worth $2,000 for a potential $1,000 profit. A stock's price will generally appreciate when investors believe the company's future prospects for increased profits look favorable.

Additionally, many companies will pay out a portion of profits to the shareholders. These payments are referred to as dividends. Dividends are typically paid annually, quarterly, or occasionally both. Dividends are usually expressed as a given amount per share, for example, $0.25 per share. In an instance where you own 1,000 shares in a particular company that pays a $0.25 dividend per share, you'd receive $250 each time dividends were dispersed.

While it is possible for a stock to both pay consistent dividends and have significant potential for price appreciation at the same time, it's not common. Stocks with the most potential to increase in price are typically less established companies who are focused on growth, so instead of distributing dividends to shareholders, it's more sensible for them to re-invest their earnings back into the company to help continue their growth. Also, each time a dividend is dispersed, the stock's price will be reduced by roughly the amount of the dividend. This makes sense when considering that the price of a stock is based on the company's potential future value. If that company pays out $0.25 per share, the company would essentially be $0.25 per share less valuable because it's $0.25 per share poorer.

The downside to any individual stock is that if the company goes out of business, you can potentially lose your entire investment. Investing in individual stocks takes diligence.

How to Pick Which Stocks to Buy
Individual stocks can be one of the best ways to earn high rates of return on your investments, but there is a real risk of losing significant amounts of money. Unfortunately, there is no way to guarantee that any stock will be a good investment, but by taking some time to evaluate a number of different stocks and spreading your investments over several companies, you can lower the risk of losses.

Start With Your Goals
First, determine what you want your investments to do for you. Do you want to maximize how much your money grows, or are you more interested in steady returns? Your greatest potential for large gains over time is through investments in companies with the potential to grow. Popular growth companies today include Meta (Facebook/Instagram), Alphabet (Google), and Amazon, but we don't know what the best growth companies of the future are yet. If you're interested in more consistent returns, investments in established dividend-paying companies make sense. Coca-Cola and McDonald's are good examples of companies with long histories of paying dividends with limited risk.

Learn The Fundamentals

You'll need to know some of the basics behind what drives a stock's price. Here are some ideas on where to start.

Dig Into Public Documents

All public companies who offer stock must provide details about their finances, including how they use their money. You'll need to become familiar with reviewing these statements each quarter. Here you'll see how much debt a company has, what its expenses are, how its revenue is growing, and more. You'll need to get to know any company you invest in. Use these statements to determine whether the company appears to be trending in a positive direction or if trouble is on the horizon.

10-K

Don't worry, it has nothing to do with running! The 10-K is a report every public company must file annually, and it includes five sections: business, risk factors, selected financial data, financial statements, and management's discussion and analysis. One of the best places to start when analyzing a company is in the business section of the 10-K. The business section gives a description of what the business actually does and how it expects to make money. If you don't think the business makes sense as an investment after reading this, you can move on without digging any further. Reading through the risk factors and management discussion can also provide you with invaluable insights as to what took place within the company over the prior year. If the company missed expectations for the year financially, does their explanation of the events sound valid to you or are they just making excuses?

10-Q

A 10-Q form has similarities to the 10-K but is filed after every quarter. The report contains updated financials with a management discussion and analysis over the period. When the 10-Q is released, the company will typically hold an earnings call available for investors to listen in on. The earnings call provides additional discussions about the prior quarter and the steps the company plans to take in the near future. The earnings call may also take questions from investors which can result in more insights and clarification of data in the 10-Q.

Balance Sheet

The balance sheet lists out the various assets and liabilities a company holds at a certain point in time, such as on December 31st or the end of the most recent quarter. Assets include cash on hand, inventory, property, investments, the value of trademarks and patents, and anything else the company holds that has value. Liabilities include unpaid bills, pending wages, required dividend payments, and traditional debts such as loans. The balance sheet will help you understand where the company's money is tied up and what type of debt the company owes. Reviewing how these numbers change from quarter to quarter or year-over-year can help you determine the direction of the company in question.

Income Statement

A company's income statement reports the income and expenses for the company over a specific period of time, typically over the course of a quarter or year. The income statement will break down the different types of income the company receives. It includes operating income, which covers revenue related to selling the company's products and services. The statement also includes non-operating income such as interest, income from investments, income from strategic partnerships, and other miscellaneous income. As important as income is, the expenses reported on the statement include incredibly valuable information. If profitability is down, is it related to excessive expenses or a slowdown in revenue? If expenses have increased, which expenses in particular have increased, and was the increase justifiable? Are debt payments too onerous for the company to improve its future prospects?

Cash Flow Statement

The statement of cash flows is fairly similar to the income statement. However, it is specifically focused on the receipt and outflow of cash through the company. A major difference between the cash flow statement and the income statement is that the two utilize different accounting methods. The income statement uses a method known as the accrual method. As a simplified explanation, the accrual method accounts for income when an invoice is sent and accounts for expenses when the bill is received, not when cash changes hands. So the income statement will report income that has not yet been received and expenses that have not yet been paid. The income statement can also include other accounting adjustments to income and expenses that are non-cash expenses such as depreciation, accrued interest, or changes in inventory to name a few. The cash flow statement excludes these types of accounting adjustments and gives a clear picture of exactly how much cash was moving in and out of the company, where it came from, and where it went during the reported period.

When reviewing any of the company's financial documents, look for footnotes. Footnotes are used to explain uncommon income and expenses that may be one-time events. These footnotes can give you additional insights into whether the company's current trajectory will continue. After reviewing the company's public documents, there are a number of other specific areas to focus on which will help you select the right investment.

Revenue Growth

Revenue is the amount of money a company has coming in before deducting expenses. Even though profit is ultimately what investors want to see, growing revenue consistently is a good indicator that profits will increase in the future. Profits can vary due to things like cost-cutting or one-time events, but continuously increasing revenue is a sign of a healthy company. Look for companies with several years of revenue growth.

P/E Ratio

The price-to-earnings ratio (P/E) helps you examine how expensive or inexpensive a particular stock may be based on the company's earnings. To determine the P/E ratio of a stock, you'll first need to look up the company's earnings per share as well as the stock's price per share. Then divide the price per share by the earnings per share, and you'll have the P/E ratio. Many online resources will complete this calculation automatically when you research a stock. The average P/E ratio over time is around 20, so an average stock with a P/E ratio below 20 may be considered a better value if all things are equal. However, all things are not generally equal between two stocks.

To make more sense of a particular P/E ratio, you'll want to compare it to the P/E ratios of similar companies in the same industry. Also, even though a lower P/E ratio can signal an investment opportunity, it may only indicate that the particular company is thought to be in decline. Likewise, a stock with an above-average P/E ratio may indicate an expectation of higher future earnings. The P/E ratio alone cannot tell you whether or not to buy a particular stock but is one of several tools that can help you get a better understanding of a given stock's price. Often an investment opportunity can be identified when a company has significantly changed its business strategy and should now be categorized as part of a different industry. If its P/E ratio is still aligned with its previous industry, and the industry they are switching to typically has higher P/E ratios, you may be able to capitalize on the change before other investors.

Dividend Yield

Another good way to help determine the value of a particular investment is by determining the dividend yield. The dividend yield is the total amount of dividends paid out per share throughout the year divided by the stock price. A dividend-paying stock can also be a sign of a company in relatively good financial health. The average long-term dividend yield is around 2%, but if the price of a dividend stock is unusually low, you may find yields of 4%-5% or even higher. Higher dividend yields can be found during stock market declines when the price of stocks is falling.

Does the Company Have an "Economic Moat"?

An economic moat means a company has staying power even through challenging times. A company with a robust economic moat has a solid history of earnings, profitability, cash flow, and debt levels. However, the business model itself also needs to be analyzed to determine the strength of the moat. The company should have a strong product that is difficult to replicate. They should have a distinct advantage over competitors, be it price, quality, or service level. Customer loyalty and a strong brand name greatly contribute to an economic moat.

Consider Macroeconomic Factors

Research how the company fits into the broader economy. Does the company operate in part of the growing or shrinking economy? Does the company serve a specific demographic, and will that demographic be willing and able to buy the company's products and services for the foreseeable future?

Invest In What You Know

Especially when first starting to invest, it's a good idea to invest in a company whose business you understand. A good way to do this is to look at companies that operate in the same industry as your line of work. You'll generally be familiar with challenges another company in the same industry might face and also be able to recognize new innovations quickly. It would also make sense to consider investments in businesses where you have an opportunity to review their operations on a first-hand basis, like retail stores or restaurants that you frequent. Sam Walton, founder of Wal-Mart stores, said in his autobiography, "If I were a stockholder of Wal-Mart, or considering becoming one, I'd go into ten Wal-Mart stores and ask the folks working there, 'How do you feel? How's the company treating you?' Their answers would tell me much of what I need to know."

If you don't know much about a company, don't be afraid to use your creativity to find out everything you can. The Los Angeles Times detailed a story of how several investors came together to share the various techniques they were using to dig up information on sales of Tesla cars. In the story, one investor flew his small Cessna airplane up to Northern California, where he knew of a large lot Tesla had leased. From over 1,000 feet above, the investor peered down at the lot below, and something caught his eye. Dozens of car-carrier trailers, over 100 in fact, all sitting empty. Could this be a sign that Tesla wasn't selling as many cars as expected? Meanwhile, a hired spy in Hawthorne, California, photographed a parking garage filled with hundreds of Tesla Model 3s. The spy observed that the cars were covered in dust and believed some of those cars had been sitting there for months. That's interesting. Other Tesla investors used remote-controlled drones or satellite images to scour for secrets about the car company's success or struggles. Many people conducting these various investigations of Tesla shared their stories and findings in an online forum. It seemed apparent to them that due to widespread findings of unsold cars stored across the country, Tesla was not selling as many cars as they expected. Many of the investors made a bet against Tesla stock by "shorting' it, meaning they could profit if Tesla's stock price fell. Soon after the reconnaissance missions above, Tesla announced that they had delivered substantially fewer cars than expected. Tesla's stock price fell over 10% that day and nearly 40% in the next two months, creating a healthy profit for the investigating investors. It can certainly pay to do your due diligence when investing.

Renowned investor, Peter Lynch explained that he made as much as a 1500% profit by investing in Dunkin Donuts. His decision was based on the fact that he stopped in for coffee and thought the coffee was pretty good. He figured that if he thought the coffee was good, other people probably would too. He noticed the stores in his area were always busy, and after reviewing the company's finances, bought the stock. It was as simple as that.

Get To Know the People Who Manage the Company
You'll need to know a company is in good hands before becoming an owner. Look into the top executives. Learn about their abilities and what they've accomplished in the past. What adversities have they overcome in business and how have they responded in a crisis? Were they involved in prior scandals?

Consider the Opinions of Professional Analysts
You can learn a lot of details about a particular stock without doing all the research on your own. Numerous stock analysts' opinions can be found on various investor websites and blogs. Analysts study the above and more on various stocks for a living. Frequently they produce ratings on individual stocks such as "buy", "sell" or "hold". Ratings of buy or sell are pretty clear, but I've always found the hold rating fairly curious. The hold rating simply means if you own the stock already, you shouldn't sell, and if you don't own the stock, you shouldn't buy. But, all things considered, if a stock is good enough to hold onto, shouldn't it be good enough to buy? A better way to look at a hold rating is to think of it meaning that the analyst doesn't expect the stock to perform any better or worse than the stock market as a whole.

If you begin to study analysts' recommendations, you'll quickly find that many analyst's opinions on a given stock are often at odds with each other. One analyst sees a stock as a strong buying opportunity, while another thinks you should sell. This is often more helpful than everyone agreeing because you can learn arguments for and against the company. An analyst's explanation underlying their rating can be much more valuable than the rating itself.

Take analysts' "buy" ratings with a grain of salt. Analysts have an inherent need to hand out "buy" ratings over "sell" ratings. Investors are searching for which stocks to buy, not which stocks to avoid. If an analyst only produces sell ratings, investors will move on to an analyst who can recommend something to buy.

There is a deeper and more nefarious conflict of interest for analysts. Most investment analysts work for major financial institutions whose retail investment arms must work in concert with their institutional investment banking and underwriting arms. Investment banking is the sector of banking that handles major business events such as mergers and helps corporations and governments issue new stocks and bonds to the public. The fees for these services can be hundreds of millions of dollars. Needless to say, these investment banks want to keep their customers happy, and a negative public rating from one of their analysts certainly wouldn't do that.

Before the Trump Taj Mahal Casino opened in Atlantic City, Analyst Marvin Roffman told the Wall Street Journal that the bonds used to finance the casino's opening were a bad investment. When the newspaper published the story, Roffman's boss received a fax from Donald J. Trump himself, instructing the research firm to publicly change their opinion or fire Roffman. Roffman refused to change his opinion and was fired on the spot. The casino filed for bankruptcy the year after it opened.

Henry Blodget was the head of the global Internet research team at Merrill Lynch during the early 2000's. "I can't believe what a POS [piece of shit] that thing is," Henry said, describing Lifeminders stock in the year 2000 through private company emails. Publicly, Merrill Lynch told a different story saying, "We think LFMN (Lifeminders) presents an attractive investment." Merrill gave the company a "buy" rating. A different stock, Infospace, was internally discussed by Merrill Lynch as a company that is "very important to us from a banking perspective, in addition to our institutional franchise." While Blodgett thought the stock was a "powder keg" and a "piece of junk," it was given a high "buy" rating and listed on a "Favored 15" list of stocks. Blodget and Merril Lynch were sued shortly after the Dot Com crash of the early 2000s when the internal discussions became public.

When reviewing analysts' positive opinions, take some time to look into the company they work for. Were they the underwriting company for that stock? Do they own many shares of the stock they are recommending? Both factors are required to be disclosed in the research report. While you don't need to agree with an analyst's opinion about buying or selling a given stock, analysts' reports are a terrific source of information regarding a company's strengths, weaknesses, competition, and future potential. They can add new insights you can weigh against your opinion of a particular company.

Legendary investor Warren Buffet says, "It's far better to buy a wonderful company at a fair price than a fair company at a wonderful price." When deciding to invest in a company, you need to have the mindset that you're going to buy part of that company. Make sure it's a company you want to own, not just a stock you buy hoping to see a spike in its price. Once you own a company, be diligent about watching how that company is running, not only whether the price of a share is moving up or down.

Diligently studying one stock won't be enough. You'll need to spread your investments over several companies because no one can predict when a sudden event may decimate any single stock. For example, a 2015 illness outbreak at several Chipotle Mexican Grill restaurants drove its stock price down almost 50% in just sixty days, and three years later, Chipotle shares were worth just 30% of their pre-outbreak value. After being named "America's Most Innovative Company" for six consecutive years, a complex accounting scandal its own executives hardly understood brought Enron's stock price from $80 to $0.26 per share in just a few months. Even good companies can have something unpredictable go wrong.

Spreading your risk over several different stocks is known as diversification. There isn't a specific rule regarding the appropriate number of stocks you must invest in to remain diversified. Generally, the number is considered to be anywhere from 20 to 50 different stocks. Researching and monitoring 20 or more different stocks is a challenge; most people find this pretty intimidating. However, with a bit of practice and experience, you'll find that once you've selected good companies to invest in, you can monitor their performance in just a few hours a week. We'll cover more on diversification later in the book when we discuss strategies, but diversification involves more than just picking a bunch of stocks to invest in. You may also want to diversify your money into different types of investments like the ones we cover in the rest of this chapter.

A LENDING HAND

Bonds are another of the most common investments available. Most investment plans recommend the inclusion of bonds as part of your investments. One way to classify bond investments is to think of them as a type of investment that is somewhere between CDs and stocks. They have the potential to provide somewhat higher rates of returns compared to CDs but not as high as stocks. They are also a more stable investment than stocks but less secure than CDs.

Similar to stocks, companies can use bonds to raise money for operating their business. Additionally, government entities frequently use bonds to fund various projects like building roads and schools. A bond represents a loan taken out by either a corporation or a government entity. You can think of a bond as an I.O.U. which includes the details of the loan and the payments you'll receive. Also, if a company goes bankrupt and is forced to sell off its assets, bondholders must be paid before shareholders.

A bond has a due date for when the loan needs to be paid back to you (known as a maturity date), similar to a CD. Bonds can have a wide range of maturity dates, from one year to thirty years or more. Like a CD, bonds pay you interest at a specified rate, known as the coupon rate, on a regular basis. The term "coupon" is used because old physical bond certificates had coupons attached which investors used to redeem their interest payments. Most commonly today, interest is paid semi-annually, but some bonds pay interest monthly or quarterly. Like CDs, utilizing a bond ladder to strategically invest in bonds with a variety of maturity dates can be a useful strategy to improve your rate of return and maintain flexibility.

The interest rate a bond pays is based on a few factors, but like CDs, bonds with longer terms will typically pay higher rates. However, the biggest factor determining a particular bond's coupon rate is the ability of the issuing entity to pay back the bond. You can think of it the same way banks do when considering a loan applicant. If a person applying for a mortgage has a good source of income and a high credit score, the bank feels confident that the loan will be repaid, and they are willing to lend for a low interest rate. However, if the applicant has a low credit score and a less reliable source of income, the bank knows that the risk of that loan not being repaid is higher. In order to make this higher-risk loan worth their while, they issue the loan with a higher interest rate.

When investing in bonds, you are the bank. Bonds issued by entities that have the best ability to pay you back will also offer the lowest interest rates. For example, bonds issued by the U.S. treasury offer fairly low interest rates, but you can be very confident that the loan will be repaid (because the U.S. Treasury can just print the money they need to pay you). Conversely, bonds issued by entities that may be struggling financially can pay very high interest rates, but you are at a greater risk of the loan not being repaid.

Bond Ratings

Bond ratings are a shortcut to understanding how risky a particular bond may be. You can think of these as the bond's credit score. While there are several rating agencies, the three most referenced are Moody's, Standard and Poors, and Fitch. Each has its own method for scoring credit worthiness of bond issuers, and each has a slightly different rating system.

They all generally use the following grades:

	Quality	Bond Ratings	
Bond		S&P/Fitch	Moody's
Ratings	Highest Quality	AAA	AAA
	High Quality	AA(+/-)	AA(1,2,3)
Bonds are rated by several agencies	Upper-Medium	A(+/-)	A(1,2,3)
based on the ability	Medium	BBB(+/-)	Baa(1,2,3)
of the issuer to repay your	Speculative Medium Grade	BB(+/-)	Ba(1,2,3)
investment. Ratings start at	Speculative Lower Grade	B(+/-)	B(1,2,3)
AAA and go as low	Speculative Risky	CCC(+/-)	Caa(1,2,3)
as D.	Default Imminent	CC	Ca
	In Default	D	C

Figure 5.1

The rating agencies utilize + and - symbols or the numbers 1, 2, and 3 to rate bonds in more detail. For example, an A+ is better than an A. However, this system can occasionally cause confusion because we assume an A+ is very good, but in reality, an AA- is a better grade than an A+.

Bond ratings are only one way to measure the stability of a bond. In order to really understand your investment, you'd have to do much of the same research needed to buy a stock.

Bond Prices

The subject of bond prices is where bonds can act more like stocks. Similar to stocks, bonds are issued at a certain price, most commonly $100 or $1000 each. Like stocks, the issuing entity collects money from the initial sale of the bonds. Once bonds are purchased from the issuing entity, they can be resold on the open market. Why would someone want to sell a bond on the open market?

A bond's price may vary from its original issue price for a number of reasons. Most commonly, changing market interest rates will affect a bond's resale value. For example, if you purchase a bond that has a 5% interest rate for $1000, and one year later, interest rates for newly issued comparable bonds have fallen to 3%, you may be able to sell your bond for about $1,200 on the open market. Because the higher 5% rate of return is harder to find, investors may be willing to buy the 5% bond for a premium price. It's important to point out that rising interest rates would have the opposite effect on bond prices. The price of that same 5% bond could fall to around $800 if interest rates for new comparable bonds rose to 7%.

So, bond prices can have some up and down movement similar to the stock market, however, the movement of bond prices tends to be somewhat muted compared to stock market volatility. Interest rates generally change gradually, and because interest rate changes are the main factor contributing to changes in overall bond market prices, the movements in bond prices are also relatively slow.

There are additional factors that also affect the price of bonds. An individual bond's price may be affected by the performance of the company issuing the bonds. When a company begins to struggle financially, owning bonds they've issued can become a risky investment, and if the coupon rate is too low, investors won't be interested in owning the bond unless the selling price is very low.

Also, the overall bond market can be affected by the economy. When the economy is doing well or expected to do well in the near-term future, the prices of bonds can fall as investors place more of their money into the higher potential returns of stocks. However, when the economy begins to perform poorly or is expected to perform poorly, bond prices can rise as investors sell off their risky stocks and invest more money in safer bonds. This isn't always the case as sometimes bond and stock market prices can increase or decrease in unison. We experienced this scenario for a brief period during the onset of the coronavirus pandemic in 2020. Both stock prices and bond prices were rapidly falling for several weeks as investors struggled to interpret the impact of an unprecedented scenario.

Types of Bonds

Treasury Bonds - These are issued directly by the U.S. treasury and are considered the safest of all bonds because the government can simply raise taxes or print money to pay you back. Because of their security, their interest rates are typically among the lowest available. Treasury bonds come with a variety of maturity dates. Treasury bonds with maturity dates anywhere from four to fifty-two weeks are called Treasury Bills (T-Bills), those with two to ten-year maturities are known as Treasury Notes (T-Notes), and those with thirty-year maturities are Treasury Bonds (T-Bonds). The treasury also offers inflation-protected bonds which increase in value as inflation increases, but these bonds pay a lower rate of interest.

Other U.S. Government Bonds - Bonds issued by government

agencies to fund their operations can be an attractive alternative to treasury bonds. Bonds issued directly from a U.S. agency are backed by the full faith and credit of the U.S. government like treasury bonds, but due to the small political risk that the rules around these agencies could change, agency bonds pay a slightly higher rate of interest compared to treasury bonds.

Usually lumped in with government agency bond discussions are government-sponsored enterprise (GSE) bonds. GSEs are technically private entities whose bonds are not guaranteed by the federal government, however, because they are government-sponsored, it's generally believed that the federal government would not allow a GSE to default on their bond obligation. Because a government guarantee is only implied, GSEs are considered somewhat riskier than true agency bonds and therefore offer a slightly greater interest rate.

Investment-Grade Corporate Bonds - These are bonds issued by corporations in good financial condition with a bond rating of BBB or higher. The risk of investment-grade corporate bonds defaulting on their repayment is relatively small. Because they have no government guarantees, however, investment-grade corporate bonds pay a significantly higher interest rate relative to treasury bonds or other government bonds.

High-Yield Bonds - These are bonds with ratings of less than BBB. They can carry a substantial risk of default. These bonds have much more price volatility as compared to higher-rated bonds. High-yield bonds are often referred to as "junk bonds." Investors frequently use bond investments to lower the risk of their investment portfolio, however, high-yield bonds don't offer that benefit. In fact, high-yield bonds can increase overall risk for many investors as they carry risks similar to investing in stocks. They do have a place in many investors' strategies as the added risk comes with higher interest rates. High-yield bonds can often pay double the rate of investment-grade bonds.

Municipal Bonds - Municipal bonds or Muni bonds are issued by state and local governments as well as their agencies to finance their various projects. These bonds can be either investment grade or high-yield depending on the financial condition of the issuer. Interest from muni bonds is tax-free at the federal level, and in most cases, munis issued in your home state are exempt from state income taxes as well. Because of the tax benefits, municipal bonds offer lower rates than comparable taxable bonds. A decision to invest in munis would have to take into consideration your tax bracket. It almost never makes sense to invest in municipal bonds within a tax-deferred account like an IRA or 401(k).

BUYING IN BULK

When someone says the stock market is up 200 points, what the heck are they talking about? When it comes to American stocks, when a person references the stock market, they're most likely referring to either the Dow Jones Industrial Average (the Dow for short) or the Standard & Poor's 500 Index (S&P 500). Both the Dow and the S&P 500 are known as indexes that provide a simple way to observe the average performance of a group of investments over time.

The Dow Jones and the S&P 500 average are most commonly referenced because they are designed to help us take the pulse of the American stock market as a whole. There are thousands of indexes that focus on determining average performance for just about any type of stock or bond you can imagine. Examples of categories tracked by indexes include company size, geographical region, country of business, type of industry, precious metals, social responsibility, and much more. According to the Index Industry Association, there are well over three million different stock indexes. Considering that there are less than 50,000 stocks globally, this means that there are about sixty times as many indexes as there are stocks.

The Dow Jones Industrial Average comprises thirty of the most prominent American companies. Each of these companies has been specifically selected to represent a particular industry within the U.S. economy. Every company in the Dow 30 gives us a clue into how the overall economy is doing. For example, as part of the Dow average, the performance of Wal-Mart stock helps us understand how much shopping Americans are doing. The performance of Caterpillar, which manufactures heavy equipment like bulldozers and dump trucks, can help us understand how much construction is happening in the country. Disney stock is a clue into how much Americans spend on entertainment. Other Dow stocks include top technology, medical, finance, oil, and food companies. The particular stocks included in the Dow can change from time to time with shifts in the economy and changes in the performance of individual companies for better or worse.

Calculating the Dow Jones Industrial Average is a straightforward process. First, the share price for each of the thirty companies is totaled. That total is then divided by a number known as the Dow Divisor. Initially, the Dow Average was simply calculated by dividing the total of all companies' share prices by the number of companies in the Dow. However, this method resulted in fluctuations in the Dow Average that didn't necessarily reflect the performance of the included companies. One example of an event that could disproportionately affect the Dow average using the simple average method would be a stock split. Occasionally, it makes sense for a company to split its stock into smaller pieces. With a 2-for-1 split, everyone who owned one share of a company's stock would now own two, each at half the value of the original share. So, if a company within the Dow Average had a share price of $100 and executed a stock split, the new price of the shares would be $50 each. If a simple arithmetical average were used to calculate the Dow Jones Industrial Average, this price change from $100 per share to $50 per share would bring down the average even though there was no real change in the company's value. The Dow Divisor is used to prevent these types of non-economic events from altering the numerical value of the Dow Average. As of this writing, the Dow divisor is 0.1492. This number will be adjusted as necessary to maintain a meaningful continuity to the Dow Jones Industrial Average. It can change as frequently as four times a year or not at all for several years at a time.

The S&P 500 average is more commonly referenced by financial media and professionals, while the Dow Jones Average is more frequently referenced in the mainstream media. The S&P 500 consists of 500 of the largest American companies. Its average is calculated similarly to the Dow; instead of basing the average on each company's share price, the S&P 500 average is based on the companies' market capitalization (the total value of all outstanding shares).

Indexes like the S&P 500 are commonly used to provide a benchmark for investment performance. Investors can take a look at how the market has performed based on the S&P 500 average and see how their investment performance compares. Most investors hope the performance of their investments beats the performance of the market, but unfortunately, most individual investors underperform the market.

Mutual Funds/ Exchange Traded Funds

If you're starting to think that selecting and monitoring a few dozen stock and bond selections might be a little more work than you're up for, mutual funds or exchange-traded funds (ETF) may be right up your alley.

A mutual fund or ETF takes individual stock and bond selection out of your hands. Both mutual funds and ETFs typically work by creating a portfolio that can contain hundreds of different stocks, bonds, or other investments. As an investor, you can purchase a share of the mutual fund or ETF and effectively own a small part of the fund's underlying investments. This gives you the ability to invest in hundreds of companies with a minimal amount of money and personal effort. A few small differences exist between a mutual fund and an exchange-traded fund.

Mutual funds have existed for about a hundred years but rose to popularity in the 1950s. For decades, mutual funds have been known as a simple way for everyday investors to invest their money with a professional investment manager. Mutual funds allow investors to pool their money with a fund manager who selects, monitors, and makes changes to the investments on their behalf. This type of fund is known as an actively managed fund. With an actively managed fund, investors hope the professional management can provide them with returns that are superior to what they could achieve by investing on their own.

Like selecting stocks, selecting a mutual fund also requires due diligence. You'll want to review the fund's performance history and compare it to similar funds. Research the fund manager and what type of success they've had in the past. You may find in your research that nearly all mutual funds have a strong performance record. It's not because they are all managed by stock geniuses. Poor-performing mutual funds are typically merged into other funds or closed altogether instead of being allowed to remain as a blemish on the mutual fund company's reputation. That's right, poor-performing funds are forced to disappear. Meaning that mutual funds only perform well until they don't.

Mutual funds can come with a variety of fees. The management fee is what you pay for having your investments managed. This fee covers the fund manager's salary and other expenses related to handling the fund's investments. Fund management fees occur on an annual basis. Typical management fees for an actively managed fund are from 1%-3% of the invested assets.

Additionally, there can be what's known as a sales charge or sales load depending on how you purchase the mutual fund. I covered this briefly under the types of advisor section, but I wanted to provide a little more detail. A sales load is a one-time fee used to pay the broker or person selling you the mutual fund. There are a few different types of loads. The Front-End load is a fee equal to a certain percentage of your initial investment. As I said earlier, the fee can be 5% or more of your entire investment in the fund, meaning if you invested $100,000, the front-end load would eat up $5,000, leaving only $95,000 to be invested. Front-end loads are typically associated with "Class A" mutual fund shares. Another type of load is the back-end load or contingent deferred sales charge. The back-end load charges no upfront fee, allowing you to invest all your money upfront. The back-end load applies when the mutual fund is sold and is typically reduced gradually over five to six years until eventually reaching 0%. This may seem like a good way to avoid paying a sales load if you plan to keep the investment for several years, but mutual fund shares with a back-end load typically charge higher ongoing management fees which often makes them more expensive than a front-end load over time. Back-end loads are most frequently associated with "Class B" shares. There are also "Class C" mutual fund shares frequently available. The class C shares won't have a front-end load but usually have a small back-end load and charge the maximum 12b-1 fee. The 12b-1 fee is an ongoing or trailing fee typically paid to the person who sold you the mutual fund for as long as you continue to own it. Class A and B shares will also have 12b-1 fees, but Class C will typically have the highest, maxing out at 1% of your total investment. The sum of the management fee, 12b-1 fee, and any other ongoing charges are referred to as the fund's expense ratio.

All of these fees, as well as the mutual fund's investment objective, will be disclosed in the fund's prospectus. If you're a current mutual fund owner and haven't looked at your fund's prospectus, now is a terrific time. Summaries of the fees charged by a fund can also be found by looking up the fund on Mornigstar.com.

As I've said earlier, these loaded mutual funds are falling out of favor. Most mutual funds now offer no-load versions and focus on lowering expense ratios. Today, a reasonable expense ratio for an actively managed fund is about 1%. A slightly higher fee is acceptable for funds focusing on foreign investments or investing in small businesses because of the additional challenges in managing those types of investments.

Aside from actively managed funds are passive funds. Passive funds don't require an expert fund manager to analyze and pick the best potential stocks for the fund like an actively managed fund does. Instead, a passive fund typically mimics the performance of a specified index, for example, the S&P 500. The passive fund achieves its goal by purchasing shares of the companies that comprise the specific index. So in the case of an S&P 500 passive fund, the fund would invest in 500 companies based on the percentage of the total S&P 500 index each company makes up. If the S&P 500 goes up 15%, so does your investment, less some fees.

Speaking of fees, the highlight of passive funds is their low fees. Whereas actively managed funds typically charge 1% annually for their services, passive S&P 500 index funds might only charge 0.015%. Over the course of many years of investing, this small difference in fees can result in a substantial difference in your overall returns.

Exchange Traded Funds, or ETFs, are relatively new compared to mutual funds as they first appeared in the 1990s. ETFs are very similar to mutual funds, and they too can be actively managed or passively managed however, most ETFs fall into the passive category. There are two main distinctions between an ETF and a mutual fund. First, the exchange-traded fund, as its name says, is traded on an exchange and can be bought and sold throughout the day. An ETF's price is updated based on the price of its underlying securities every 15 seconds, whereas a mutual fund's price is only updated once at the end of each day. An order to buy or sell a mutual fund will only be processed at the end of the day, so if you submit your order to buy after an early morning stock market crash, and the market rebounds by the end of the day, your mutual fund purchase will be made at the higher recovered price. A second benefit to ETFs is that they are typically more tax efficient, assuming your investments are outside of tax-favored accounts like IRAs or 401(k)'s. Because of their ability to be sold on an exchange, ETFs don't need to buy and sell as many of their internal investments as mutual funds do. This is because when an ETF holder wants to get rid of their shares, they sell them to another investor through an exchange, and the ETF fund itself doesn't need to sell any of its underlying stocks. Conversely, when mutual fund holders want to cash out their investment, they redeem their shares with the mutual fund company directly. This redemption can require the mutual fund to sell off some of its underlying stocks which can trigger capital gains. A mutual fund must distribute capital gains to its shareholders at least annually, creating a tax liability. ETFs may occasionally distribute capital gains, but typically, the distributions are less substantial.

HEDGE FUNDS

It's likely you've heard of hedge funds as having a negative connotation. The first hedge fund was created in 1949 and utilized a strategy to minimize risks based on the stock market overall. Essentially, the fund worked to select stocks that would outperform the stock market but at the same time made equal bets against stocks that were expected to fall. This created a hedge against market losses. Hedge funds have a bad reputation because they are known to cater to wealthy investors, charge high fees, and have often made enormous profits during market crashes while average investors lost their shirts.

Hedge funds have some similarities to actively managed mutual funds in that a group of investors pool their money to have it managed by a professional money manager. Hedge funds are arranged quite differently compared to mutual funds, however. In most cases, a hedge fund is established as a partnership with investors considered limited partners and the investment manager considered a general partner. Hedge funds are not publicly traded and typically take more aggressive investment positions than ordinary mutual funds. Hedge funds are able to sidestep many SEC regulations because they are generally only available for investment to accredited investors deemed to be able to sustain greater investment risk. An accredited investor is an individual who earns more than $200,000 per year or has a net worth exceeding one million dollars (excluding the value of a primary residence).

Hedge funds usually attempt to earn investment profits whether stock markets are up or down. Hedge funds can use complex investment strategies or buy alternative investments that mutual funds are prohibited from utilizing. Some hedge fund strategies today don't even involve hedging at all. They will often use borrowed money to help boost investment returns, but this strategy also amplifies risk.

During the first few decades of their existence, hedge funds produced incredible results that far outperformed the stock market. Based on stellar results, hedge fund managers were able to charge astonishing fees that remain standard practice today. Hedge fund managers typically use what's known as a two-and-twenty fee structure. The fund manager collects 2% of all assets invested in the fund as well as 20% of investment profits. For example, a hedge fund with $100 million in assets which earned $25 million this year would pay the manager $2 million in fees based on the account values plus $5 million out of the investment earnings, and the fund investors would share the remaining $20 million in gains. However, over the last decade, hedge fund performance has fallen flat. A large part of hedge funds' recent downfall is a result of more money managers and even individual investors having attempted to adopt the same strategies en masse, diluting the opportunities to find undervalued or overvalued stocks to place aggressive bets on. Given their high fees, it's hard to imagine a long-term future for hedge funds without substantial retooling of their costs.

-CHAPTER SUMMARY-

- The types of investments you utilize will depend on your scenario in life and what you'll need to use the invested funds for.

- Traditional investments have a role to play in every investment plan.

- Selecting individual stocks is more challenging than selecting CD's or Savings, but the potential for vastly superior returns is worth the effort.

- Using bonds can provide returns with potentially less volatility but will result in lower long-term returns.

- Index funds and mutual funds provide a short cut for investors who want to avoid all the work of researching companies and creating their own diversified portfolio.

- Hedge funds may be on their last leg and don't provide investors with the results they could in the past.

CHAPTER SIX

Classic Investments

"I love simplicity." – Zendaya

SOPHISTICATED INVESTMENT OPTIONS like stocks, bonds or even savings accounts haven't always been available. Even today, many people around the world don't have access to the investment vehicles most of us take for granted, and in the absence of modern investment tools, there have always been people who understood the importance of investing for their futures. In societies with less sophisticated investment markets, purchasing building materials and supplies with their surplus funds became a common practice for future-minded individuals. In this way, over the course of a month, they would obtain enough to construct a section of a wall. After enough months, they would have constructed a room, and after the course of steady investing for a few years, they'd have built an entire home. Once their working days are over, they have a home to live in which they can eventually pass down to the next generation.

GET REAL

Today, buying real estate is the sexiest investment out there. Real estate investment not only comes with the potential for terrific returns and special tax breaks, but it also comes with an elevated feeling of status that many investors crave. Investing in real estate has unique pros and cons that make it appealing for some but terrifying for others.

The Appeal

Over the past hundred years, real estate investments have appreciated by about 5% per year, whereas broad stock market investments have gained 10% on average. There are several reasons why most Americans prefer real estate investment over stock investments despite real estate appreciating at half the rate of stocks.

People understand what owning a house, land, or office building means. It's a simple concept; it's tangible. They can see and touch it. There's something very comforting about investing in something that's real. It will essentially take an act of God for you to lose an investment in a building, whereas it feels like an investment in stocks could potentially vanish out of thin air. The price of real estate is relatively stable, and while booms and busts do happen, they're far less violent or frequent compared to the crashes that occur in stock markets.

Due diligence when it comes to real estate investments can seem simpler to understand than what it takes to analyze the value of a stock. Most people have heard the old cliché, "Location, location, location!" when it comes to buying real estate. Yes, you'll need to thoroughly evaluate the property itself, but what will have the greatest effect on the long-term appreciation of your investment will be its location.

Generally, you'll do best in real estate investing by determining a great geographical area, then narrowing it down to a particular neighborhood. Researching the growth and development of a potential area will be a key to investment success. Localities with a surging population tend to indicate a bright future for real estate investment. Successful real estate investors know they need to become experts on the real estate in the neighborhood they've selected. They need to know what subtle differences cause one three-bedroom house to rent for $200 more per month than another three-bedroom house on the same block. After understanding the neighborhood, the investor needs to know the street and the lot.

There's a saying that to make the best investment, one should buy the worst house in the best neighborhood. While that may not always be true, it's probably a better strategy than buying the best house in the worst neighborhood.

Once a real estate investor is an expert on the market they're working in, they'll be able to identify an appropriate value for a given property.

The top determinant trait of a successful real estate investor is the ability to buy properties for less than their worth. This can mostly be accomplished through diligence and patience. There are certain circumstances that require homeowners to sell urgently and the patience to find these types of sellers will give you better odds of profitable real estate investing. In the book *The Millionaire Real Estate Investor*, the authors note that once an investor has narrowed their list down to thirty properties that meet his criteria for investment, ten of those will be worth investigating thoroughly, three will be worth making an offer on, and only one of those offers will be accepted.

Beyond the price appreciation in real estate, investors also have the opportunity for steady "passive" income. People always need a place to live. By renting out your property, you can generate a predictable stream of income that can be hard to achieve with other investments. Additionally, rent tends to increase by 3%-5% every year. So not only will your property appreciate over time, but your rental income potential increases year after year as well.

Additionally, investment real estate can utilize special tax rules to help keep more of your money invested. One of the most valuable tax breaks is the ability to transfer the gains from selling an old investment property into a new one. This procedure is known as a like-kind exchange or 1031 exchange. Typically, when you sell an investment, you'll need to pay capital gains taxes on the profits, leaving you with less cash to purchase another investment. When it comes to real estate, you have the option to use a 1031 exchange to defer taxes on your gains by purchasing another investment property with the proceeds. This procedure will allow you to reinvest more of your money and hopefully upgrade your investment holdings and potential rental income.

Note that a 1031 exchange will not eliminate your taxes, it only defers them. If you sell the subsequent property, you'll count both the gains from the sale of the original property and the gains on the second property as taxable income. Of course, it would be perfectly legal when selling the second property to utilize another 1031 exchange and purchase more investment properties deferring your capital gains again. You could effectively repeat this maneuver until you die. Whether your heirs will have to pay taxes on those properties or not is dependent on pending proposals to change the law. Your investment properties could be passed down to your heirs, income tax-free, even after a 1031 exchange. My old accounting professor explained that one of the best ways to avoid taxes is to "Delay, delay, delay, then die."

Perhaps the most appealing part of investing in real estate is the ability to finance the purchase easily. It's quite common to purchase an investment property with only 20% of the cost or less. This is especially appealing when interest rates are low. It's pretty difficult to buy a $250,000 property upfront, but coming up with $50,000 might be doable. Investing $50,000 to own a property that can generate over $15,000 in income from year one seems like a pretty good deal.

Why Isn't Everyone Doing It?

If everything above sounds like a dream, don't forget that every investment has downsides. Real estate is an incredibly expensive investment. Not only are the upfront costs to purchase the property significant, but the ongoing costs are higher than any other major asset class. You'll need to pay for the mortgage interest, property taxes, insurance, maintenance, association fees, significant repairs, and possibly hire property management. Because of these high costs, rental properties typically lose money for several years before they generate a profit for their investors. Additionally, the transaction costs of buying and selling real estate are extremely high when compared to other investments. Closing costs such as title fees, appraisals, commissions and more can cost 2%-5% of the sales price for buyers and 6%-10% for sellers. Even when you have the ability to purchase real estate with a partial down payment, you have to consider the opportunity cost of that money. How much could you be earning with other investments while you wait for the rental property to become profitable?

There's also a substantial amount of time involved. It takes work to ensure you rent to the right tenants and that they pay their rent on time. You may also need to spend time handling their requests, making repairs, or replacing appliances. Also, owning a rental property makes preparing your taxes more complicated, and you'll need to keep good records of your expenses throughout the year.

If owning a rental property sounds like too much work, you may be considering buying a vacation home as an investment. Considering the high ongoing costs, in almost all cases, real estate that isn't used as your main home or rented out to tenants winds up being a very poor investment that would struggle to keep up with inflation. There are exceptions, but real estate must generally be occupied if you want a good return on your investment.

Speaking of inflation, real estate has historically been seen as a hedge against inflation, meaning investors have viewed real estate as a good way to protect their money during times of high inflation. This appears to have been true for a century from 1900-2000, with the prices of homes increasing only 0.25% per year when adjusted for inflation over that period. During this time, real estate prices only increased about the same as the inflation rate. This also meant that real estate prices surged during the inflation crisis in the late 1970s, sheltering investors from rising prices throughout the economy. After the year 2000, however, this tight relationship between home prices and inflation deteriorated.

Homes had traditionally been seen as a place to live, so the primary buyers were people who intended to live in them. In that scenario, it makes perfect sense that home prices would rise at about the same rate as inflation because prices were based on what a buyer could afford to live in the home. However, when people started looking at homes with a motive to profit, the dynamic changed. Homes became less about maintaining living arrangements and more about wealth building. People became less concerned about the short-term costs and more interested in the potential for gains. Between the years 2000 and 2021, the percentage of homes bought for investment purposes increased from 6% to 14%. A few factors probably contribute to the breakout of real estate as an investment commodity rather than mere living accommodations. For one, interest rates had been historically low for nearly twenty years. Since access to financing is such a big draw for real estate in general, it's easy to understand why the surge in investment purchases has occurred. Another factor to consider is the success of HGTV (Formerly Home and Garden Television). HGTV debuted on cable in the mid-1990s and has since grown to become one of the most-watched networks in all of television. Some of the most popular shows on HGTV involve buying houses, making repairs, and then quickly reselling the property for impressive profits in a process commonly referred to as "flipping". Flipping was already around for many years amongst real estate professionals, but HGTV brought the idea into the mainstream and made it look easy. This shift in attitudes from homes being purchased to serve as family residences towards being purchased as a means to make quick profits has created a housing market that's less likely to follow inflation and more likely to act like stock markets.

This trend towards a more volatile housing market will continue. Technology and changes in real estate transactions will make buying and selling a home much faster. Websites like Zillow and Redfin help buyers quickly compare and identify potential properties, reducing the time it takes sellers to find a match with a buyer. These sites also make it simple for homeowners to quickly estimate what their home could sell for in the current market, possibly enticing more homeowners to sell during pricing booms or panic sell during real estate market downturns.

Other technology firms are using automated underwriting systems to identify well-qualified buyers. The firms then use cash to buy the home of their customer's choice and sign the homes over to the customer. This allows the transaction to close in just a few days instead of taking a month or more, as with traditional home financing. Eventually, technology will allow real estate transactions to close in just a few minutes as more of the process becomes automated. Additionally, advancing technology will lower the transaction costs for real estate deals. The system will eventually have enough automation that fees for real estate agents will be all but eliminated.

One of the main factors that has historically kept housing prices so stable is the difficulty and expense of buying and selling properties. While there will always be some degree of stability in real estate because it's difficult to physically move people in and out of homes, as the speed of real estate transactions increase and costs fall, the volatility of the housing market will accelerate to look more like stock markets. The long-term future for real estate is one where transactions are almost instantaneous with little to no cost, making investors far more likely to buy or sell based on gut reactions to the market's direction.

Alternatives to Buying Property Directly
When you don't have the cash or the patience to buy real estate

directly, there are a number of options available that will allow you to invest in real estate on a smaller scale.

REIT

A real estate investment trust (REIT) offers a means to invest in various real estate sectors without a significant outlay in cash. REITs can be thought of in a similar light to mutual funds and ETFs. A REIT is a company that purchases and owns real estate. Investors pool their money with a REIT, and the REIT's management selects properties to buy or sell, manages those properties, and collects rents. REITs are required to distribute 90% of their income to shareholders each year. The dividends you receive as a REIT holder typically qualify for a special business tax deduction, saving you up to 20% on taxes.

REITs can own virtually any type of real estate you can think of. Apartments, offices, self-storage, cell towers, pipelines, timber, and billboards are all examples of real estate a REIT might own. Typically, a particular REIT will focus on one type of property, but there are REITs that focus on a diversified mix of real estate.

REITs can help add a steady income stream to your investments and modest appreciation over time. It's common for REITs to provide higher dividends than common stocks. Another benefit to REITs is that they're incredibly easy to buy and sell. A couple of the downsides are that REITs typically have higher fees than mutual funds or ETFs, and their growth potential is limited. Because REITs must pay out 90% of their profit each year, they don't have much money to reinvest and expand.

REIG

Real Estate Investment Groups (REIG) differ from REITs discussed above. Most REIGs are operated as private partnerships, and shares cannot be purchased through a stock exchange. REIGs typically require a substantial amount of money to join. In most cases, a REIG will construct or buy property such as apartment complexes or condos, and investors will purchase one or more of the individual properties through the REIG as a partner. The REIG will handle the management of the property, such as maintenance and filling vacancies for a share of the rent collected. REIGs are less regulated than REITs which could be both a pro and con.

Other Exposure
Aside from the options previously discussed, there are various other ways to ensure some of your investments are tied to real estate. Several real estate-focused mutual funds exist. These funds may invest in real estate construction companies, lenders, or a mix of REITs. You can also participate in the housing market by investing in a roundabout way by buying mortgage-backed securities. Typically mortgage-backed securities are offered when a bank buys up a large lot of mortgages from another bank. The new bank then sells securities to new investors backed up by homeowners' interest payments on their mortgages.

In 1948, Richard and Maurice McDonald launched an innovative restaurant in San Bernardino, California that used an assembly line kitchen and served food in paper wrappers with no utensils. It was the birth of fast food. At the time, no one had seen anything like it, and people traveled for miles to try it. After a few successful years, they had built a new custom-designed restaurant and were working on franchising their business model.

By 1954, the brothers had six franchised locations. Ray Kroc, then a salesman for Multimixer, heard the brothers were using eight of his company's milkshake machines in their San Bernardino restaurant and decided to visit the store to see what they were up to. Kroc was excited by what he saw at the restaurant and convinced the brothers to put him in charge of franchising the business nationally. Ray was off and running for the next few years, but he became frustrated. He couldn't open new stores as fast as he wanted, and despite the recent expansion, the company was in a precarious financial situation.

Around this time, Ray met Harry Sonneborn, who suggested that Ray work to own the land and buildings the franchisees would operate and then collect rent from the franchise operators. This new model made starting a store accessible to more people, and the company's expansion skyrocketed. Today, McDonald's is one of the largest real estate owners in the world, and as surprising as it may be, its profits from real estate exceed the profit it generates from the sale of food.

Not only does this story highlight that real estate can be an incredible investment, but it also helps illustrate a second point: by investing in major companies, you're also investing in the real estate those companies own.

GOLD/ COMMODITIES

The Oak of the Golden Dream

Fransico Lopez had spent the early part of the day helping his niece herd cattle on her ranch about thirty-five miles north of present-day Los Angeles. He broke for lunch, and after spending hours in the sun, he sought out the shade of an oak tree. There, Lopez stretched out and fell asleep. As the legend goes, he dreamed about a river of gold. When his siesta ended, he recalled that he promised his wife he'd return home with wild onions. Fortunately, wild onions were in the vicinity of the oak. Lopez used his knife to dig up a bunch, but when he lifted the onions up from the ground, he was amazed when he could see tiny particles of gold entangled in their roots. He proceeded to dig further where he discovered subsequent and more substantial deposits of gold. The date was March 9, 1842, and marked the first discovery of gold in California. The lesson for men is, don't forget your promises to your wife.

Several years after Lopez's discovery, John Marshall would discover gold in Northern California at Sutter's Mill which set the 1849 Gold Rush in motion. Just six months after Marshall's discovery, nearly three out of every four men in San Fransisco left town in search of gold. As word spread across the country, people (primarily men) began to make the journey to California at any cost, borrowing, mortgaging their properties, or burning through their life savings.

By the end, it's estimated that over 300,000 people migrated to California dreaming of riches, and over 750,000 pounds of gold were pulled out of California mines. The Gold Rush also sped the development of California's cities and helped fast-track the region into statehood. Of course, by the time most forty-niners arrived, the easy pickings were gone and many of them were forced to become laborers for more established mining outfits.

Today, gold still has its luster. Most gold today, around 78%, is used to create jewelry because of its malleability, appearance, and resistance to tarnishing. Additionally, a small percentage of gold is used in various high-tech industries such as the manufacturing of computers, cellphones, aerospace components, and space equipment. Nearly 20% of gold is held for financial purposes primarily by government banks but also by individual investors.

It's believed gold was first used in transactions 6,000 years ago and the first gold coins were created over 2,000 years ago. Gold has long been used as a form of money because of its scarcity, durability, and because it is relatively easy to divide. Throughout history, many governments utilized a gold standard, meaning that printed money could be redeemed for a set amount of gold. The United States partially utilized this method until it was entirely abandoned in 1971. Once the U.S. ended the gold standard, the U.S. dollar became what's commonly referred to as a fiat currency. The country was able to print as much money as it wanted since it no longer needed additional gold to back it up. As the treasury printed more money, inflation spiked through the 70s, and by 1980, inflation reached 14%. Today, there are no countries using gold to back up their currencies.

The primary lure of gold from an investing standpoint is the protection it provides from the devaluation of a fiat currency. As a country prints more of its currency, its value and purchasing power decline. At the same time, gold tends to hold its purchasing power no matter what the U.S. dollar is worth. The price of gold can spike during times of high inflation or during financial crises when the treasury prints large sums of money to stimulate the economy. This was the case during the 2008 financial crisis as well as the 2020-2021 Covid-19 pandemic. Gold can easily be exchanged for another currency or some other items of value as it has been for thousands of years.

During World War I, Germany financed their war efforts entirely through debt and printing more of its own currency under the assumption it would win the war and force the defeated allies to make reparation payments. Well, they lost, and reparations were imposed on Germany instead. Because of the falling value of Germany's currency, reparation payments were required to be paid in either gold or foreign currency. Germany's strategy was to print their own money and use it to buy the other foreign currencies required to make their payments. However, they eventually missed a reparation payment because their currency had so little value no one would accept it in exchange for gold or other currencies. France and Belgium sent troops to Germany's industrial center to collect goods as payment instead. The German government effectively ordered their workers to go on strike in protest of the occupation, but Germany kept paying workers by continuing to print money.

The price of a loaf of bread in Berlin rose from about four German Marks in 1921 to over 200,000,000,000 Marks in 1923. This phenomenon is known as hyperinflation. The currency was losing value so quickly that anyone who received it tried to spend it as fast as possible. Many grocery store shelves were empty as Germans bought all the food they could find. Ultimately, the currency became so worthless that it was used in some instances as kindling for fire or to fashion children's toys. People were forced to switch to accepting payments in foreign currency or to barter for goods and services.

The story of hyperinflation in Germany served as a valuable lesson to countries across the world, yet dozens of nations still fell into the trap of hyperinflation in the time since. A hundred years later, Venezuela experienced an inflation crisis that some considered even worse than the crisis in Germany. Venezuela's economy is strongly dependent on the production of oil. While the country had struggled with high inflation for decades, once the price of oil started falling globally in 2014, Venezuela's government was unable or unwilling to cut back its spending. Like Germany in the 1920s, Venezuela resorted to the continued printing of money to keep up with the bills.

Beginning in 2016, Bloomberg published its "Cafe Con Leche Index," which tracked the price of a cup of coffee in the Venezuela Bolivar. In 2016, one coffee cost 0.01 bolivars. After just two years, a cup of coffee was over one thousand times the price at 14.00 bolivars. By July of 2021, one cup of coffee was approaching 7.8 million bolivars. The paper money had become so devalued that it was cheaper to wipe with bolivars than it was to use them to buy toilet paper, with one roll costing millions. Venezuela introduced a one million bolivar bill which was worth about 52 U.S. cents at the time.

Today, U.S. Dollars have a distinct advantage over other currencies. After World War II, America emerged as the dominant economic force in the world. In addition, our dollars were linked to the stockpile of gold the U.S. accumulated in exchange for supplying the allies through both world wars. This allowed other countries to feel extremely confident in the stability of the U.S. dollar and in 1944, the Bretton Woods agreement was signed by forty-four countries willing to link their currencies to the U.S. dollar. Since, at the time, the U.S. dollar was as good as gold, other countries began to hold U.S. dollars in their reserves in place of gold. The Bretton Woods agreement was eventually disbanded when the U.S. ended the gold standard in 1971, but despite the gold standard ending, the U.S. dollar still held onto its status as the reserve currency of the world.

Today, over 60% of foreign bank reserves are held in U.S. denominations. Because most countries are comfortable transacting with dollars, most commodities are bought and sold in dollars regardless of which country is buying or selling. For example, when Saudi Arabia sells oil to Japan, Japan pays Saudi Arabia with U.S. dollars. This arrangement gives the United States the unique ability to print money to buy foreign imports and also lets the U.S. print money to pay off debts. Both actions allow the U.S. to effectively export inflation to other countries that hold dollars.

Obviously, not everyone appreciates that the U.S. has the special privilege of stewarding the main reserve currency of the world. Both China and Europe have made efforts towards reducing the U.S. dollar's global status by working to increase transactions utilizing the Euro and Yuan respectively. It's unlikely that either one will be able to dethrone the dollar anytime soon. The dollar's use still dominates international transactions and, in several countries, the dollar is the only form of currency used at all. However, increasing U.S. debt and the continued expansion of the U.S. money supply will eventually start to erode international confidence in the dollar. If other countries lose confidence in the dollar, they'll be less willing to hold dollars in their reserves and be less willing to purchase U.S. treasuries.

A lack of demand for U.S. dollars internationally would result in a spike in interest rates as investors would demand a higher rate of return for an investment they are less confident in. Additionally, with less demand, the value of the dollar would fall, which effectively raises prices for everyone using them. When foreign countries stop holding the U.S. dollar in reserves, that money may flood back into the United States leaving the country with a glut of cash and skyrocketing inflation. The Dutch Guilder and the British Pound each had nearly hundred-year reigns as the reserve currencies of their time. The U.S. dollar has held its status as the world's reserve currency for over seventy-five years. Its time will eventually end but predicting exactly when is anyone's guess.

From an investor's perspective, the value of gold as an investment should be viewed as protection against runaway inflation or the outright collapse of modern currencies. Other than the preservation of purchasing power, an investment in gold does not pay interest, dividends, or grow over time relative to inflation. There are several ways to invest in gold.

Physical Gold

It would be hard to beat the feeling of reassurance you'd get from owning physical gold if the world went belly-up tomorrow. Once you own physical gold, you're not dependent on the security and stability of another institution to keep it safe. Hackers won't be able to steal your gold from under your nose with just a password and a few security questions. Also, owning gold can give you privacy. No one needs to know how much gold you own besides you. Gold won't deteriorate and is durable enough to survive a house fire. Physical gold allows you to store substantial value in a small space. $50,000 worth of gold would fill less space in your home than an iPhone. In addition to all that, it's shiny!

When thinking of physical gold investments, you probably imagine big shiny bars locked in a vault. This is known as gold bullion, and it comes in many sizes from several grams to 400 ounces. The most commonly sold bullion size is a one-ounce bar which is similar to about half the size of a credit card and worth around $2,300 at the time of this writing. Smaller bars are easier to transact with due to their lower values but also cost more per ounce due to additional minting costs. Gold coins are also another popular choice for holding gold. Coins will typically cost more than bullion due to increased minting costs as well as premiums due to collectability.

For those who want to own physical gold, but aren't interested in bullion or gold coins, investing in gold jewelry may be an option. Buying gold jewelry gives the owner some usability out of the investment which is a benefit over keeping it locked away. Be sure to make note of the jewelry's purity, as any jewelry that is less than 24 karats has been mixed with other metals for practical purposes. Jewelry would clearly be the most expensive option to purchase gold as an investment because of the high additional costs of design. While many times the premium paid for jewelry design can carry over to resale value, over time, changes to fashion trends in jewelry mean older jewelry may not be worth any more than the gold it's made from.

Some of the benefits of owning physical gold can also cause headaches. You'll have to sort out how to secure it. If it's in your home, you're at risk of losing it in a robbery or even simply misplacing it. Stories of new homeowners discovering stashes of gold forgotten by previous owners are commonplace. Storing gold at home requires additional insurance while storing gold in safe deposit boxes or other special depository requires additional fees. Purchasing physical gold takes diligence, just like any investment. Finding a reputable gold dealer is important to ensure your purchase is authentic and isn't "lost in shipping."

Alternatives to Physical Gold

If your interest in gold investments is more about hedging against inflation and less about doomsday prepping, a couple of other options might make more sense for you.

Investing in companies that mine and process gold is a roundabout way to invest in gold itself. Gold mining stocks will typically fluctuate with the price of gold but are also dependent on the overall fundamentals of the company itself. Both ETFs and mutual funds which work to emulate investments in gold or other valuable metals are widely available. Some gold funds track the price of gold directly while others may invest in a group of mining stocks. These investments are easy to buy and sell and don't require the extra responsibility of owning gold bars.

While gold is seen as a source of long-term security and stability, it's a speculative investment at the same time. The price of gold can fluctuate significantly over short periods and prices may take many years to return to a high after falling. Absent any crisis, investments in gold result in missed returns in other sectors. From 2010 to 2020, an investment in the broad stock market would have resulted roughly in a quadrupling of your money while the value of an investment in gold would have remained worth roughly the same amount as where you started.

About twenty years after Fransico Lopez discovered gold in California, Ramon Peria was hunting deer just ten miles west of Lopez's precognitive golden dream under the oak tree. Peria had wounded a buck, and while tracking the deer down, he arrived before an oil spring. He observed that the oil seemed unusual and thought it could be valuable. He gathered some of the oil in his canteen to have it analyzed, and it was determined to be valuable indeed.

Peria was given a share of ownership in the oil company that would establish drilling operations on the site. He reportedly exchanged his ownership stake for a barrel of booze and a twenty-dollar gold piece. Ultimately, his oil discovery led not only to the first profitable oil well in California but to the most successful oil well in the state's history, pumping oil from the site for over a hundred years.

Interestingly (for me anyway), my office is located almost precisely between these two historic sources of wealth, with Lopez's gold discovery about five miles to the East and Peria's oil discovery five miles to the West. I'm hoping that's a good omen.

Face it, you and I are not going to discover oil and become wealthy because of it. Still, the opportunity to profit from oil and other commodities is available to the typical investor. The commodities markets offer investments in various types of physical goods from oil to cattle to soybeans. The most common way an investor would participate in pure commodity investing is by using futures contracts.

A futures contract is a commitment to buy a certain amount of goods for a stated price on a specific date. For example, a contract could require you to buy 5,000 bushels of corn for $4.27 per bushel on July 14th. You'd want to buy a futures contract if you thought the price of corn would increase before the contract's expiration date. Once the price increases, you can sell the contract you own for a marked-up price. You're probably thinking 5,000 bushels is a lot of corn to have to buy, especially if you don't even like eating corn. Most commodity brokers will automatically sell the contract on your behalf if you fail to do so before the expiration date, so you won't be required to purchase the goods.

Futures contracts are typically utilized by sophisticated investors to speculate on changes in the prices of commodities. However, due to technological advances in trading, this type of investing has become available to mainstream investors. With that being said, futures contracts are highly speculative and high risk. One should not venture into this area of investing lightly.

Like investing in gold, you can invest in commodities without the complications of dealing with futures contracts. To benefit from price increases in oil, for example, you might consider investing in companies that drill, refine, or transport oil. Mutual funds and ETFs exist that follow the ups and downs in various commodity prices, allowing you to easily capitalize on rising commodity costs.

-CHAPTER SUMMARY-

- Real estate investing can result in substantial investment returns while also offering an often sought after sense of prestige to investors.

- Real estate investments come with favorable tax advantages.

- Investing in real estate typically requires access to a significant sum of money for the initial investment as well as substantial ongoing costs, so it's not for everyone.

- Gold and other precious metals give investors protection against the demise of major financial systems which is a concern that grows with the expanding U.S. National Debt.

- Holding physical gold presents its own challenges such as storing the assets and protecting them from theft.

- Investing in commodities and gold through ETFs can give investors the opportunity to capitalize on growth of the assets with fewer challenges.

CHAPTER SEVEN

Alternative Investments

"New ideas that fly in the face of conventional wisdom of the day are always greeted with doubt and scorn, even fear."
– John C. Bogle

STOCKS, ,BONDS, AND REAL ESTATE have all stood the test of time when it comes to investing. That's why they've been used by your parents, grandparents, and great-grandparents. Any investment portfolio needs to utilize the traditional investments we covered in the last chapters, but as technology continues to advance, new ways to invest become available to us. This chapter will cover some of the less conventional investment options as well as investment opportunities developed as a result of technological advancements.

CRYPTOCURRENCIES

Cryptocurrencies or digital assets have quickly pushed their way into mainstream investing in the years following Bitcoin's invention, making many early adopters extremely wealthy. First of all, what is Bitcoin?

The origins of Bitcoin are still rather mysterious. Satoshi Nakamoto is the name used on the 2008 documents proposing the creation of Bitcoin as the first digital currency, however, it has never been verified if he was a real person, a fabrication, or a group of people acting together. There have been many speculations as to who Satoshi Nakamoto could really be, but the truth has yet to be confirmed.

Bitcoin was designed as an alternative to traditional currency. The idea is that governments influence the value of their money through various tactics, like printing too much of it. Governmental control over money can be considered a negative for citizens, especially if you consider past examples of hyperinflation. Alternatively, Bitcoin doesn't have a central bank, central command, or any single entity controlling it. It's what's referred to as a "decentralized" commodity. Instead of being controlled by a government entity or a CEO, Bitcoin follows a computer code.

It is a "currency" that exists only in digital form, so there are no physical Bitcoins. You may have seen artists' renderings of a Bitcoin, but nothing exists in a tangible form. Bitcoin exists on a digital network of volunteer computers spread across the globe. In a process known as "mining", these computers process Bitcoin transactions and update the digital records on the Bitcoin network. The owners of these computers are rewarded with transaction fees and Bitcoin of their own.

Each group of transaction records added to the network is called a block. Each of those blocks contains information that links it to the previous block on the network creating a blockchain. You can think of the blockchain as the history of all transactions. Because the blockchain exists on a network of independent computers, it is virtually impossible to delete or falsify. For example, if one of the computers was compromised, the records stored on the rest of the network would quickly invalidate any inaccurate or manipulated blockchain data coming from the compromised computer. For comparison, if a major bank wanted to delete your account and all of your account history, they could technically do it because their records are centralized giving the bank full control. On a decentralized blockchain, no one has the power to delete history.

Why is Bitcoin valuable? The number of Bitcoin that will ever be available is capped by design at about 21 million. Because the supply is limited, as more people become interested and compete to buy Bitcoin, its price will increase.

The price of Bitcoin is extremely volatile. After its trading value hovered around a few hundred dollars for years, in 2017, the price of Bitcoin saw its first major breakout and surged from around $1,000 to nearly $20,000 in a span of only eight months. When the selling price of Bitcoin first broke through the $1,000 level, it drew attention to the digital currency, and that created more demand. As more people saw the price of Bitcoin rising, more of them thought it was a good opportunity to profit. This created a sort of reverse panic. Speculators started to believe that there was no limit to how high the price could go, and if they didn't buy Bitcoin as soon as possible, they would regret it for the rest of their lives. Of course, the price came crashing down just a few short months after reaching that high. Two years following that crash, Bitcoin was surging again, reaching a peak of over $60,000 in 2021 before falling nearly 75% over the twelve months that followed. Bitcoin does not produce anything and pays no dividends, so when a person buys Bitcoin, they're generally hoping they'll find someone else to buy it back from them at a higher price down the road.

A general distrust and dislike of government control has helped spur the rise of Bitcoin. There are now many cryptocurrency zealots who seem certain the global financial markets as we know them will collapse, leaving only digital currencies remaining.

Eccentric millionaire founder of McAfee anti-virus software, John McAfee, pledged in 2017 during Bitcoin's first major price run-up that if the cryptocurrency's price didn't surpass $500,000 by the year 2020, he would eat his own genitalia on television. Talk about conviction. Well, eventually he was convicted. McAfee wound up sentenced to prison for tax fraud where he later died in 2021.

Bitcoin has yet to surpass $500,000, and it's believed that McAfee's privates remained intact up to his passing. Lofty price predictions for the currency are frequent and numerous. However, it's impossible to predict how high or low the price of Bitcoin may move, because there is nothing tangible backing it and no precedent for this type of asset in history. Unlike stocks which can be analyzed by evaluating the performance of the underlying business or real estate which can be compared to other properties to determine price, cryptocurrency pricing remains a guessing game. To predict the future price of Bitcoin, one must predict how much interest in Bitcoin will grow.

The interest in Bitcoin will undoubtedly grow from where it is today and with it the long-term price. However, it seems hard to imagine a scenario where the interest in Bitcoin expands indefinitely. For something to be valuable financially, it must not only possess characteristics of rarity but must be useful or carry intrinsic value. It's apparent that Bitcoin has no intrinsic value as it does not exist in physical form, but is it useful?

Bitcoin was designed to be used as an alternative to traditional currencies; however, it's not very good for buying or selling anything that isn't illicit. Unfortunately, very few merchants accept Bitcoin directly, and those who do accept it do so primarily as a means to generate publicity. Processing Bitcoin payments is complicated and expensive. The Bitcoin network can currently process up to seven transactions per second. Compare that to the Visa network, which can process up to 65,000 in a second, and you can start to see how far behind Bitcoin is as a payment system. Additionally, confirmation of a Bitcoin payment takes about ten minutes on average, but, in some cases, you could end up waiting days.

What's worse is as the number of transactions on the network increases, the slower they'll be processed. At the 2018 North American Bitcoin Conference, organizers ironically announced that they would no longer accept Bitcoin as a form of payment for tickets, citing high costs and complications with accepting the digital currency.

The ability to make purchases utilizing Bitcoin has increased recently but only thanks to opportunistic third-party companies who have stepped in to facilitate Bitcoin payments in a more expedient manner. Businesses partner with a cryptocurrency payment processing company to accept Bitcoin payments on their behalf. In most cases, the customer would transfer an amount of Bitcoin to the third party and the third party would then transfer cash to the business they've partnered with. The Bitcoin payment processor would either charge an upfront fee to the customer, convert the Bitcoin to cash at less than what it's worth while pocketing the difference, or both. Having to utilize a middleman payment processor to use Bitcoin for ordinary purchases highlights how poorly it functions as a currency. If you can find someone willing to accept Bitcoin as payment directly, you could face a transaction fee of nearly $60. That kind of fee might be a good deal if you are transferring $10,000 to a friend in the Philippines, but it certainly won't work for paying the babysitter, especially with a number of free peer-to-peer payment options available today like Venmo, Cash App, Zelle, and FedNow. Bitcoin transaction fees fluctuate depending on how many people are requesting transactions at a particular time. The busier the network is, the higher the fee.

Its failure as a usable currency alternative hasn't deterred many long-term Bitcoin investors who see it as a potential store of value. As discussed in the prior chapter, the U.S. dollar has served as the world's reserve currency for decades and we know it's a matter of time before that status changes. Many Bitcoin enthusiasts believe Bitcoin has the potential to take that mantle away from the dollar. There is a pretty good rationale for this argument. Bitcoin cannot be manipulated by any single government, and every country who used it as a reserve would theoretically be on a level playing field. They'd be unable to manipulate their own currency but also not be forced to endure the monetary whims of more powerful countries. When Venezuela lost control of its currency through massive hyperinflation, many citizens and businesses began transacting in Bitcoin in place of their native currency. To date, El Salvador and the Central African Republic have adopted Bitcoin as legal tender. More countries will follow.

In a scenario where Bitcoin becomes a global reserve currency, the price per Bitcoin could easily jump into the millions or billions of dollars. However, an event like that would force a stiff, nearly impossible uphill battle. Major governments like China, the European Union, and the United States, would fiercely fight to protect the control of their currencies, including waging all-out war. Many pundits have suggested that the numerous U.S. wars in the Middle East have been waged not for the liberation of innocents but to protect the oil production in the region. The U.S. cannot afford to lose its influence in the region, as the country is highly reliant on keeping major commodities priced in dollars as we discussed in the last chapter. Oil is the king of commodities. If oil decouples from the U.S. dollar, most other commodities would follow. Saudi Arabia recently threatened to end the pricing of oil in dollars as a protest against proposed U.S. legislation. The proposed legislation was withdrawn as a result. While the U.S. has helped battle tyranny in the Middle East, it's clear that the country was fighting for its own financial interests as well and would certainly do so again. I also wouldn't rule out major countries using Bitcoin as a type of shadow reserve currency or back up currency. I can imagine scenarios where governments hold Bitcoin in secret while still standing behind their native currency publicly.

Still, even if Bitcoin does not become a global reserve currency, it may serve some role as a type of digital gold or perhaps a reserve currency of the crypto world. Since the advent of Bitcoin, thousands of other cryptocurrencies have been developed. Many of these other cryptocurrencies try to solve what's known as the Blockchain "trilemma" by trying to strike the best balance between decentralization, security, and the ability to scale enough to serve the entire world. Bitcoin has been successful at remaining decentralized and is considered quite secure, but it is not very scalable due to transaction processing speed and expense. Many of the cryptocurrencies created after Bitcoin have addressed some of its shortfalls. Despite other cryptos having better functionality, Bitcoin remains the highest valued and is the cryptocurrency investors are most confident in. It's possible that a future scenario exists where multiple cryptocurrencies co-exist in a useful way and Bitcoin serves as a stabilizer or safe haven in the market.

Digital currencies may play a larger role in developing countries where access to traditional banking is limited. Over the past several decades, developing countries have been able to adopt modern technologies by leapfrogging outdated systems. For example, many African countries never developed extensive land-line phone infrastructure but went straight to cell phone adoption. Digital currencies may provide an opportunity for developing countries to leapfrog traditional banking systems in a similar fashion. However, many experts believe that current central banks will link blockchain technology to their existing currencies. This could essentially eliminate the usefulness of private digital currencies.

How risky are cryptocurrencies? They're one of the riskiest investments you can find. The prices of various cryptocurrencies are highly speculative and volatile because no one has the ability to calculate a reasonable value for any of them. When there is no way to determine a reasonable value, the price can only be based on how many people hope its price will continue to rise, and that number of people can change on a whim. Additionally, crypto-currencies are essentially unregulated. Under present laws, anyone can establish a new cryptocurrency without the need to file an application with the Securities and Exchange Commission like companies would need to do when issuing stocks or bonds to the public. Cryptocurrency creators adopted the phrase Initial Coin Offering or ICO to indicate the sale of a newly created cryptocurrency. Because there was no regulation, 98% of ICOs issued between 2016-2018 are now worthless. Many businesses were using ICOs to raise funds for their company as a way to sidestep SEC disclosure requirements. Ultimately, the SEC ruled that this process was illegal.

One of the biggest challenges with investing in cryptocurrencies is that everything having to do with it is fairly new, unknown, and rapidly evolving. This combination leads to rampant fraud. Few digital coin intermediaries have existed long enough to establish a dependable reputation that investors can rely on. It's easy to be drawn into a scam suggesting a new, special technique or "hack" for making money with crypto that no one else seems to know about because investing in crypto in any way is new. Tens of billions of dollars have already been lost to outright scams driven by cryptocurrencies. Due to its lack of regulation, cryptocurrencies are subject to much more price manipulation. For example, in early 2021, Tesla CEO Elon Musk announced that his car company had purchased $1.5 billion worth of Bitcoin and would begin to accept the currency as payment soon. This announcement helped accelerate a Bitcoin rally to an all-time high of over $60,000. Just a few weeks after the original announcement, Musk tweeted that Tesla would no longer be accepting Bitcoin as payment due to environmental concerns related to the high electricity requirements needed for Bitcoin mining (an issue he was undoubtedly aware of before making the first announcement). Bitcoin's price fell over 50% from its high in the ensuing weeks. Elon Musk has a history of promoting various cryptocurrencies, and after he makes favorable online posts regarding a specific digital coin, a price surge typically follows. Whether Musk has intentionally influenced the price of cryptocurrencies for personal gain or not isn't known, but the events serve to highlight that, while Bitcoin is not managed by a central bank, all it takes is one person with enough money to influence the entire crypto market. Pump and dump schemes involving cryptocurrencies are not technically illegal, yet. As long as the promoted cryptocurrencies are not tied to some underlying value or otherwise considered a security, they are not covered under existing securities laws.

Eventually, comprehensive cryptocurrency regulations will be passed. As that begins to happen, regulations will act somewhat like a double-edged sword. Fraud and manipulation risks of investing in cryptocurrencies will be reduced. At the same time, cryptos may lose some of their appeal since the independent, "Wild West" nature of the cryptocurrency market is a major part of its draw.

Additional regulations are also one of the most substantial risks to cryptocurrencies as a whole. China, which keeps tight controls over the flow of money in and out of the country, has consistently ramped up restrictions on crypto-currencies over prior years. China banned ICOs early on and has also banned crypto exchanges which allow investors to buy and sell various cryptocurrencies. Additionally, businesses and banks in China are not allowed to offer cryptocurrency-related services. China has also banned cryptocurrency mining. While Chinese citizens are still permitted to own crypto, many experts believe an all-out ban may be coming to the nation soon. India, the second most populous country in the world, has placed similar restrictions on cryptocurrencies and is currently considering a full ban. Try to contemplate the outlook of cryptocurrency investments if both China and India, whose citizens makeup over one-third of the global population, ban the ownership of digital currency.

Other Cryptocurrencies

While there are thousands of cryptocurrencies in existence, most are simply irrelevant. Let's talk about some of the more popular alternatives to Bitcoin.

Ether

Ether is the primary digital currency of the Ethereum network. The Ethereum network functions in a manner similar to Bitcoin. Ethereum utilizes its own Blockchain with a network of miners who verify transactions to earn a reward paid in Ether. However,

Ethereum is designed to accomplish much more than Bitcoin ever was. While Ethereum does have the ability to process payments and does so much more efficiently than Bitcoin, it's also designed to support "smart contracts" and "decentralized apps." These two features are what make Ether the second most valuable digital currency today.

Many business experts believe smart contracts will have a massive impact on the way transactions work in the future. However, smart contracts are not what we typically think of when we hear the word contract. A smart contract can be thought of as a program that executes a predetermined outcome once specific conditions are met. In 2017, French insurance provider AXA started utilizing smart contracts for their flight delay insurance. The smart contract was linked to air traffic data, and if a flight was delayed or canceled, the customer would automatically be compensated. The procedure for customers without the smart contract required them to call the insurer to report the flight delay. Once reported, the insurer would verify the status of the flight and then send payment to the customer. Eventually, AXA shut down this smart contract as a result of low demand, but the company remains committed to exploring and experimenting with smart contracts on a broader scale. It's expected that smart contracts will eventually be used to automate and streamline even the most complex transactions like buying or selling a home.

Ethereum also supports decentralized apps. Typically, websites and apps are hosted on a single server. This makes traditional websites and apps subject to potential censorship shutdowns or unintended downtime if those servers fail. Decentralized apps are essentially hosted by the entire Ethereum network and are not dependent on a single authority to remain operational. This arrangement may be particularly appealing in countries with governments that take an authoritarian approach to what content should or shouldn't be shared online.

To utilize any services on the Ethereum network, the user must pay a fee using Ether based on the complexity of the desired task. This is where Ether's value comes from. Proponents of the Ethereum network believe that it has the potential to play a massive role in society's future. As more entities begin to adopt services on the Ethereum network, the demand for Ether will soar, and investors hope that demand will cause exponential growth that could potentially surpass the value of Bitcoin. However, unlike Bitcoin, there is no limit to how much new Ether can be created. If the creation of additional Ether keeps up with increased demand, there would be no fundamental reason for its price to increase.

Because cryptocurrencies are created by computer coding, their functionality can be frequently altered. For major cryptocurrencies, changes and upgrades aren't as simple as computer programmers typing in a few new lines of code. Suggestions for improvements are generally presented to core developers, who decide if the changes are worth implementing, but the final word doesn't rest on a small group of developers. For a broad change to take effect, a consensus of miners needs to agree to begin using the new software, otherwise the currency may "fork" into two separate tokens with one set of users utilizing the updates and others refusing the changes.

Forks have happened several times to Bitcoin, Ethereum, and others. Forks are why you'll find spin-off cryptocurrencies like Bitcoin Cash, Bitcoin Gold, and Ethereum Classic. In a project originally labeled Ethereum 2.0, developers are currently working to improve the network's processing time to handle up to 100,000 transactions per second.

As with any emerging technology, it's difficult to say if Ethereum will maintain its lead in developing a successful infrastructure for smart contracts or if some other network will evolve, making Ethereum irrelevant. There is a growing consensus that blockchain technology will play a significant role in the near future, and while Ethereum is used by more developers than any other network, the usefulness of smart contracts is still mostly theoretical as there has been very little real-world use at all.

Dogecoin

In late 2013, software engineer Jackson Palmer launched a website mocking the growing cryptocurrency investment speculation. His website announced a new cryptocurrency based on a popular Internet meme featuring a Shiba Inu dog and its internal dialogue written in broken English, including an intentional misspelling of the word dog: "doge." Like the meme, his website displayed flashes of random words and phrases such as "much profit," "many coin," and "amaze," while prominently featuring the famous Shiba Inu at center stage in coin form. The tagline read, "dogecoin is an open-source, peer-to-peer cryptocurrency, favored by Shiba Inus worldwide."

Like Bitcoin, Dogecoin would have a cap on the total number of coins that could be created, but instead of the 21 million limit tied to Bitcoin, Dogecoin listed the absurd limit of 100 billion coins. The coding for the currency was developed in a joint effort between Palmer and engineer Billy Markus.

The joke caught on, and Dogecoin began to develop a devoted community of followers. In keeping with the lighter spirit of Dogecoin, followers have successfully led efforts to raise $30,000 to help send the Jamaican Bobsleigh team to the 2014 Sochi Olympics, helped fund the construction of a well in Kenya, and successfully raised funds to sponsor a NASCAR driver whose car would race with "Dogecoin" emblazoned across its hood and rear fenders. The car was nicknamed the "Moonrocket," a reference to the hopes that the price of Dogecoin would shoot to the moon and make its holders rich.

Today, Dogecoin has evolved into much more than a joke, having reached a cumulative value of over $70 billion at one point. Billionaires Mark Cuban and Elon Musk have repeatedly touted Dogecoin as a cryptocurrency that works especially well for accepting payments. Mark Cuban, who owns the Dallas Mavericks professional basketball team, announced special pricing on team merchandise for customers who paid with Dogecoin. Cuban cited the currency's robust community as a reason for its value. Dogecoin's billing as the "fun and friendly" internet currency helps keep people engaged, and as long as enough supporters believe Dogecoin is valuable, it will have value. Despite its praise by prominent billionaires, Dogecoin is technologically inferior to other cryptocurrencies and has lacked dedicated developers that other major cryptos depend on. Originally, Dogecoin's website stated that the creation of new coins would be limited to 100 billion, a number neither creator ever thought the joke currency would remotely approach. To keep the currency functional, Dogecoin's programming now allows for the creation of unlimited coins, and billions of new Dogecoin are released each year.

In order for Dogecoin to increase in value, interest and adoption of its use must continuously expand more quickly than new coins are generated. Proponents of Dogecoin's increasing supply believe that this feature will prevent the hoarding of the currency (as seen with Bitcoin) and help to maintain its usability as a currency. However, if the supply of Dogecoin expands too rapidly, investors will see the value of their Dogecoin falling due to inflationary pressure.

Cardano

After a disagreement with his fellow Ethereum co-founder about the future direction of the platform, Charles Hoskinson broke off to start his own crypto platform. Hoskinson started development of the Cardano platform in 2015 and officially launched it in 2017, making it a fairly new arrival to the scene. Cardano is designed to help address some of the shortcomings of other digital currencies. The Cardano network is built for speed and security and, like Ethereum, was specifically created to support smart contracts and decentralized apps. The Cardano network utilizes a cryptocurrency called Ada in a manner similar to how the Ethereum network uses Ether.

To be clear, Ethereum has the jump on Cardano in this market.

Ethereum already has thousands of apps built on its network, and Cardano is still in its infancy as far as getting apps built. Hoskinson emphasized the fact that the Cardano network is taking the time to ensure that the system is able to function in a real-life way that provides value to those who use it while Ethereum is still operating in a somewhat hypothetical marketplace. The Ethereum network has already experienced reduced speeds and increased transaction costs, highlighting the challenges it faces in trying to scale into widespread acceptance. Cardano is designed to work faster and more efficiently. Additionally, the Bitcoin and Ethereum networks require massive amounts of electricity to operate the computers that keep their networks running. Cardano has also addressed this issue and is considered an environmentally friendly cryptocurrency. For these reasons, Cardano investors believe it has the potential to eclipse Ethereum as the second-largest cryptocurrency network in the market.

Stablecoins

The value of digital currencies is known to fluctuate as much as 10% on any given day. A category of cryptocurrency known as stablecoins has changed that. A stablecoin is typically tied to another familiar asset like gold, the U.S. dollar, or the Euro. A stablecoin is designed to replicate the value of its underlying asset, so a stablecoin tied to the dollar will typically be worth about a dollar, regardless of how the crypto markets swing. You don't purchase stablecoins expecting any price appreciation like you'd hope for from other digital currencies.

A part of cryptocurrency's appeal to so many is that it allows for transactions outside traditional financial institutions, but this can lead to a gap between traditional financial institutions and those that specialize in digital currencies. Many cryptocurrency exchanges deal only in crypto and don't process transactions in fiat currency like dollars. In other cases, exchanging dollars for cryptocurrency may take days. Stablecoins allow investors who want to quickly move in and out of various cryptocurrency investments to do so without having to deal with fiat currency conversions. Stabelcoins give investors a place to hold their cryptocurrency when they don't want to be subjected to the wild ups and downs in the market. Additionally, stablecoins help address transactional issues that arise with volatile cryptocurrencies. Imagine placing an order on Amazon and paying with a cryptocurrency only to have the price change while in the middle of checkout because your cryptocurrency of choice lost value over the last five minutes. Stablecoins help to alleviate this problem. Stablecoins could likely play a role in countries without developed financial systems or whose currencies are experiencing a crisis. Stablecoins can offer an alternative currency to any person in the world. Two of the world's most used digital currencies are stablecoins Tether and USD Coin (USDC), which both mirror the U.S. dollar.

More Crypto Investments

Other notable cryptocurrencies today include Polkadot, which is developing a system to link various blockchains and allow them to work together, Solana, which focuses on decentralized apps for finance as well as smart contracts, and XRP, used on the Ripple digital payment network for fast and efficient payment processing.

Aside from the smart contracts and decentralized apps we discussed earlier, blockchain technology can secure a chain of custody from beginning to end for anything from works of art to election ballots, making it nearly impossible to pass off counterfeits and frauds as the real thing. Nike, for instance, has developed blockchain technology to ensure the authenticity of their shoes. Each pair of shoes would be assigned a unique code linked to a buyer's personal code after purchase. If the owner decided to sell those shoes to another party, the shoe's code would then be linked to the new buyer. On the Blockchain there would be a traceable history documenting the original buyer receiving the shoes from the factory, then a record showing the transfer from the original owner to the second owner. A potential third buyer would be able to review the blockchain to confirm the shoes were authentic. Nike frequently produces rare and sought-after shoes. The high demand for these shoes entices large-scale counterfeiting by merchants who sell their reproductions online or on the street as authentic. By utilizing blockchain technology to verify the origins of a particular shoe, every buyer would know whether they were purchasing a genuine article or a fake.

Digital assets are sold and tracked similarly to how Nike can track shoes using what are known as Non-Fungible Tokens, or NFTs. Some examples of assets sold as NFT's are digital images, written works, or unique music. This concept may be a little harder to grasp than cryptocurrencies in general. The ability to accurately trace a digital asset to its origin and verify its authenticity as an original can substantially increase its value. One way to think of it would be to imagine an artist creating an original painting and many other artists creating perfect replicas. If you can prove you own the original, it would be much more valuable than any copy. While it's very easy to copy and distribute digital images, NFTs now provide a way to own original or unique creations of digital art because of their traceability. Many NFTs, like other rare items, have become status symbols for their owners. This makes sense in an increasingly digital world. Instead of hanging fancy art on their walls, NFT owners can show off their assets through their social media platforms or other online presence. The role of digital personas will exponentially increase for younger generations.

Consider today that video game fans spend billions of dollars a year to upgrade characters they'll use in online gameplay and the idea of valuable digital assets starts to make sense. Many cryptocurrency investors see NFT's as another way to invest in blockchain technologies.

You may be curious about how much a digital piece of art can really sell for. The "CryptoPunk" series will clue you in. CryptoPunks are a set of 10,000 rudimentary digital portraits created using computer algorithms in 2017 and distributed through the Ethereum network. No two CryptoPunks are the same. Originally, all 10,000 were given away for free as part of a movement to advance the use of NFTs for original art. Today, their history as one of the earliest NFT art projects has made them extremely valuable to NFT art collectors. In 2021, CryptoPunk #7523, which is one of only nine Alien punks and wears a facemask similar to those worn during the COVID-19 pandemic, sold for $11.8 million. Many other CryptoPunks have sold with multi-million-dollar price tags. Larvalabs, the creator of CryptoPunks, says that the average selling price of a CryptoPunk during 2021 was over one hundred thousand dollars. Those numbers have definitely gotten the attention of investors, not just art collectors.

How much more is there to know about cryptocurrencies? A surprising amount. Each set of systems governing each particular currency is very complex. Add to that the task of comparing the inner workings of dozens of digital currencies while monitoring the potential changes to their programming, and you can easily become overwhelmed.

The landscape changes so quickly that reliable resources are difficult to find and the information surrounding digital assets could easily fill several books. The challenge is that by the time a book is written and published, a significant amount of the content will be outdated. There are many terms and concepts relating to cryptocurrencies that are beyond what it makes sense to cover here. If you're sincerely interested in learning more about the inner workings of crypto, I've included common terms and definitions in the back of the book for your reference. The best resources will be found online on websites like Cointelegraph.com and from non-traditional resources like social media platform X.

The crypto market is still rapidly developing and changing quickly. It's possible all the coins I've talked about may no longer exist in just a few short years. While it is extremely difficult to know which specific cryptocurrencies will have value over the long term, it's becoming increasingly clear that the underlying blockchain technology will have long-lasting, widespread use in the near future.

I used to compare choosing which cryptocurrency to invest in to choosing which number on the roulette wheel to bet on. Chances are you'd lose everything you bet, but you'd have a small chance of winning big. Today, I see investing in the cryptocurrency market as much more like betting on a horse race. You can look at the horse's racing history, look at its opponents, observe track conditions, and you don't even need your horse to come in first to do well. You can also bet on a fringe horse with lousy odds and cash in big if it pulls off an upset. No matter how much research you do, you'll need some luck to win, and you have to hope horse racing isn't outright banned while your bets are out. Investing in cryptocurrencies is high risk, but there's still potential for high rewards. Many investors today can benefit from investing a small portion of their portfolio in cryptocurrencies. For most people, this amount is probably from 1-10% of their total portfolios, depending on investment timelines and tolerance for risk. The majority of people would fall into the low end of that range, but in any case, a crypto investment should not be an amount more than someone can afford to lose.

BE THE BANK

Money deposited at a bank isn't simply locked away in a giant vault at the back of the building. Generally, banks are only required to keep 10% of deposits on hand. The other 90% can be invested or lent to other customers. Depending on the type of credit given, a bank might charge customers anywhere from 5%-30% interest to borrow money. To thank you for allowing them to earn interest on the money you've deposited, the bank will pay you from 1%-5% interest on your deposits and pocket the difference. Understanding this one-sided arrangement can help make it clear why eight of the ten tallest buildings in Los Angeles are all presently or previously named after banks.

Wouldn't it be nice if there was a way to have those buildings named after you instead? There's now a way to cut out the banks as the middlemen and become a lender yourself. Peer-to-peer lending, sometimes called P2P lending or social lending, is a relatively new option to earn interest income. Peer-to-peer lending utilizes Internet platforms to match individual borrowers with potential investors. Instead of earning the paltry 1% interest banks had been paying for over a decade, peer-to-peer lending investors averaged a 5% annual return over the same period. Investors can earn as high as 36% rates of returns on some loans but not without risks.

Peer-to-peer lending platforms each have their own systems and investor requirements. Some have modest income requirements investors must meet and most have minimum deposit requirements to begin investing. P2P platforms generally categorize loan applicants from low to high risk based on various criteria such as the applicant's income, credit scores, and purpose for the loan. It's up to the investor to choose which loans they'd like to provide funding to. As an investor, you can sort potential loans to fund based on criteria you choose such as rate of interest, various borrower information, and the length of the loan.

Since you're the lender, you're also taking on the risk that the borrower never pays you back. Most peer-to-peer platforms have a system in place to deal with borrowers who stop making payments, however, there's a real chance that the loan ends up being sold to a collection agency for a fraction of your initial investment. Loans with higher interest rates are more likely to default, but there's no guarantee that high-quality borrowers will pay back the entire loan either. With that being said, the default rate for P2P lending has been about 2% of all loans which is similar to what traditional banks experience.

Another downside to investing with peer-to-peer lending programs is that you generally must keep your money tied up for some time as most loans carry a two to three-year term, however, five years or longer is also common. Additionally, as the borrower repays your loan, the interest you earn on the loan will gradually decrease as the principal is reduced. You'll need to actively reinvest loan repayments with new borrowers to keep your returns flowing.

Peer-to-peer lending provides an opportunity for investors who are willing to take a little more risk to earn higher rates of return. P2P can be a good option to fill the gap between low-risk, low-return bank investments, and high-risk, high-return stock investments. Utilizing peer-to-peer lending platforms also allows investors to be more hands-on in their investments, which can be appealing to many investors in contrast to letting that money drably sit at the bank.

BE THE SHARK

Shark Tank is the hit television show that puts aspiring business owners looking for investments for their business in front of shrewd millionaires and billionaires eager to cash in on a deal. On the show, entrepreneurs present their most compelling pitch for their business idea before asking the investors for the cash they need to fund their dreams. The Sharks all have long histories of business success and have access to large sums of investable capital. Typical Shark Tank deals involve hundreds of thousands of dollars in exchange for a share of ownership in the burgeoning company. If the businesses take off, the Sharks frequently wind up with 30%-40% of future profits. One of the biggest Shark Tank success stories resulted from a deal between Shark Daymond John and high-quality sock manufacturer Bombas. After a tense negotiation, Daymond was able to purchase 17.5% of the company for a $200,000 investment. Since the deal, Bombas has generated over $225 million in sales. Daymond's initial investment may now enable him to make millions of dollars a year due to his 17.5% early ownership in Bombas. The ability to invest in a company during its infancy can result in exponential returns.

ly mean you lose money because the additional money raised by issuing stock should theoretically increase the value of the company. Instead of owning 2% of a $1 million company, you could own 1% of a $2 million company. Lastly, crowdfunding opportunities are more easily manipulated with fraud due to the level of difficulty involved in researching a startup. To reduce fraud risks, only make crowdfunding investments using platforms that are registered with the SEC to facilitate the transactions.

Equity crowdfunding gives investors a chance to swing for the fences with at least some of their capital. Most of the time you'll miss, but occasionally you'll hit one out of the park. Like peer-to-peer lending, investing through crowdfunding is a good fit for investors who want to be involved with their investments. Being there from the beginning and helping a company move to the next level can be its own intrinsic reward. While investing is meant to grow your money, there's no reason not to invest in a way that makes you feel good at the same time.

WHEN ROBOTS TAKE OVER

Technology expands exponentially, meaning, the more advanced technology becomes, the faster it continues to advance. For consumers, this usually translates into more convenience at lower costs. The downside, of course, is that automation through technology ultimately replaces people. This is true even in occupations with high levels of skill, including financial advisors.

So-called robo-advisors have emerged over the last decade as a valuable option for many investors. Robo-advisors are computerized investment advisors developed to help investors who either don't have access to an investment advisor due to costs or simply don't want another person to handle their investments. Robo-advisors are programmed with the help of investment experts and work with modern investment theories in mind. Based on well-developed algorithms, the robo-advisor will automatically select investments based on the investor's answers to various questions.

Until recently, you'd have to be an accredited investor with millions of dollars for startup investing to be a viable option, but thanks to special exemptions that came into effect in 2015, small companies may now accept investments from everyday investors. Crowdfunding platforms have helped flip the script when it comes to investing in startups. Instead of seeking a large sum from a wealthy investor, startup companies can now seek small amounts from large numbers of ordinary investors.

The two most well-known crowdfunding platforms are Kickstarter and Indiegogo. Both were started in 2009 to give inventors, artists, and entrepreneurs opportunities to raise money for their projects through small contributions from the masses. Both companies utilize a system that prevents a project from starting until a funding goal is met. If fundraising falls short of the goal, all previous contributors will be refunded. Kickstarter and Indiegogo both utilize a system of specific rewards for contributors rather than giving away an ownership percentage of the new business. This serves those who are excited about a certain project and want to do their share to get it off the ground, but it doesn't provide any value for someone looking to gain ownership in an up-and-coming business.

To use crowdfunding for investment, you'll need to work with platforms that offer "equity crowdfunding." While "equity" has several definitions in terms of finance, in this case, it refers to ownership. Part of what has made Kickstarter and Indiegogo so popular is their altruistic business models which are aligned with the potential for viral promotion through social media. While equity crowdfunding campaigns allow you to support projects you believe in, they're also about making money for yourself, and self-promotion is generally perceived as tacky. This is one of the reasons that the most popular equity crowdfunding platforms are not household names. Top equity crowdfunding platforms today include AngelList, MicroVentures, Fundable, and StartEngine who employs Kevin O'Leary from Shark Tank as a strategic advisor and spokesman.

With popular equity crowdfunding platforms, individuals can invest in startups with as little as $250. Like peer-to-peer lending platforms, equity crowdfunding requires investors to select investments on their own. Notable companies that were open to investments through crowdfunding platforms before becoming publicly traded include Uber, Facebook, Postmates, and Spotify. Optimally, when one invests in a startup company, the hope is that the company will either be bought out by another large company or that the company goes public and completes an initial public offering (IPO). In either case, early investors will be rewarded handsomely. The variety of startup investment opportunities available today tests the limits of imagination, ranging from artificial intelligence developers to sustainable burger chains.

Naturally, there are downsides to investing in startups. The truth is most startups flop, and only a tiny share make it big. When you invest through equity crowdfunding, there is a high likelihood that you'll lose 100% of your investment on any given venture, so you're dependent on investing in multiple companies and hoping that one out of ten is successful enough to cover losses from the other nine. Additionally, waiting for a startup investment to pay off may take many years. Some crowdfunding platforms give you the ability to offer your investment for sale on a secondary market, but there's no certainty someone else would be willing to buy it from you. In most cases, once you invest in a startup, that money remains tied up for an extended period.

Furthermore, it can be challenging to find enough information about a start-up to make an informed investment decision. You can't find professional analysis of startup companies as easily as you can find an analysis of a public company, that is, if you can find any analysis on a particular startup at all. In order to offer investment opportunities through a crowdfunding platform, a company must file information with the Securities and Exchange Commission (SEC). Included in those filings is a document

known as an "offering circular." The offering circular will generally be thirty or more pages long and details various aspects of the business such as financial standing, names of top executives, number of employees, previous sales of equity, and near-term plans for the company. Reading through the entire circular is just the starting point for your decision to invest in that startup. You'll want to research the history of people involved with running the company and the company's mission. Have the startup's leaders managed other companies that have been bought out or gone public? Were they involved in any controversies? Does the company solve a real problem? What are their competitors offering? What are they going to do with the additional cash they're raising with your investment?

There are a number of other issues to be aware of when investing through equity crowdfunding. Regulations limit how much any individual may invest with crowdfunding during a twelve-month period based on income and net worth. The limits are occasionally adjusted for inflation. Currently, anyone can invest at least $2,200, but that limit may increase to either 5% or 10% of either annual income or net worth depending on the investor's financial scenario.

When exploring crowdfunding investments, be on the lookout for an option referred to as a SAFE (simple agreement for future equity). A SAFE is an agreement between you—the investor—and the company in which the company promises to give you a future equity stake based on the amount you invested. It also involves some kind of triggering event that must take place in order for you to get your future equity stake. The triggering event may be the company's initial public offering or another round of financing, but it's important to note that the triggering event may never occur, leaving you with no equity in the company. Also, future rounds of fundraising by a company you've invested in may dilute your ownership stake. For example, if your initial investment gave you a 2% ownership stake, a future issuance of stock could reduce that ownership to 1%. This doesn't necessari-

What makes these robotic advisors valuable to individuals is their ability to simplify the investment selection approach. Studies have repeatedly shown that a major contributing factor as to why more people don't contribute to retirement accounts is their concern about their ability to select appropriate investments. Often, those who contribute without understanding their investment options wind up allocating all of their contributions to simple money market accounts, crippling their ability to grow their investments. Robo-advisors help solve this problem by providing customized investment selections based on the individual's circumstances.

Most robo-advisors aim to set up investment portfolios that utilize a selection of passive exchange-traded funds (ETFs). As you deposit more funds into your account, your money will automatically be invested into the predetermined allocations, for example, 60% stocks and 40% bonds. If one particular category of your investments grows substantially faster than others, the robo-advisor will automatically make adjustments to bring your portfolio back to its original mix of investments. This is referred to as automatic rebalancing and helps prevent your account from drifting into becoming either too risky or too conservative in relation to your goals over time.

A handful of robo-advisors have adopted a more active approach to investing. Australia-based "unhedged" is a robo-advisor that utilizes a more speculative momentum algorithm to systematically buy and sell stocks based on whether those stocks have been recently trending upward or downward in price. Other robos manage their investments by mimicking what top hedge funds are investing in or simply offer actively managed ETFs as part of their offerings.

Robo-advisors can also help investors automate a strategy called tax-loss harvesting. Tax-loss harvesting can be used by investors who own stocks in taxable accounts (accounts outside of retirement accounts) by selling at a loss before year end to lock in a tax deduction. Capital losses can be used to reduce capital gains from other investments, and as much as $3,000 in losses can be used to reduce other taxable income. Robo-advisors can automatically identify and sell investments at a taxable loss and then reinvest your money after harvesting that loss.

Typical fees for robo-advisors are around 0.25% of your invested balance on an annual basis, however, a few are offering investment management for free hoping to build a book of clients who will pay for other services. While robo-advisors were initially conceived as competitors to human advisors who typically charge significantly more, the robo-industry initially struggled to gain traction. They were caught between two types of customers. Those who wanted help with their investments wanted to work with a person, while people who felt confident in handling their own investments didn't see the value in having a robo-advisor select investments for them. Eventually, most robo-advisor firms pivoted to providing a hybrid offering: robo-investment selection with access to professional human advisors on a limited basis.

Betterment, one of the earliest and largest robo firms, has put a substantial focus on marketing its system for use by professional investment advisors over the last several years. Currently, my firm utilizes the Betterment platform to manage investments for a portion of our customers as it allows me to spend less time with manual work like buying or selling investments and automates several other tasks. The Betterment platform has allowed me to reduce the fees we charge and enables us to efficiently serve customers with smaller account values.

Robo-advisors typically have a limited selection of investments. You generally will not have the ability to buy or sell any specific stock but must invest in their offering of ETFs or mutual funds. This may not necessarily be a bad thing as having too many investment choices can stop people from investing at all. Additionally, when robo-advisors offer access to a professional planner, the help they can provide is rather limited. Generally, you can connect on a phone call or virtual meeting to have some of your questions answered, but the professional will not be able to provide you with comprehensive advice or a full financial plan.

The use of robo-advisors will continue to grow. Ultimately, virtually all workplace retirement plans will utilize robo-advisors to help employees receive the full benefit of their retirement accounts. At some point, robo-advisors will effectively replace many index funds by allowing investors to directly buy a fractional share of each and every stock in a particular index through "direct indexing". Direct indexing provides better opportunities for tax-loss harvesting, so can be valuable for individuals in higher tax brackets. However, the fees for direct indexing range from 0.30%-0.40% while fees for index funds can be as low as 0.03%. Eventually, there will be no discrepancy between the fees for direct indexing vs. fees related to index funds as technology improves.

So far, robo-advisors have not been able to eliminate the need for human advisors, but as the technology improves and artificial intelligence learns to empathize with the emotions tied to investing, human advisors will no longer be required.

ROBINHOOD

"Then they vowed that even as they themselves had been despoiled they would despoil their oppressors, whether baron, abbot, knight, or squire, and that from each they would take that which had been wrung from the poor by unjust taxes, or land rents, or in wrongful fines. But to the poor folk they would give a helping hand in need and trouble, and would return to them that which had been unjustly taken from them. Besides this, they swore never to harm a child nor to wrong a woman, be she maid, wife, or widow; so that, after a while, when the people began to find that no harm was meant to them, but that money or food came in time of want to many a poor family, they came to praise Robin and his merry men, and to tell many tales of him and of his doings in Sherwood Forest, for they felt him to be one of themselves." -*The Merry Adventures of Robin Hood*, by Howard Pyle

Vladimir Tenev and Baiju Bhatt met as roommates at Stanford. After graduation, they both moved to New York to develop and sell stock trading software to hedge funds. After gaining experience in the financial industry, they realized that big Wall Street firms paid nearly nothing to buy or sell stocks, but most Americans were charged commissions for every trade they made. They decided it was time to create a platform that provided everyone with access to the financial markets, not just the wealthy. While developing their platform's mission to level the playing field between the rich and everyday Americans, the pair recognized a resemblance between what they were building and the passage above. They named their company Robinhood, hoping it would become a platform that could even the odds for the little guy.

Robinhood officially launched in 2015 as a mobile app with the revolutionary concept of allowing customers to buy and sell stocks for free. At the time, publicly available trading platforms charged individuals $5-$10 for each trade. Along with eliminating fees, Robinhood focused on ease of use and educating its users, many of whom bought and sold stocks for the first time in their lives using the app. Before long, Robinhood also supported trading on the web and currently has over 21 million users. Robinhood isn't an investment itself, but it's certainly changed the way people look at investing, so I've included it in this section.

Without fees, how does Robinhood make any money? Robinhood makes some revenue by lending their users money to invest in stocks and charging them interest on those loans. They also have some income from fees they charge for their premium services. However, the lion's share of Robinhood's revenue comes from earnings through transactions. Interesting for a platform that boasts no transaction fees. When a Robinhood customer places an order to buy or sell a stock, Robinhood forwards that request for processing to another firm. The firm that processes the transaction receives both buy and sell orders for the same stock at various prices and by matching up lower-priced sell requests with higher-priced buy requests, the processing firm can realize a profit on the difference. The firm that processes the requests gives some of its profits back to Robinhood. This arrangement was originally pioneered by Bernie Madoff and is now known as "payment for order flow". While the gains may be small per transaction at less than one cent per share, over the course of nearly a billion trades in a year, these payments result in hundreds of millions in revenue for Robinhood. Unfortunately, the SEC recently found that Robinhood's payment for order flow arrangement had cost its customers over $34 million after determining that customers would have been able to buy stocks for less and sell them for more through other brokerages, even when factoring in trading fees at the other firms. They were required to pay a $65 million fine and faced a class action lawsuit for the infraction.

While its founders say it was designed to help everyone invest, the Robinhood platform encourages frequent buying and selling which typically results in smaller investor profits over the long-term. The app interface utilizes bright-colored charts and graphics that turn green when your investments are positive for the day and red when they're negative. You'll also get pop-up notifications on your phone if investments you're watching are experiencing significant price movements that day. Robinhood also offers novice investors access to complicated trading instruments known as options (a topic we'll cover later in the book) which are used to speculate on short-term price movements. Buying and selling through Robinhood is easier than posting on social media. You could now buy and sell stock while sitting on the toilet. Additionally, Robinhood provides very little information for each individual stock relative to other brokerages. For example, Robinhood provides five data points for a given stock whereas TD Ameritrade provides 489. This requires

Robinhood users to rely more heavily on gut instincts than critical analysis when buying or selling a stock. All these factors promote increased trading activity, which helps increase Robinhood's income.

Alex Kearns had been using the Robinhood app for just a few months before he started making risky options bets while home from the University of Nebraska. He studied management in college and had been recognized repeatedly for academic and community achievements throughout high school. In June of 2020, he opened his account to find a shocking negative balance of -$730,165.72. Alex contacted Robinhood customer support through email for clarification because phone support did not exist. At first, he received a generic automated response that didn't answer his questions. Later around 3 a.m., he was notified by Robinhood through another automated email that he needed to take "immediate action" to deposit $178,612.73 within five days. He made a number of other attempts to contact Robinhood the next morning but was unsuccessful. Later that day he left home on his bike but never returned. Alex decided the best resolution was to jump in front of an oncoming train.

"If you're reading this, I am dead. How was a 20 year old with no income able to get assigned almost a million dollars' worth of leverage? The puts I bought/sold should have canceled out, too, but I also have no clue what I was doing now in hindsight. There was no intention to be assigned this much and take this much risk, and I only thought that I was risking the money that I actually owned. If you check the app, the margin investing option isn't even 'turned on' for me. A painful lesson. Fuck Robinhood.

I was starting to look forward to my future, too, before I hit this pretty large speedbump. I cannot imagine the amount of pain this has caused you. Please understand that this decision was not made lightly. You could fill an ocean with the amount of tears I've shed typing this. Please, please take care of yourselves. The amount of my guilt I feel as I commit to this is unbearable – I did not want to die."

I have to imagine Alex was not only feeling hopeless about having to pay back over $700,000 but also feeling ashamed that he could have made such a terrible mistake. As it turns out, the only mistake he made was not understanding what he was looking at when he logged into his account. Robinhood never released the details of the trades Alex made, but it's believed he had purchased offsetting bets, one which would allow him to purchase shares at a given price and another that would allow him to sell at a set price. These bets could be purchased for a fraction of what the shares themselves would cost. When Alex looked at his account, it only reflected one side of his transaction as the offsetting option was still being processed. A day after his death, a message from Robinhood stated he no longer owed any money. In fact, despite the app displaying his account was severely negative, his true balance was a positive $16,176.14 at the time he wrote his suicide note. Alex was correct in believing that his trades canceled out, but his lack of experience with the complex investments paired with the confusing readout on his Robinhood screen left him doubting himself.

Since Robinhood launched its no-commission model, most large brokerage firms have followed. Today almost every brokerage firm utilizes the payment for order flow arrangement to eliminate commissions, although most brokerages take a smaller cut than Robinhood and pass savings on to their customers. While other brokers have adopted the no-commission structure, they've generally avoided turning their investment platforms into the type of high-stakes video game Robinhood has been accused of creating. Robinhood has largely succeeded in its mission to bring investing to everyone, whether that's truly a good thing or not remains to be seen.

GRAB A PARTNER

Another investment option to consider is a publicly traded limited partnership. Typically, publicly traded partnerships are focused on various natural resource sectors. Some examples include logging, oil and gas drilling or transportation (including pipelines), mining, and the general processing and storage of natural resources. Many partnerships are available to invest in through various stock exchanges just like buying a stock.

Publicly traded partnership investments don't provide a great opportunity for growth because they typically operate in developed industries. However, the trade-off for limited growth is lower risk and regular cash flow. Investments in publicly traded partnerships are a good investment for people who are interested in receiving regular income payments from their investments as they typically pay higher yields than stocks or bonds.

Similar to buying stocks, investing in a partnership makes you a partial owner or a limited partner. Like stocks, you become a business owner, but the form of ownership is slightly different. Partnerships don't issue shares, instead, investors buy "units" of the partnership. One reason why publicly traded partnerships can pay higher yields when compared to ordinary stocks is that the partnership itself pays no taxes. All profit is passed down to the partners based on the number of units each owns, and the partners will then pay taxes on their share of the earnings.

The special tax treatment of a partnership is good and bad news for investors. The good news is that the initial cash payments you receive from your partnership (usually paid quarterly) are considered a return of your initial investment and not considered taxable income. This arrangement is helpful for someone looking to reduce their taxable income for a period of time. However, the downside is that your tax filings can become much more complicated. As a limited partner, each year you'll receive a K-1 tax form that lists your share of the partnership's total income, expenses, deductions, and credits, each of which may need to be reported on separate forms in your tax return. These forms are notorious for making otherwise simple tax returns difficult. To add to the drama, most K-1 forms aren't sent until mid-March at the earliest, requiring many partnership investors to request extensions to file their taxes. Additionally, you'll need to maintain a record of your basis in your partnership investment for as long as you own it. Basis generally means how much money you've paid to purchase the investment. Your basis will be reduced each time you receive a distribution, but it will also be affected by various information reported on the K-1 form. When you sell your partnership investment, you'll need to report the correct basis to determine your taxable gain. If your basis reaches zero, all distributions after that point will be considered taxable income.

If you already work with a professional accountant or are proficient in complicated tax matters, publicly traded partnerships can be a good fit for you. They are easy to buy and easy to sell while also offering the ability to delay some taxes and offer better investment yields than typical stock dividends.

COLLECTIONS

After working twenty years in the toy industry, Ty Warner decided to start his own toy company in 1986. His first successful toy was a unique plush cat which was deliberately under-stuffed to give it a flexibility that ordinary stuffed animals were missing. As it gained in popularity, he added new varieties. His stuffed animals sold for anywhere from $10-$20 each, but he was interested in developing a product that would sell for $5 which a child could buy with his or her allowance money. By 1993 he introduced nine new creatures at the World Toy Fair in New York: Spot the Dog, Legs the Frog, Brownie the Bear, Squealer the Pig, Flash the Dolphin, Splash the Whale, Patti the Platypus, Chocolate the Moose, and Pinchers the Lobster. The toys were smaller and filled with a mix of traditional stuffing and plastic pellets allowing them to be posed in various positions. He named them Beanie Babies.

The new toys first went on sale in 1994 with limited success. Interest in the toys steadily grew as new editions were released gradually throughout the year, generating an anticipation for what kind of character might come next. Within a year, demand was escalating rapidly, partly due to an artificial scarcity.

Ty only sold Beanie Babies to smaller stores and shunned large toy chains. He also limited each store to receiving only thirty-six of any particular Beanie Baby per month. Once the store was sold out, customers would need to wait until the next month's delivery. Beanie Babies became a craze in 1996 when Ty began announcing that production would be permanently stopped on certain creatures. Assuming these retired varieties would become extremely rare and valuable, collectors started buying every one they could find. When collectors realized there was no way to know which Beanie Baby would be retired next, they began to buy out every variety. Hard-to-find varieties began to sell on secondary markets for thousands of dollars. During the peak, Beanie Babies made up 10% of all sales on eBay.

Buying a collectible can be a rewarding investment. Some examples of collectibles that have historically held value over a long period include rare postage stamps, coins, toys, fine art, and oddly enough, sneakers. Other collectibles that have experienced periods of high value have included comic books, vintage alcohol, trading cards, and rare historical documents. Investing in a collectible item brings with it the benefit of getting to own something tangible worth admiring. In the case of art, your investment can decorate your home, while potentially growing in value. Sharing the story of a collectible with family or friends can be an enjoyable experience.

What makes a collectible valuable? First and foremost, the item needs to have some unique characteristics or be quite rare. Manufacturers have obviously caught on to the perception that rare items are more valuable, so they've mass-produced "limited editions" by the millions making them limited by title only. Rarity can occur by mistake. An error on a 1996 twenty-dollar bill allowed it to be auctioned for $396,000. Midway through its printing process, a Del Monte sticker from a banana adhered to the bill causing the treasury seal and serial number to be printed across the sticker. The bill made its way to circulation with the sticker still in place. The bill was sold previously in 2003 for $10,100 and again in 2006 for $25,300 before selling for nearly sixteen times that amount in 2021.

Aside from being rare, a collectible must be desirable. There must be enough people interested in the item to give it long-term value. In 2005, I purchased two dolls based on my favorite movie, "Edward Scissorhands", intending to sell at least one of them for profit in the future. Only 2000 of these dolls were ever created. Their original pricing was around $40, but I paid $60 each on the secondary market. I held onto both dolls for about eight years, one safely tucked away and the other on display. When I sold, I was able to collect $450 for one that was kept pristine and $300 for the one that had been displayed. Over a decade has passed since I sold those dolls, yet the resale price today is still about the same as it was when I sold them. Even though there are undoubtedly fewer of the dolls available today, the audience for people interested in buying them is also declining which prevents the price from climbing.

Once the conditions of rarity and desirability are met, other factors may impact the value of a collectible. Does it have historical interest? Has it been authenticated as genuine by an expert? What condition is it in? How old is it? The answers to these questions can determine how valuable the item may be.

There are a number of cons to buying collectibles as an investment. You'll need space to physically store them. As with any physical item, there's great risk that the item can be destroyed or damaged, especially if kept over a period of many years. If you're collecting expensive items, you'll need insurance to protect them. Additionally, gains from the sale of collectibles don't get the same capital gains tax treatments that other investments receive. Instead of the 15% or 20% long-term capital gains tax rate, collectibles may be taxed at 28%. Also, it can be extremely difficult to determine what will be valuable years down the road.

Chris Robinson produced a documentary titled, "Bankrupt by Beanie Babies" which tells the story of how his father spent $100,000 buying Beanie Babies in the late 90's as an investment towards his sons' college education. He planned to hold the Babies for a few years and cash out for a huge profit, but the Beanie Baby craze ended as fast as it started. The Robinsons never sold their collection, estimated to be 20,000 dolls in all.

With hundreds of millions of beanie babies in existence today, even "rare" Beanie Babies sell for just a few dollars, and common varieties sell for ninety-nine cents or less, shipping included[2]. This is always a big risk when using collectibles as an investment. The reality is that someday, no one will want them anymore. If you decide to invest in collectibles, choose items that you enjoy anyway, and don't spend your entire life savings on them no matter how hot the market is.

---

[2] If you search online today, you'll still find many listings for rare Beanie Babies on sites like eBay selling for tens of thousands of dollars apiece. The high dollar listings can be found side by side with listings for the identical characters in excellent condition selling for only a few dollars. It's speculated that the highly priced listings are used for some type of fraud. For example, two parties may agree to process the payment for an elicit transaction through a fake Beanie Baby purchase instead of paying each other directly or the transactions could be related to money laundering. The website operator wouldn't know anything about agreements made between buyers outside of their platforms. The hype surrounding the original Beanie Baby craze was so substantial, that a $10,000 price on a Beanie Baby still seems plausible to many, but if you still have Beanie Babies in your attic, don't let these spurious, high-dollar listings get your hopes up.

-CHAPTER SUMMARY-

- Cryptocurrencies are a rapidly evolving and volatile investment class which will experience wild price swings for the foreseeable future, but they have the opportunity for significant gains.

- Blockchain technology has the potential to dramatically change the marketplace and value of digital assets.

- New opportunities like peer-to-peer lending and equity crowdfunding have made institutional type investments available to everyday investors.

- Advancing technology is changing the way we think of investing. Robinhood has brought complex investing options to the palm of inexperienced investors' hands, and robo-advisors are helping to eliminate mundane investing tasks.

- Investing in collectible items can be fun and rewarding but comes with unique challenges and risks.

PART III

STRATEGY

CHAPTER EIGHT

Lessons

*"History never looks like history when
you are living through it."*
– John W. Gardner

IT'S HARD TO IMAGINE today, but for most of the 17th century, the Netherlands was the leading economic power in the world. Despite being a tiny country geographically, they became the center of global trade by utilizing the world's first publicly traded company, the Dutch East India Trading Company, which handled over half of all the shipping in Europe. During this period, the Dutch also formed the first central bank and the first stock exchange. They also experienced the world's first documented financial bubble.

The Dutch were showered with new and desirable goods from around the world, including spices, textiles, and unique plant life as a byproduct of their extensive trading. Among these were rare, vibrant, and delicate tulips. The combined beauty and scarcity of tulips quickly made owning them a symbol of wealth through various parts of Europe including Holland and France. The wealthy would plant them in their gardens and use them to adorn their clothing. Some would use mirrors in their yards to exaggerate how many tulips they owned. The rarity and high demand for tulips caused their prices to rise steadily through the early part of the 1600s.

Tulips are typically grown from bulbs. Once mature, the tulip plant will produce smaller bulb offsets buried beneath the ground. These offsets can eventually produce a genetic replica of the original flower and generate offsets of their own. Like most flowering plants, tulips can also be grown from seeds, but it may take five years or more before a tulip plant grown from seed is strong enough to produce a flower. Additionally, tulips grown from seed will generally be a hybrid of two plants due to a necessary cross-pollination process. This means that a grower would have no guarantee of what a flower grown from seed may look like until after it blooms. Therefore, when a scarce and desirable flower was produced, its bulbs became very valuable as the only means to replicate it.

Generally, tulip bulbs should remain in the ground for most of the year to help them spend as much time as possible growing and producing new offset bulbs. That meant for most of the year, any buying or selling of tulip bulbs had to be done utilizing a type of futures contract, as the physical bulbs were unavailable to be transferred. Traders would sign a contract to exchange a specified bulb or set of bulbs for a set price on a particular date. This arrangement made it very easy to buy and sell tulip bulbs as no one had to deal with transporting or storing them each time they were sold.

The Dutch market for tulip bulbs was traditionally limited to professional growers until ~1634, when more of the general population joined in speculating on how high the prices of tulip bulbs could climb. Tulip bulb prices steadily rose through 1636 until reaching manic levels in January of 1637.

Between January and February that year, it was common for the price of bulbs to increase by 1,000% or more as investors felt they could quickly resell their contracts for a profit to the next fool who came along. A particular contract may have exchanged hands as many as ten times in a day. One of the most desirable varieties, the Semper Augustus, saw its price increase to 10,000 guilders for a single bulb. As historian Mike Dash described, "It was enough to feed, clothe and house a whole Dutch family for half a lifetime, or sufficient to purchase one of the grandest homes on the most fashionable canal in Amsterdam for cash, complete with a coach house and an 80-ft (25-m) garden – and this at a time when homes in that city were as expensive as property anywhere in the world."

The wildness of Tulipmania gave birth to many stories of lore which have been embellished or otherwise fabricated, such as the popular story of a sailor who mistook a valuable Semper Augustus tulip bulb resting on a merchant's counter for an onion. The myth has the traveler eating the tulip bulb as a relish for his herring breakfast and later being imprisoned for the act.

As rapidly as prices rose, their fall was even quicker. When fewer interested buyers than expected showed up to a traders' meeting in early February, fear set in that contract holders would be unable to unload their bulbs for a profit. A massive sell-off ensued. Before February was up, tulip bulbs had lost as much as 95% of their value compared to just a few weeks prior. While it's not difficult to imagine why people tend to make speculative investments, it's interesting to note that the rise and fall of tulip prices occurred during the peak of a particularly severe outbreak of bubonic plague in Holland. Perhaps in the face of heightened mortality, investors became more willing to take risks, hoping to get rich quickly. This theory draws parallels to the enormous increase in the number of speculative stock and cryptocurrency investors during the 2020-2021 coronavirus pandemic.

Ultimately, the tulip bulb boom and bust never wound up growing into a large-scale economic crisis in the Netherlands. Many individual speculators experienced severe personal losses both to their finances and reputation. Dutch artists who prolifically painted popular floral scenes seemed to pause the creation of such pieces from 1630-1640, possibly as the perception of floral elements soured through the mania. Still, for the most part, the country went about its business as usual. Today, comparisons to Tulipmania pop up just about any time investors seem to speculate irrationally.

THE SOUTH SEA CO.

In the early 1700s, Great Britain found itself buried in debt after decades of fighting to expand its empire. It soon became apparent that the country could not repay their debts. By 1711, the British government had devised a scheme that would allow them to unload much of their debt by creating the South Sea Company. England's government gave the South Sea Company monopoly trading rights with South America and its surrounding waters to enhance its appeal to investors. The company was also the beneficiary of a propaganda campaign touting the tremendous economic potential for trade in the South Seas to spike interest. In exchange, the South Sea Company would take over portions of the government's debt in stages.

Britain would pay the South Sea Company 6% annual interest on the debt, a fee which would then be passed on as dividends to shareholders of the company's stock. Holders of government debt would be allowed to exchange their government notes for shares in the new company at an amount equal to the value of their debt holdings. Understanding the precarious state of the government's finances and the relative difficulty of cashing in their government debt holdings, many people jumped at the opportunity to exchange their government debt for shares in a company that could easily be sold through a stock exchange and also provide the potential for future returns as a result of its trading monopoly in the South seas.

Initially, the South Sea Company's shares were valued at £100 each, which meant that debt notes worth £100 could be exchanged for one share of South Sea Company stock. Chief executive of the South Sea Company, John Blunt, understood that if the price of the stock increased, the company would need to offer fewer shares in exchange for the debt notes. For example, if the company's stock price rose to £200, one share would be enough to wipe out two £100 debt notes. Any shares left over after the exchanges for debt notes were completed could then be sold by the company on the open market allowing the company to pocket any additional proceeds. With this in mind, Blunt started working to raise the price of South Sea Company shares.

In 1711, when the South Sea Company was formed and given monopoly trading rights by England in the South Seas, the country was at war with Spain, who incidentally controlled the ports in South America. Spain blocked the South Sea Company from trading until the war ended several years later. Even then, Spain only granted the company rights to handle the slave trade in the region, a practice that was not only questionable morally but also financially. In addition to the slave trade, the South Sea Company was granted permission to send only a single ship per year for the trade of goods while the already well-established East India Trading Company was sending fleets to trade in the region. With limited trading prospects, the promises of great returns from the South Sea Company seemed dubious early on.

Despite the company's challenges, John Blunt was able to keep up the public's interest in the South Sea Company by naming leading members of parliament to the company's board of directors, appointing the king's son as "Governor" of the company, even convincing King George to become an investor. With so many members of the government personally vested in the company's ongoing success, public confidence was bolstered.

As the government remained strapped for cash, it could not make its interest payments to the South Sea Company. The company agreed to forgive the payments in exchange for the right to sell additional shares to the public. After the expanded stock offering, the South Sea Company had 10 million shares of stock issued. At the time, South Sea Company stock represented roughly half of all stock issued in the entire country despite the company having little to no profits. Soon, King George took over the role of Governor of the South Sea Company, and its stock price began to rise. Pointing to the early success of the plan and with many of them receiving additional shares as bribes, government officials decided to unload even more debt through the South Sea Company, a move which called for an additional 31 million shares of stock to be issued.

As details of the deal to issue the additional stock were ironed out, the company was busy pumping up the share price by spreading rumors of the riches that would come from the South Sea trade and sharing the names of government officials who owned shares in the company (whether those officials paid for their shares or not) to improve the company's legitimacy. The stock price rose from £128 in January of 1720 to £330 in March. In April, however, the stock price hit some turbulence, falling slightly. Since the company wasn't making money trading, it relied on issuing new shares at continually increasing prices to generate income and make its dividend payments. To halt the April price decline, the South Sea Company began to allow investors to buy shares by making payments every other month after a 20% down payment. Later, stock was issued for a 10% down payment, and no additional money was owed for four years. At one point, the South Sea Company was loaning investors £3,000 each so they could buy more company stock.

All this at a time when educational resources about stock investment were almost impossible to come by. Most stock buying and selling was done in an informal, unregulated environment. London coffee shops in Exchange Alley became unofficial stock exchanges and home to most of the South Sea Company stock speculation. Nobility, women, brokers, and servants could all be seen trading their investments in the alley.

Other companies were formed attempting to capitalize on the same type of hype and scheme the South Sea Company successfully leveraged. New companies rushed to issue stock hoping to grab a share of the cash that seemed to be flowing freely from investors. Most companies forming at this time may have been legitimate, but many weren't. One such company described itself as "a company for carrying out an undertaking of great advantage, but nobody to know what it is." Another wanted to create a device to draw vapors out of human brains. The South Sea Company saw these new ventures as a threat that would siphon away the money they needed from investors. In June 1720, the government passed the Bubble Act (with support from the South Sea Company), which made all companies that issued stock without government approval illegal and void.

Initially, the Bubble Act helped push South Sea Company Stock to nearly £1000 per share. However, the peak was short-lived. Those who invested in companies that were shut down by the Bubble Act wanted to make up their losses, and with South Sea Company stock at an unbelievable high, they started selling. The South Sea Company, desperate to stave off a major price crash, promised investors an absurd 30% year-end dividend with 50% dividends to follow annually for a decade. Investors saw through the impossibly generous offer and realized the game was over. Like Tulipmania, the sell-off was rapid. By October, five months after the Bubble Act, the stock had fallen nearly 90% from its peak, bringing other stock prices down with it.

Issac Newton who had invested and lost money in the South Sea bubble, remarked, "I can calculate the motions of the heavenly bodies, but not the madness of people." Interesting thoughts from the man who understood better than most that what goes up, must come down. While the South Sea bubble had broader implications than the Tulipmania bubble in Holland, it didn't result in a more severe financial downturn for the broader economy. For the most part, the economic impact was limited to those who invested after the stock price had already gained substantially, especially those who borrowed to buy the stock. The South Sea Company remained operational for over a hundred years. Britain eventually re-acquired its debt from the company, which it finally paid off in 2015.

MISSISSIPPI COLONIES

While the South Sea bubble was inflating in England, a very similar story was playing out in France. Like England, France found itself impoverished and deep in debt after long involvements in wars. Looking for creative ways to improve their financial situation, they turned to John Law, an experienced Scottish financier. Law was given permission to form a bank with the power to print money backed by silver and gold. Law hypothesized that increasing the supply of money would help boost commerce and therefore the economy of France, and printing paper money was the easiest way to increase the supply. Paper money was a new concept for the French as they were accustomed to exchanging gold or silver coins as currency, but the country was facing a coin shortage, forcing citizens to barter for goods. To help boost confidence in the new bank, the regent of France arranged to have one million Livre (France's currency) worth of gold deposited in a public display during the bank's busiest time of day. Before long, the people of France were more willing to use paper notes over coins.

It appeared that the increased supply of money had stimulated the economy as Law suggested. Based on this success, Law founded a trading company and was given a trading monopoly with France's colonies along the Mississippi River spanning from present-day Louisiana to Canada. Later, Law took over the companies that had French trading rights with Africa, China, and the East Indies and merged those with the Mississippi trading company. Around this same time, France bought out Law's bank but left him in charge. Law proceeded to open branches throughout France. Law soon purchased the rights to mint coins and collect taxes on behalf of France, meaning one man effectively controlled all of France's trade and finances.

Law had initially raised the money to develop this empire by selling shares in the Mississippi company. Similar to the South Sea Company, John Law allowed holders of French debt to exchange their government notes for shares in the company. After the first stock issue was mildly successful, Law prepared to issue additional shares, but in order to buy one of the new shares, an investor would need to own four of the company's old shares. This restriction was designed to boost the demand for old shares, driving the prices up even higher. When Law issued a third round of shares, he required buyers to own shares from both the first and second issue. As the company's capacity expanded to include more trade routes as well as managing the country's finances, its stock price rose, and as the price rose, more people became interested in owning shares.

Law's bank was initially established as a private venture started with capital from investors. Before the bank was bought out by French royalty, Law maintained tight control over how much money was printed knowing he would be required to answer to the bank's investors if they thought his decisions weren't prudent. Once the bank was purchased by France and became a royal venture, that oversight was effectively wiped away and Law would follow guidance from the regent of France. There was no longer anyone stopping money from being printed far in excess of the bank's reserves. Money printing picked up in earnest, and without enough gold and silver in reserves, Law decided that the money should also be partially backed up by shares of the Mississippi Company. The bank loaned money at a low rate of only 2% interest. Stock in the Mississippi Company could be used as collateral for the loans, and the loans could be used to buy additional Mississippi Company shares. Later, a deal was arranged which allowed the Mississippi Company to buy out France's debt. As new issues of stock continued, the bank printed more money to ensure that the public had the funds needed to continuously purchase new shares.

The price of Mississippi stock surged. After starting at 500 Livre per share, the price had skyrocketed to 10,000 Livre each in less than a year's time. It was common for people to sell their homes and possessions in order to buy shares and make it big.

Even the relatively poor capitalized on the craze. Servants carrying out sell orders for their masters found that by the time they reached the market, prices rose, and they could sell off their employer's shares for more than they expected. They used the difference to buy shares for themselves. So many people became wealthy that a new word was created; millionaire.

The new colony in North America struggled to produce anything of value. The French people were reluctant to journey to the new land which needed people to develop it, while many of those who decided to move died on the trip or shortly after arriving. Law rounded up the poor, prisoners, and prostitutes and shipped them off to populate the Mississippi colony with no success.

With share prices reaching amazing highs, investors began to sell their shares. Many pulled their money out of the country completely, and some reinvested their capital gains in England with the South Sea Company. As selling intensified, the bank printed money to buy up the shares investors were dumping in an attempt to keep prices from crashing. The banks were successful in propping up share prices for a few months. Slowly, people began to request gold or silver in exchange for their paper currency. Knowing that only a tiny fraction of the precious metals were available in relation to the amount of paper currency they had printed, Law began passing a series of restrictions meant to limit the outflow of gold and silver, but the restrictions couldn't stop what was coming.

With people realizing that too much paper currency had been printed, they began to question its value. Law decided to destroy large sums of the notes in a public bonfire, a move that was meant to show that the money supply was being controlled. Instead, it accelerated a panic. Dozens were trampled to death during the ensuing run at the bank to withdraw any remaining gold or silver. The share price fell over 95%, crime skyrocketed, and France's economy went into a recession. When Law was ultimately chased from the country, he left behind substantial assets and carried just enough gold coins to travel with. His money was confiscated at the border as a result of his own laws.

The Mississippi Bubble carried some similarities to the South Sea Bubble, however, its story is more an example of things unintentionally going wrong in contrast to a case of blatant fraud. While John Law is still not well known, economists today view his experimental ideas as revolutionary for the time while the lessons of the period help shape policy today. The current scenario in the U.S. has drawn comparisons to the Mississippi Bubble. The Federal Reserve Bank has been creating massive amounts of new money which it used to purchase trillions of dollars worth of Treasury Bonds (U.S. government debt) and mortgage-backed securities to create an artificial demand. Since the artificial demand for these securities is so high, the issuers don't need to offer high interest rates to attract investors. Because the interest rates on mortgages and other lending are directly influenced by the interest rates of U.S Treasuries, the Federal Reserve's purchases created an artificially low interest rate environment that spurs borrowing, spending, and investing. Has the Federal Reserve created too much money too quickly?

RAILWAY MANIA

Let's travel back to Great Britain one hundred years later. England was in the midst of an industrial revolution. During this time, the steam-powered locomotive was developed, and for the first time, people could travel well beyond their local region with relative ease. The first iterations of passenger carriages were rudimentary, offering nothing more than a wooden bench on an open-air car leaving riders exposed to wind, the sun, dust, and soot from the engine. Despite the lack of basic comforts like a restroom, traveling and transporting goods by rail became an unequivocal financial success for railway developers. When the Liverpool and Manchester Railway Company started paying shareholders dividends of 9.5%, the potential for profits caught the eye of investors and entrepreneurs.

It would take some time for the growth of railways to really pick up steam. Opening in 1830, the success of Liverpool and Manchester came despite a relatively slow British economy. Each new rail line required authorization by Parliament, and by the mid 1830's, fifty-nine new railways were approved. Share prices rose nearly 120% over a twelve-month period prior to steadily declining by 37% between 1836 and 1841. At the time, investment in railways was hampered by high interest rates as institutional investors like banks preferred to invest in government bonds.

This dynamic changed as the Bank of England lowered interest rates from 5.1% to 2.5% between 1839 and 1845. The reduction in interest rates made government bonds less attractive and pressured investors to seek out better rates of return. At the same time, the economy began to improve as the government moved towards a pro-business attitude. The Bubble Act, formed at the height of the South Sea bubble, had been repealed, allowing new companies to more easily sell shares to the public. Along with low interest rates, railway companies allowed investors to buy shares with a 10% down payment. From 1843 to 1845, the price of railway shares doubled.

Parliament never developed a cohesive railway plan, meaning they approved each railway on an individual basis without consideration of how each line would integrate with others. Also, concerned with preventing monopolies, Parliament allowed competition. This often resulted in multiple railways connecting the same cities with competing lines. The city of Wells, which only had a population of around 4,000 people, wound up with three train stations built by three different rail companies. In 1844, Parliament received requests for 199 new railways and an additional 562 requests in 1845. The number of railway companies listed on the London Stock Exchange quintupled in 1845 alone. Between 1842 and 1852, 4,600 miles of rail would be constructed, a staggering accomplishment. Compare that to a current 109-mile rail project started in England in 2012 with a planned completion date of 2029, seventeen years later.

Railway stock prices reached their peak in mid-1845. Once rail companies started collecting additional payments from investors who started with 10% down payments, many investors decided to sell their shares rather than keep their investments. At the same time, interest rates began to climb. In six weeks, railway stocks fell over 16%. It began to become apparent that many of the rail projects underway would never be financially viable. Railway stock prices would lose 67% of their value over the coming five years. Failed rail companies would either be cannibalized by larger successful companies or abandoned outright. The rise and fall of rail stocks pale in comparison to some of the previous bubbles as far as how substantially and rapidly prices rose, yet it still provides us with a valuable perspective of a time when investors were too optimistic about the potential of an investment.

THE GREAT DEPRESSION

Two decades into the twentieth century, America experienced one of its biggest economic booms. The Roaring Twenties represented a vibrant and prosperous era for the country. The rapid advances in technology changed the way the country worked, lived, and played. The electrification of the country improved remarkably through the decade with the number of homes that used electricity increasing from 35% in 1920 to nearly 70% in 1929. Electricity in factories helped spawn the mass production of goods, including automobiles, which helped bring prices down. The cost of a car in 1920 was $940, but by 1929 a car was just $290. Mass production boosted consumption as well as employment. Talkies and in-home radio programs became popular entertainment. Mass marketing had caught on as mail-in catalogs and chain stores spread across the country. Sears and JCPenney experienced exponential growth. Travel by air picked up, and

Charles Lindberg completed the first solo pilot flight across the Atlantic Ocean in 1927. Americans were extremely optimistic as there seemed to be no limits to what the country could accomplish.

Before the twenties could start roaring, World War I lifted the U.S. out of recession and started the economic boom. For most of the war, the United States avoided direct participation but manufactured and sold supplies to European countries. This meant vast sums of money flowing into the country. When the U.S. ultimately entered the war in 1917, government spending took off. Three million people were added to the military, which drew citizens who weren't previously working into jobs like manufacturing. The unemployment rate fell from 7.9% to 1.4%.

There are two reasons why World War I is so important to this story. For one, it serves to show how the U.S. arrived at having such a strong economy in the 20s, but secondly, the huge sums of government spending led to the widespread introduction of war bonds to cover the costs. Liberty Bonds were introduced in the Spring of 1917, and the response to the first issue was fairly tepid with most purchases being made by financial institutions. In response, the government launched the largest marketing campaign in history, producing millions of pamphlets and advertisements promoting the bonds as a patriotic purchase as well as providing education about how the bonds worked as investments. The Boy Scouts and Girl Scouts were enlisted to sell bonds to friends and family as well as play significant roles in marketing materials. Celebrities promoted the bonds in public appearances, and Charlie Chaplin even made a short film to help sell Liberty Bonds. Americans were encouraged to cut their expenses and use the difference to buy bonds.

New issues of Liberty Bonds were met with enthusiasm by American citizens who saw the investments as a civic duty to support the country and the soldiers fighting in the war. At least a third of adult Americans purchased bonds. For most, the purchase of a Liberty Bond was their first experience investing in any type of security, something previously believed to be appropriate for only the wealthy or professional Wall Street investors. For the first time, Americans became accustomed to investing their savings someplace other than their local bank.

With the U.S. and its allies emerging from war victoriously in November of 1918, it was time for the American economy to keep rolling. The emergence of the use of credit contributed to growth in consumer spending and rising stock prices. Not only could Americans now buy homes and cars with credit, but they could also buy everyday items for their homes such as washing machines and vacuum cleaners, and they could pay for them later. Americans also learned how to buy stocks on credit. Stock market regulations were minimal and certainly weren't designed for an American public who was suddenly ready to invest their savings into stocks for the first time. The stock market showed steady gains each year starting in 1921.

As stock market gains continued, more people became interested in buying stocks. It looked like easy money, after all. Brokerage offices opened all over the country to serve ordinary Americans who were ready to buy stocks but didn't know how. By the mid-1920s, around three million Americans had investments in the market. Telegraph ticker tape machines provided stock price updates across the country, giving investors the chance to watch their investments climb or fall as price swings happened, saving them from waiting for updates in tomorrow's paper.

With the belief that stock prices would continuously rise, buying stock with margin debt became increasingly popular. Investors could regularly buy stock for only 25% of the purchase price out of pocket, but in some cases they'd only need to put up as little as 10%. Investors saw little risk in this tactic. If they bought a $100 share with just $20 out-of-pocket, and the share price rose to $200, they'd experience a 500% return on their $20 investment even though the stock itself only rose 100%. By the late 1920s, nearly 40% of all lending was for margin purchases.

Between 1921 and 1929 stock prices increased sixfold, and the number of Americans investing in stocks had grown to over twenty million.

In his March 1929 inaugural address, President Hoover stated, "We have reached a higher degree of comfort and security than ever existed before in the history of the world. Through liberation from widespread poverty, we have reached a higher degree of individual freedom than ever before...I have no fears for the future of our country. It is bright with hope." Stock prices reached an all-time high in September of 1929. At the start of October, Yale economist Irving Fisher declared, "Stock prices have reached what looks like a permanently high plateau."

But there were growing concerns about speculation on Wall Street and a slowing economy. Days after Hoover's optimistic address, investment banker Paul Warburg had warned that a depression may be imminent. Behind closed doors, Hoover had serious concerns about the stock market and the economy. After a volatile September stock market, Hoover reached out to the head of J.P. Morgan Bank, Thomas Lamont, to voice his concerns. Lamont assured Hoover that there was no need for concern and no need for government intervention, closing his response with, "The future appears brilliant."

Five days after Lamont's reassurances, the market opened to intense selling, falling by 11% in the first few hours of what came to be known as Black Thursday. The selling was so fierce that ticker tape machines could not keep up with the volume, and updates to traders outside of the stock exchange were hours behind. Thousands of people gathered outside the doors of the New York Stock Exchange hoping to find out what was happening inside. Four hundred mounted police were sent to control the crowd. Hoping to avoid further panic, the major banks agreed to pool $250 million to strategically and publicly purchase specific stocks by midday. The banks paid more than the asking price, and investor confidence was stoked. The market climbed back from its bottom, ending the day down just 2%. The New York

Daily's front-page headline declared, "Stock Market Crisis Over." Trading on Friday resumed without incident.

When investors bought their stock with margin debt, the shares they purchased served as collateral for the loan. Brokers require margin investors to maintain minimum ratios between the value of their stocks and the amounts of their margin loans. The difference in the value of the stock and the amount of the margin loan is known as equity. For instance, at a broker who required a 25% ratio, an investor with $1,000 worth of stocks would need to ensure that he maintained at least $250 in equity ($1,000 stock value x 25%). In the above scenario, an investor could own $1,000 worth of stock with a margin loan of $750 and he would meet the 25% requirement. However, imagine the value of that investor's stock fell to $750, equal to the amount of his margin loan. Suddenly he would have $0 equity. The broker would make a "margin call" and request that the investor deposit an additional $187.50 ($750 stock value x 25%) to increase his equity and meet his margin requirement. Given that this amount would have been over half the price of a new car in the 1920s, you can imagine that many investors would have a hard time coming up with the cash, especially with the value of their investments falling. If investors were unable to meet the margin call with extra cash, the broker would sell the investors' shares without their consent. This led to a precarious situation on Wall Street. If stock fell, margin calls would force investors to sell more. As investors sold to meet margin calls, the prices would fall even further, inducing additional margin calls. It was a vicious cycle.

When the markets reopened the next week, selling resumed. The market fell 13% on Monday. Tuesday didn't fare any better, and, despite attempts to pump up stock prices by financial institutions and financial giants like the Rockefeller family, the market lost another 12%. In the months following, stock prices would see a temporary recovery posting steady gains through the Spring of 1930. However, over the next two years, stock prices steadily declined. By the Summer of 1932, stocks had lost nearly

90% of their value since the 1929 peak. Many banks struggled after losing both money they lent to investors and money they had invested directly in the markets. People began to lose confidence in their banks after it was discovered that several banks didn't have enough money to pay their depositors back. Americans pulled cash out of financial institutions en masse. Over 3,000 banks were forced to close. The country entered the Great Depression, and it wouldn't be until 1954 that the stock market reached its 1929 high again.

Comedic star and avid stock investor Groucho Marx had been shooting a movie that mocked investors in a recent Florida real estate bubble while the 1929 market was climbing to its peak. He was known to call or visit his broker every day for updates as he had invested his entire savings in the market, with margin. When asked by a friend why the market kept climbing, Groucho said, "I don't know, but my broker down in Great Neck tells me that it's because there's a worldwide market for American goods, and it's never going to go down, that the market'll just keep going up and up and up." However, once the crash was underway, Groucho got a call from that same friend, "Groucho, the jig is up." Groucho lost hundreds of thousands of dollars in the market, equivalent to nearly $4 million today. He later went on to say, "I would have lost more, but that was all the money I had."

EBBS AND FLOWS

Following the Great Depression, stock markets generally experienced routine ups and downs for the next several decades. In 1962, the markets experienced a 20% decline over a six-month period. Optimism over John F. Kennedy's election in 1960 and a growing interest in small electronics had pushed stocks higher, however, after the dip, the markets quickly rebounded. By the mid-1960s, the U.S. economy was booming.

After President Kennedy's assassination in 1963, Lyndon

Johnson became president. Johnson announced policies to create a "Great Society." Some of these policies included expansions to Social Security and food stamps programs. In 1965, the U.S. entered the Vietnam War. In short, the country was spending money out the wazoo. The strong economy and expansion of government programs slowly started to cause prices to rise. By 1968, inflation had reached 4.2% and began to concern policymakers.

Richard Nixon took over as president in 1969. While he was aware of the inflation concerns, Nixon weighed the political costs of both, remarking, "We'll take inflation if necessary, but we can't take unemployment." Within a year, he had more of both as the economy began to sputter. Growing concerned with the 1972 election, Nixon fired the chairman of the Federal Reserve and replaced him with his economic advisor. This allowed Nixon to pressure the Federal Reserve to keep interest rates low despite the high inflation in hopes that it could pump up the economy. Meanwhile, foreign countries whose currencies were tied to the value of the U.S. Dollar became concerned that the U.S. was printing too much money to cover their expenses. When foreign governments started to trade their dollars for gold, Nixon abruptly ended the gold standard and the Bretton Woods agreement (discussed in Chapter 6). This caused the dollar's value to fall compared to many foreign currencies, resulting in higher prices for imported goods. Nixon eventually announced a price and wage freeze to halt inflation. The measure was popular at the time among voters.

Nixon pumped the economy enough to triumph in a landslide election, winning forty-nine states, but the best days for Nixon were behind him. His price freezes temporarily slowed inflation, but once they were lifted, price increases accelerated to make up for lost time. Poor weather helped lead to even more significant price increases in food, and an oil embargo from the Middle East caused added spikes in energy prices. Before his second term was underway, concerns about inflation and unemployment could no longer be ignored by stock market investors. Troubled by numerous challenges in the economy along with Nixon's Watergate scandal and eventual resignation, from 1973-1974, the market fell 44%. The market had a modest rebound in 1975 but stayed relatively flat for about a decade, and with high inflation, a flat market effectively meant investments were losing value.

By the end of 1980, a one-hundred-dollar bill could only buy about forty dollars' worth of the goods it would have purchased in 1970. With no end in sight to relentless inflation, newly appointed Fed Chairman Paul Volcker decided that interest rates needed to rise dramatically to slow down the flow of money into the economy. He felt that raising rates would help break the current mindset of Americans who believed prices would continuously rise forever. The federal funds rate rose from around 6% for most of the 70s to 20% in 1981. With the federal funds rate so high, private banks had to raise their interest rates. Mortgage rates reached 18.5%, nearly three times what they are today. As a result, it was harder for businesses and consumers to borrow. The country went into a recession, and unemployment spiked. Volcker came under intense political pressure and was the target of several protests. However, he held firm. Inflation came under control within two years and remained low for four decades.

With inflation under control, the stock market took off with several years of 20% or higher gains during the 80's. In 1987, the stock market rose 43% through the first eight months. On Wednesday, October 14th, a new proposal by Congress to eliminate a business tax deduction spooked investors, causing stocks to fall more than 10% over the following three days. While trading was closed over the weekend, many mutual funds allowed investors to redeem their shares over the weekend at Friday's price. The redemptions would require the mutual funds to sell off assets once the stock market re-opened on Monday. Other investors realized that this would cause selling pressure as soon as Monday morning trading began, so they, too, put in orders to sell at the open. Adding to selling pressure was the emergence of computer-controlled trading, which, through automation, accelerated selling as stock prices fell. The market fell 22.6%, the most significant single day drop in history on what came to be known as Black Monday. The selling was utterly chaotic.

Amongst the panic, one trader interviewed by the Los Angeles Times told them, "I'll tell you how I feel, but you can't use my name because I don't want my customers to know how scared I am." By the end of the day, Tom Sosnoff, founder of financial network Tastytrade and a floor trader on Black Monday, had made more trades than any other day of his career and ended his workday with a feeling of imminent doom. Battered by a relentlessly brutal day of screaming and shouting through a crowd of traders, Sosnoff stopped by his favorite hot dog stand near the end of the night. No one there had a clue about what had happened in the market that day; this helped give Tom some perspective that the real world would keep moving on.

Like 1929, investors were leveraged with margin debt, and the rapid fall of stock prices meant large margin calls would be required. Wanting to avoid a repeat of 1929, the Federal Reserve made it clear that it would provide all the liquidity the markets needed to remain operational and pressured banks to continue lending. The New York Stock Exchange issued a moratorium on computerized trading, hoping to bring sanity back to the exchange. Still, when markets opened the next day, the sell orders continued to be relentless. The problem now was that there was no one willing to buy what others were selling. While the stock exchange opened at its regular time, the trading in many stocks was delayed for hours or stopped altogether while attempting to find buyers to match with sellers. The New York Stock Exchange was considering temporarily halting all trades until order could be restored. Concerned about the possibility of a NYSE shutdown, the Chicago Board Options Exchange and Chicago Mercantile Exchange, which trade futures contracts, temporarily closed.

Before the exchange closures, Blair Hull, founder of Hull

Trading Company, one of the computerized trading firms at the time, couldn't Google what he wanted to know in 1987, so he sent an employee to the library to quickly research what had happened when markets had been temporarily closed in the past. When his employee returned, the research he shared helped Hull feel confident enough to make his way to the floor of the Chicago Board of Trade, a smaller futures and options exchange that remained open, as one of the only people placing consistent buy orders. This move paved the way for other traders to start buying again. The CBOE and CME reopened, and the NYSE avoided a shutdown. Stock prices surged for the rest of the day, resulting in one of the most extensive single days of gain in the market's history. Despite a 22% single-day loss late in the year, the Dow Jones ended 1987 in positive territory.

The 1960s, '70s, or '80s didn't necessarily endure any major bubble-like booms or busts. Despite this, each decade experienced its own significant stock market declines, all due to the unique circumstances of their time. The falls in the 1960s and 1970s seem to be reasonably well explained by changes in the economy, while a short-term panic perpetuated the 1987 crash. In each of these instances, the recovery for stock markets was relatively quick.

JAPAN

The steps taken in America to curb inflation at the start of the 1980s resulted in steadily strengthening the U.S. dollar through 1985. A strong dollar meant that goods priced in dollars were more expensive globally compared to goods priced in foreign currencies. This created challenges for U.S. manufacturing as price discrepancies led to the country importing more and exporting less.

In a period recognized as the "Economic Miracle," through the decades leading up to the 1980s, Japan had developed itself into one of the premier manufacturing countries in the world. Since the end of World War II, Japan's economy had grown to be the second largest on Earth. While Japan's economic growth began to slow from all-time highs in the 1980s, it was still booming, boosted by groundbreaking products like Donkey Kong, Super Mario Brothers, and Walkman cassette players. Japan's currency, the yen, was substantially weaker than the U.S. dollar, and this allowed Japan to dominate the global export markets. The differences in currency values were part of what helped the country become one of the top economic powers in the world. With political pressures from the manufacturing industry in the U.S. growing, the United States pressed for an agreement that would help moderate the exchange rates of currencies in the top countries in the world. The agreement became known as the Plaza Accord and was signed in 1985.

The agreement had the desired results for America: the dollar began to weaken, and the Japanese yen strengthened. In anticipation of losing some of their exchange rate advantages, Japan acted to stave off a potential slowdown in their economy. The government worked to lower interest rates, reduce regulations, provide business tax incentives, and promote increased lending. At the same time, concerns about becoming over-dependent on exports pushed Japan to develop a more robust domestic service economy.

With an economy that was already booming, aggressive pro-growth policies should have led to inflation. However, inflation was practically non-existent in Japan through the 1980s. Instead of the Japanese spending more liberally, money flowed into assets, specifically stocks and real estate.

Corporations could establish their own tax-advantaged investment funds or investment companies known in Japan as *tokkin*. Corporations typically used these funds to make speculative investments. The investments they made reflected on the company's balance sheet, and therefore gains in their speculative investment funds would raise the value of the company making the investment, in turn, raising the price of the corporation's stock.

Another arrangement, known as *keiretsu*, has two or more companies buy shares of each other's stock. *Keiretsu's* are typically
used when companies are working together. For example, an au-
tomotive manufacturer like Toyota would own shares in the
companies that produce the myriad of parts needed to build their
cars, and those part-producing companies would own shares in
Toyota. *Tokkin* and *keiretsu* investments effectively meant that
the fate of many Japanese companies' stock prices were inter-
twined. One company's share price could not fall without bringing down the share price of the companies that invested in it.

At the same time investments in stocks were rising, Japanese
real estate began to boom. In the early 1980s, Japanese banks
became more aggressive in issuing loans. It was quite easy for
any landowner to borrow money at low rates using their property
as collateral. The price of land in Tokyo increased 10.4% in
1986, 57.5% in 1987, and 22.6% in 1988. As the value of the
land increased, so did the value of the collateral, allowing borrowers to take additional loans backed by properties they'd previously borrowed against. These loans were issued on the prem-
ise that land prices would continuously rise. Loan proceeds were
frequently used to buy additional land or invest in the stock market. By 1989, the value of Japanese stocks represented 44% of
all stocks around the globe. In 1991, Japan's land value reached
$20 trillion compared to $4 trillion for all the land across the
United States. At the peak, the land in the city of Tokyo alone
was more valuable than the land in the entire United States. Japanese investors, flush with seemingly limitless funds and with a
Japanese currency more closely valued to the U.S. dollar, began
to snap up valuable assets in America, from golf courses to movie studios like Columbia Pictures to iconic buildings like Rockefeller Center in New York, even world-class art at inflated prices.

By the end of 1989, the Bank of Japan became concerned that
land prices were accelerating too quickly, so it decided to start
raising interest rates, which made it more challenging to borrow

money. To keep up the payments of their previous loans, Japanese investors had become reliant on continuously borrowing more as their asset prices increased. Now that the cost of loans was becoming more expensive, investors began to sell off their stock investments to make up the difference. With the stock prices of so many companies tied to one another, there were no safe stocks to invest in. The market fell nearly 39% in 1990. However, land prices remained high for the time being. The Bank of Japan made the decision to further increase interest rates, which again led to fervent stock selling. By 1992, Japan's Nikkei stock market index was worth just 36.7% of its peak value in December of 1989. Ultimately, the value of land prices began to fall. Over the next several years, land prices in Japan would steadily decline, particularly in major cities where land value eventually collapsed 70% by 2001.

GETTING ONLINE

In February 1995, my grandparents, Bev and Duke, dropped off me and my brother at the California Institute of Technology (CalTech) campus in Pasadena, California. The university was hosting a joint event with MIT to showcase the school's potential to future students. Obviously, my grandparents were far too optimistic about my academic potential. During the day, we attended a number of demonstrations ranging from earthquake detection to dropping homemade comets off of a high-rise. One segment of the day was dedicated to a hands-on demonstration of the Internet. I remember being bored out of my mind during this session. We sat in a computer lab, each of us connected to an Internet that was made up of about 5,000 websites, most of which consisted of a single page, gray background and a bit of text scrawled across it. Graphics were sparsely used on websites due to their slow loading times and forget about streaming videos or playing games. Search engines had only been around for a few months but didn't really work well anyway. Without knowing the address of the particular website you wanted to visit, there wasn't much to do on the Internet in early 1995. It was difficult to imagine precisely what the Internet had to offer.

Yahoo.com had barely launched as a manually constructed index of "popular" sites around the Internet, and Amazon.com would sell its first book a few months later, both sites adopting a gray background spattered with bright blue hyperlinks. Regardless of what we thought the Internet might be used for, people would need Internet browsers if they wanted to surf the web. In June of 1995, Spyglass, Inc., a maker of web browsers, made its initial public offering (IPO), becoming the first Internet software company to sell its shares to the public. Its IPO price launched at $17 per share and climbed to $27 per share by the end of its first day of trading. Two months later, popular Internet browser developer, Netscape, had an IPO of its own despite having never generated profits. Its starting IPO price would be $28, but during its first day, the price shot up as high as $75 per share, more than doubling in just a few hours. Now the Internet had investors' attention.

After maintaining high interest rates throughout the 80s to keep inflation in check, the U.S. Federal Reserve Bank finally saw fit to begin cutting rates in the early 90s, with rates coming down from 8.10% in 1990 to just 3.02% in 1993. Emerging technology companies benefit from low interest rates because they are heavily reliant on borrowing in their developmental years. Later, in 1996, regulations were eased with the specific goal of bolstering the rapid development of communications technologies. Those regulations were followed shortly after, in 1997 with a reduction in capital gains tax rates. Each of these developments made investing in Internet stocks more appealing.

Investments in Internet-related stocks accelerated to a frenzied pace. Like in previous periods, margin debt steeply increased in the second half of the 90s—huge, quick returns from Internet IPOs continued. When The Globe.com went public in 1998, the price of its stock gained 606% on the first day. The two co-founders of the company, Stephan Paternot and Todd Krizelman, were still in their early 20's, but now each had a net worth of over $100 million. Paternot was soon quoted as saying, "Got the girl. Got the money. Now I'm ready to live a disgusting, frivolous life." In 1999, 457 IPOs were completed with 117 of those doubling on their first day. Investing in Internet companies seemed like a sure bet.

Most Investors had little understanding of how to value an Internet-based company. If companies had very little revenue and were losing money, how could someone determine what the company was worth? During this same period, investment bankers had become extremely aggressive in bringing companies to IPOs. Prior to the Dot-Com boom, businesses could spend years building their company with the help of venture capitalists or other private investors who understood risk. It was typically *after* the company became profitable that an IPO would be considered. However, during the Internet boom, most companies who issued IPOs were losing money and many struggled to generate revenue at all. Many investors failed to recognize the fact that an IPO being underwritten was not an endorsement of the company and in no way reflected the future prospects of the business for investors. Stock analysts working for investment banks who depended on blockbuster IPOs to make money became cheerleaders for Internet stocks instead of offering honest analysis. In many cases, Internet IPOs were little more than a way for company founders like Paternot of Globe.com and investment bankers to cash in on a crazed market.

Early dot-com businesses assumed each customer they acquired would be very valuable long-term, so they spared no expense trying to obtain them. Pets.com became one of the most recognizable website names in the world thanks to its aggressive marketing campaign. Pets.com bombarded the airways with its oddly enthusiastic sock puppet mascot. The puppet appeared in a Super Bowl ad, talk shows like Good Morning America, and was interviewed by People magazine and other publications. He even earned a balloon in the 1999 Macy's Thanksgiving Day parade and later became the subject of a lawsuit related to another famous 1990s K-9 puppet, Triumph the Insult Comic Dog. However, in its 1999 fiscal year, Pets.com had $619,000 in income, while spending $11.8 million on marketing. To add to the pain, Pets.com was selling their products for only about one-third of what they were paying for them. Turns out, it was rather difficult to compete on price and ship heavy bags of dog food to people's homes. Michael Barach, the CEO of Mothernature.com, said his company discovered that each of their customers had a lifetime value of around $10, but they were paying $60-$80 to attract each one. Barach believed that his company was one of the first to realize that Internet-based customers were far less valuable than investors were expecting. Pets.com, which raised over $80 million with their IPO, and Mothernature.com, which raised over $50 million, both shut down less than a year after their IPO dates. Other companies like Etoys, Priceline, and Kozmo, who followed the standard Internet business model of spending heavily on marketing and selling products or services at a loss, suffered similar fates. It almost seemed like losing money was a requirement in order for a dot-com company to be a desirable investment.

Nearing the end of 1999, it was becoming clear an Internet stock bubble had formed, however, the size of the bubble and when it could possibly burst were unknown. The NASDAQ market, where most Internet stocks traded, reached a peak on March 10, 2000. The average price-to-earnings ratio of the NASDAQ reached 200, meaning stocks were priced at $200 for every $1 a company earned per share. At the peak of the 1991 Japanese asset bubble, the Nikkei Index had a price-to-earnings ratio of 80 for comparison. Institutional investors became leery of dumping more money into companies that struggled to become profitable. From September 1999 through July 2020, dot-com insiders cashed out $43 billion while selling off their shares at twice the rate they had in 1997 or 1998. A week after the

NASDAQ peaked, Barron's released an article highlighting the precarious financial conditions of many Internet companies, bringing to light that many only had enough cash to survive a few months at best.

The NASDAQ began to have more frequent down days before bouncing back and then falling again. Eventually, the bounce backs stopped bouncing. The NASDAQ market fell 49% from its March high by the end of 2000 and continued its downward trend, which was exacerbated by a number of accounting scandals, the decision to raise interest rates, the Japanese recession, and the 9/11 terrorist attacks in 2001. By 2002, the NASDAQ had lost nearly 75% of its value. While technology and Internet stocks suffered the worst, the crash spilled over into established stocks as well. The S&P 500 index lost nearly 50% of its value during the same period. The crash wouldn't go on forever. As we know, many of the dot-com companies spawned during the boom like, Amazon and eBay, survived the crash and went on to fantastic success. Stocks, in general, had a strong year in 2003 and experienced steady gains until reversing again in the 2008 financial crisis.

NEW MILLENIUM REAL ESTATE

"We can put light where there's darkness, and hope where there's despondency in this country. And part of it is working together as a nation to encourage folks to own their own home," President George W. Bush stated in a 2002 speech.

The conditions for purchasing a home in the early 2000s were favorable, to say the least. The percentage of Americans who owned their home climbed to nearly 70%, including over 40% of those under the age of thirty-five. Ownership rates were boosted by a low-interest rate policy put in place to keep the economy moving after the Dot Com crash, but that wasn't the only reason so many people had the ability to buy a home.

Historically, the majority of mortgage-providing banks would keep an account until it was paid in full while collecting steady interest over a period as long as two or three decades. Since this was such a long investment commitment, lenders were diligent in making sure the people they lent to were likely to pay them back. Gradually, this dynamic shifted.

By the early 2000s, a type of investment known as a mortgage-backed security had gained popularity. A mortgage-backed security (MBS) is a type of investment that pools together a number of home mortgages and allows investors to own a part of that pool. The mortgage-backed security gives investors a share of the interest homeowners pay on their home loans. In return, the creator of the mortgage-backed security takes their share of fees.

It didn't take long for mortgage lenders to adjust their business models to one which, instead of holding accounts for decades of slow, steady interest payments, focused on a quick payout related to selling newly written mortgage loans to investment banks for the purpose of those banks selling mortgage-backed securities to their investors. Because the original lenders no longer had to depend on the borrowers making their payments for thirty years, they had the flexibility to get a lot more creative with whom they were willing to lend money to. The investment banks didn't have to worry about the borrowers making their payments either because the risk was passed on to individual investors.

With the risks transferred out of the hands of mortgage banks, lending standards deteriorated. Mortgages were given to applicants with lower credit scores, lower income, more debt, less documentation, and smaller down payments. In addition, more creative loans that kept payments low for the first few years but increased later were given to help people get into a home.

Home prices had steadily risen at about 5% per year on average between 1992 and 2002, however, several factors conspired in the mid-2000s to accelerate price increases. Loose lending standards not only allowed buyers with low credit scores and weak income history to buy homes but also allowed relatively well-off individuals to purchase second homes as investment properties. Those with higher credit scores were going substantially deeper into debt than those with lower scores. Housing prices spiked by double-digit percentages in 2005 and 2006. By 2007, 43% of mortgage balances for those in the top quartile of credit scores were held by investors. That same year, the poor lending standards were beginning to expose themselves as borrowers increasingly fell behind on their payments, but the worst was yet to come.

Mortgage-backed securities can typically contain a thousand underlying mortgages all with varying levels of quality. Investment banks were able to use complex financial maneuvers combined with their financial influence over credit rating agencies to ensure that their mortgage-backed securities received high AAA investment ratings despite containing significant amounts of low-quality, high-risk mortgages. These high ratings allowed large institutions like pension funds to take substantial stakes in the mortgage market with the belief that they were making a secure investment. In addition, insurance contracts known as credit default swaps were created to protect investors if the mortgage investments happened to go bad. The kicker was that you didn't need to own a particular mortgage investment to buy insurance against it. This allowed speculators to bet against the mortgage market. However, based on the high AAA ratings of mortgage-backed securities, the insurance providers saw little risk in issuing the credit default swaps, and because these contracts were unregulated, insurers weren't required to keep the cash reserves for paying potential claims like they'd need to with traditional insurance policies.

Home prices started declining in 2007 and ended the year down 7%. Banks began to tighten lending standards to minimize their risk. Home pricing declines accelerated into 2008. The government stepped in to pass a stimulus bill and lower interest rates, but it was a day late and a dollar short. Homeowners who had relied on continuously increasing home values to help them refinance out of their risky loans were now faced with higher payments they couldn't afford or owed more than their homes were worth.

Home mortgage defaults picked up steam, and as that happened, investors in mortgage-backed securities started taking losses. In March 2008, Treasury Secretary Henry Paulson repeatedly assured the American people, "Our financial institutions are strong." A few days later, investment bank Lehman Brothers was found to be heavily exposed to the mortgage market and begged Warren Buffet to provide them with $2 billion as soon as possible. Based on Lehman's financial statements, Buffet declined.

In July, California-based IndyMac Bank failed, and the dominoes only continued to fall. Lehman Brothers declared bankruptcy on September 15 after 158 years in business. The next day, insurance provider AIG was bailed out after it was determined they did not have the money to pay claims against the collapsing mortgage market they offered insurance policies for.

As bailouts continued, fear spread from the financial sector to other industries. General Motors, Ford, and Chrysler each requested bailout funds from the government. Layoffs across the country began in earnest as a recession took hold, and unemployment climbed to 10% by 2009. The stock market fell 57% from 2007 to early 2009 and took about four years to recover. Housing prices continued to fall nationally until reaching a bottom in 2011, down 33% (certain regional real estate markets like Las Vegas dropped as much as 60%). Real estate in most areas regained their 2006 peak prices by 2013, but many areas took ten years or more to recover. Once the dust settled, economic recovery was slow but steady for over a decade.

WHAT TO TAKE AWAY FROM IT

"Asset appreciation draws in people that really don't know anything about the asset and people start being interested in something because it's going up, not because they understand it. The

guy next door who they know is dumber than they are is getting rich and they aren't and their spouse is saying, 'Can't you figure it out too?' It is so contagious. That's a permanent part of the system." -Warren Buffet

Investment bubbles have a long and varied history throughout the world. The bubbles I've covered here are some of the largest in history, however, many others have grown and burst, and the rise of many more is a certainty. By taking a close look at historical bubbles, we may be able to identify future bubbles before they pop.

Recurring Characteristics of Bubbles Through History

1. Easy Access to Money- Bubbles tend to form during times when debt is expanding and credit is easily accessible. When interest rates are low, investors are more willing to borrow and speculate. Both the South Sea and Mississippi bubbles were born out of a need to handle large government debts, and in both events, investors could buy shares using unmaintainable practices (either borrowing against current shares or buying shares with a small down payment). The railway bubble was pumped up by investors buying shares for a fraction of their total cost and low interest rates. Leading up to the 1929 crash, American consumers had started using debt to purchase goods, and investors were aggressively buying stocks on margin. Low interest rates and aggressive borrowing played roles in the Japan crisis of the '90s, the Dot Com boom and bust, and of course the 2008 housing crash.

2. Steady growth followed by exponential growth - Bubbles tend to occur in assets that have seen steady growth over a period of time and suddenly catch on like wildfire, seeing their prices surge in a short period. The steady period of growth gives investors the confidence to believe the investment is unlikely to lose. The prices of tulips rose for a decade before spiking 1000% in the final few months of the bubble. The South Sea Company's stock rose for nine years, until a 500% spike hit only months before its collapse. Railway shares steadily grew for over ten years before doubling during the final two years of the bubble. During the 2008 housing bubble, prices steadily increased at single-digit rates for over a decade before the annual rate of increase accelerated in the final eighteen months of the boom.

3. New Blood- Investment bubbles draw new investors out of the woodwork near the final stages of the bubble. The concept referred to as FOMO (Fear of Missing Out) catches hold. Those who know little about the asset begin investing based solely on the fact that its price has recently risen. This was apparent in all the bubbles I've discussed so far.

4. Effort Diversion- Large swathes of people will reduce or stop their normally productive work and dedicate their time to investing in the bubble. Instead of focusing on their full-time careers, people will devote significant time to researching the latest developments in whatever market they are chasing. You'll likely experience more friends, co-workers, and acquaintances discussing the investment on a regular basis. During this period there is typically substantial media coverage around the asset as well as a surge in literature like "How-To" books, informational videos, and courses tailored to the topic.

5. New Paradigm and Suspended Disbelief- An investment bubble requires investors to detach their decisions from reality to some degree. When the price of an asset rises far beyond its tangible value, an individual must find a way to justify paying the unreasonable price. Usually, this occurs when investing in a new technology or new financial instrument. These concepts came into play during the Tulipmania, with Tulips being relatively new coupled with the development of the contracts used to invest in them, during the South Sea and Mississippi bubbles with the introduction of new financial engineering, with the adoption of trains in the railway boom and bust, with the electrification of the country leading up to the 1929 crash, and throughout the Dot Com bust. When justifying why the asset price is suddenly worth double or triple what it was just a few months ago, it's said that, "This time, it's different" (in more words or less). New investors are convinced that conventional methods for evaluating investments are out of touch and "old school" investors simply don't understand why the bubble asset is so valuable.

6. Easy Profits - Those with relatively little experience or expertise in the field are suddenly able to make substantial profits in areas where it's historically been challenging for even experts to do so.

It became apparent by early 2021 that all of these characteristics were present, forming what I call the "Stimulus Bubble". The COVID-19 pandemic that began in early 2020 led to the most extensive distortion of the U.S. economy in history. The government acted strongly by pumping unbelievable amounts of money into the system to ensure people could comply with stay-at-home directives intended to slow the spread of the disease while buying time to develop vaccines and treatment.

Among the actions the federal government took were direct stimulus payments totaling $11,400 for a family of four, enhanced unemployment benefits for those who were laid off or worked fewer hours, lower medical insurance premiums for millions of Americans, issuing $953 billion in forgivable small business loans, tax credits for getting sick, expanded child tax credits, a ban on evictions and foreclosures, and record low interest rates. Many state governments piled on with stimulus programs of their own. These programs flooded the economy over the course of two years through three phases. In hindsight, it's clear that the money was not directed to the most needed areas and became quite frivolous.

I am willing to give the government some latitude to the way the first phase was implemented because, despite what leaders said at the time, no one had a clue what was really happening. When the first round of stimulus was implemented in March of 2020, the economy was about to go off a cliff, so the nearly $2.7 trillion in aid was about quickly getting a lot of money into the hands of the people.

Naturally, with a hastily devised plan, there were many loopholes and opportunities to exploit the system. The direct stimulus payments went to everyone within certain income ranges, whether the pandemic had affected their finances or not. Unemployment benefits were expanded to include an additional $600 per week and for the first time, they included self-employed workers. In most states, if an employee was working 40 hours per week prior to the pandemic and were cut back by 10 hours, they'd then be eligible to receive the extra $600 per week in unemployment compensation (which works out to $60 per hour). Lower-wage and part-time workers were making more money being unemployed than they had been while working. Many self-employed individuals were able to "double-dip" by receiving unemployment compensation in addition to forgivable small business loans. While all of this money was being sent out, people could stop paying their mortgages, rent, and student loans. It was all within the rules of the law.

By the time the next stimulus bill passed in December 2020, Congress had a better idea of which individuals were being impacted and which industries needed the most help, yet the bill was almost a cookie-cutter duplicate of the first. The most significant change was the amount of direct stimulus payments and weekly unemployment payments being cut in half. The funds were, again, broadly targeted.

The third and final stimulus phase was completed in March of 2021. At a time when the economy was recovering and vaccines were becoming widely available, Congress passed a bill almost as large as the original (nearly $2 trillion in additional aid). Rather than dialing in the focus on those who needed the most help, the third phase *expanded* eligibility and provided the largest direct stimulus payments to date. Under this phase, even people who never worked in their lives received a $1,400 stimulus payment. In my practice, some families were able to claim a $1,400 stimulus payment three times for the same person, and it was one hundred-percent legal.

Throughout the year, I generally prepare or review several hundred tax returns, and we have a rather diverse group of clients. While the data is anecdotal, it was apparent that the majority of individuals I worked with had a financial boon in 2020 rather than a financial hardship. Those who were hit hard were owners of small retail stores and high-income individuals who were more likely to face pay cuts and downsizing.

With money flowing freely, individuals with extra time on their hands and institutional investors had to do something with their cash. From March of 2020 to March of 2021, the cryptocurrency market surged, taking Bitcoin from $5,100 to $61,000. Stocks soared, particularly those for technology companies. After several years of growth, Tesla stock surged from $85 per share in March 2020 climbing to over $1,200 per share by November 2021. Housing prices also rose 30% between early 2020 and the start of 2021 in a way that seems removed from reality. In July of 2021, I published an article warning that a crash was inevitable in the coming months.

In late 2021, a survey by Civic Science found that 4% of people over the age of 18 had quit their jobs to focus on their cryptocurrency investments. The runup in price between 2020 and 2021 certainly drew masses of new crypto investors. Again, I saw evidence of this from within my own business as the number of clients who owned crypto grew from one out of twenty customers to one out of five within a year. The cryptocurrency segment of the bubble popped at the end of 2021, leading Bitcoin to fall an incredible 72% from its peak by June 2022.

The bubble in tech stocks also burst in December of 2021, crashing over 37% by the end of 2022. Based on the share price of Tesla in August of 2022, investors still said they believed the electric car maker was worth $931 billion. To put this number into perspective, the next most valuable automaker was Toyota, worth $229 billion. Tesla's $931 billion value was more than the next thirteen car companies *combined*. That's a list that includes Toyota/Lexus, Volkswagen/Audi, Mercedes-Benz, Ford, General Motors, BMW, Honda, Ferrari, and more.

Let's look at it another way. In 2021, Toyota sold 10.5 million cars, and if the company was worth $229 billion according to its stock price, we can calculate that each car Toyota sells must be worth about $22,000 of value to the company. That number seems reasonable based on the typical selling price of a Toyota or Lexus. In 2021, Tesla sold just under one million cars. Based on investors' opinion of Tesla's value at the time, every car Tesla sold must have been worth $995,000. This is a number that had no basis in reality. Even assuming Tesla could someday expand sales by 1,000% to catch up with Toyota, based on the stock's August 2022 value, if Tesla sold 10 million vehicles, each car would still need to bring nearly $100,000 in value to the company. How can a company gain $100,000 on a car it sells for $40,000?

Tesla investors make the argument that electric cars are the way of the future, that Tesla is a technology company, and it shouldn't be compared to other car makers as an investment. In other words, "this time, it's different."

The mindset that led to Tesla's insane value carried over to other electric vehicle makers that entered the market. In November of 2021, high-end electric truck maker, Rivian, made its shares available to investors with an initial public offering (IPO). The market value of the truck manufacturer soared to $153 billion within a few days, making it one of the top three most valuable car companies.

At the IPO, Rivian projected they would produce 50,000

trucks in 2022, yet, the company hadn't actually delivered any to customers at the time. What makes it apparent that Rivian stock was a victim of too much hype around new electric vehicle makers is an introductory look at Ford who sells millions of cars per year. Not only had Ford announced that it would start selling an electric version of their F-150 (the top-selling pickup truck in America) starting in 2022, but Ford also owned part of Rivian. Yet, based on Ford's stock price, the company was worth only about half of what Rivian was. What investors were essentially saying was that Ford's stock price should be penalized because, in addition to making electric trucks like Rivian, they also make some of the most popular gas-powered vehicles in the world. This was clearly delusional. While I believe Rivian and Tesla are fine car companies, their valuations based on stock prices had certainly displayed characteristics of being part of a bubble. Rivian's stock price has since fallen over 90% from its high, and Tesla's stock price has fallen over 50% from its high. Without a major breakthrough, I'd expect Tesla stock to fall below $100 per share in the coming years.

The rapid rise in housing prices, surging 30% in less than two years after half a decade of steady 5% growth, carried trademarks of a bubble. Money was readily available with some of the lowest interest rates in history. A disproportionate number of homes were purchased by investors, either as rental properties or flipping opportunities. The common narrative was that after the 2008 real estate crash, too few homes were built in the United States, resulting in a shortage, but whenever housing prices significantly out-pace inflation, we have to look into more details. The 30% increase in prices was sudden, but did we suddenly have 30% fewer homes, 30% more people, or 30% higher incomes? There was definitely a shortage of houses listed for sale, but did that necessarily mean there was a shortage of houses in existence?

Statistically, we have about the same number of housing units per person today as we have had on average for decades. During the pandemic, many people who wanted to move put off selling their homes due to uncertainty about the future, but in addition to that, government bans on foreclosures, loan modification programs, and eviction moratoriums prevented homes that would typically be sold from coming to market. Renters could stay in their rentals without paying rent when they would have usually been forced to downsize, get a roommate, or move in with family. This locked up their property from being rented to new tenants and helped lead to a shortage of available housing rentals. Add to this a spike in demand for homes related to the changing reality around the pandemic, such as wanting more space to work from home or a yard to help avoid close contact with others in an enclosed room, and prices took off.

When prices of any asset start to appreciate quickly, it draws in new investors like a moth to a bug zapper. People were afraid to put off buying a home, so they jumped in despite fewer homes being listed. Purchasing was so frenzied that it became common for buyers to purchase properties before ever seeing them in person. Investors started piling on to get their share as well.

In the first quarter of 2022, 28% of homes were purchased by investors, an alarming number. However, housing prices must be supported by the incomes of the people living in them either through making mortgage payments or paying rent. The cost of buying a home significantly outpaced increases in income, which meant that fewer people could afford to buy. Additionally, many investors purchased homes as short-term vacation rentals like Airbnbs while the vacation market surged during a post-COVID vacation boom. Now that vacationing habits have returned to normal, many short-term rental properties are experiencing excessive vacancies.

Persistently high inflation caused largely by the massive stimulus programs forced the Federal Reserve to raise interest rates steadily. Rising rates caused an even more challenging environment for buyers trying to afford already expensive homes. Like other assets pumped up by the Stimulus Bubble, home sales abruptly slowed in June of 2022, and pricing began to fall a few months later.

Most analyses of the housing sector during the Stimulus Bubble focused on why the market was not like the market preceding the 2008 crash. Economists and real estate experts repeated the fact that buyers leading up to the 2008 crash had low credit scores, and lending standards were lax. In the early 2000s, people could buy homes they couldn't afford. In contrast, the market leading up to 2022 consisted of well-qualified buyers. However, it's often missed that the largest proportion of defaults in the 2008 crisis were from well qualified borrowers who over borrowed. In fact, by 2006, subprime borrowers made up only 39% of delinquent mortgages, which was significantly down from 71% in 2003. This means borrowers with higher credit scores are not precluded from defaulting en masse.

By the Summer of 2022, housing affordability had fallen to its lowest level since 2006. Regardless of lending standards, the fact remains that income must ultimately support the price of homes, and if housing becomes broadly unaffordable in relation to income, prices will fall. This sector of the stimulus bubble had just started to unwind during the publication of this book, but changes to home prices typically happen over a course of years. I certainly don't expect a major housing crash like we saw in 2008, but until housing affordability becomes more reasonable, housing price declines remain likely.

A financial bubble may not be very difficult to spot, but that doesn't necessarily mean you'll easily avoid losses or be able to secure outsized profits by recognizing one. There are a number of challenges inherent in bubbles. First and foremost, to profit or protect yourself from a bubble, there are multiple aspects of timing you'd need to get right, and missing just one point of timing could offset any gains you made from the points you got right.

Assuming you recognize that a bubble exists you'll need to anticipate precisely when that bubble will burst if you want to maximize profits. As we've covered, bubbles typically see the most rapid price increases in the final stages. If you pull out too early, you may miss the most significant part of the run. Many bubbles can continue inflating for far longer than anyone anticipates. Awareness of this aspect plays a role in why bubbles can get so big. Even institutional investors may recognize a bubble exists but willingly keep their chips on the table. In the Summer of 2007, Citigroup CEO Chuck Prince, after acknowledging how risky the financial markets were at the time, put it this way, "As long as the music is playing, you've got to get up and dance." Citigroup went on to require a massive government bailout the following year when the music stopped. If you can get the timing right and can milk a bubble for every cent before it bursts, you're then faced with the decision of determining when the bubble is finished deflating. Jump back in too soon, and you may face additional losses. Too late, and you may miss a substantial rebound. You're also met with deciding what to do with your money after you've pulled out from investments.

Another point to consider is that no bubble is guaranteed to pop. I define a bubble as a period when prices for a particular asset are unjustifiably high at a point in time. A bubble can avoid bursting when prices level off for an extended period, giving time for the underlying fundamental metrics to catch up. For example, when a housing bubble is present due to a mismatch between home prices and income, if incomes begin to rise rapidly while home prices remain flat for several years, the pressure on the bubble will dissipate without the need for a violent crash. After identifying a bubble, we have to consider the likelihood for the bubble to burst or if it's possible that, even if the prices are unjustifiable for the time being, those prices will be justifiable in the near future if certain other circumstances change. The most valuable lesson to learn about bubbles is to remind yourself not to actively chase after the hype when it's all around you.

-CHAPTER SUMMARY-

- History has repeatedly showcased wild speculation surrounding new and exciting investment opportunities.

- Typically, price increases accelerate fastest near the end of an investment bubble.

- Investment bubbles usually involve new technologies or new financial concepts.

- New bubbles will form. Many of them will pop, but some will result in an extended period of poor returns. Bubbles frequently burst when the easy money supporting them dries up.

- Timing an investment bubble is nearly impossible. Instead, avoid being lured into a late-stage bubble just when the hype feels futile to resist.

CHAPTER NINE

Insights

"It's tough to make predictions, especially about the future."
– Yogi Berra

IN THE 1960'S, SCIENTISTS were convinced that the rapid pace of global population growth would lead to mass starvation and economic crisis as food production and the depletion of natural resources would not keep up with the massive expanding population. A cumulation of this thinking was presented in 1968 with the best-selling book, *The Population Bomb*. The authors, Dr. Paul R. Ehrlich and his wife Anne Ehrlich, declared that the "battle to feed humanity is already lost, in the sense that we will not be able to prevent large-scale famines in the next decade."

It was suggested that strict population controls be implemented immediately, and that the government should pass aggressive tax penalties for families with too many children, including luxury taxes on items like diapers and cribs. To bring humanity back to harmony, world governments needed to set a global population target of 2 billion people by 2025. The author asked if we should consider slaughtering our cats and dogs so food production could solely focus on producing for human consumption. Many countries would need aid from developed countries, such as the U.S., on a triage basis. India was seen as being so far behind they should be denied aid in order to help salvageable countries instead.

Of course, today, we have a global population of 8 billion people, and for the most part, we are fatter than ever. In fact, we spend billions of dollars every year trying to figure out how to eat less. Today's population is roughly what scientists had predicted it would grow to in the 1960s, yet tragedy was avoided mainly by unforeseen advancements in food production and technology. India, as we know, has been one of the fastest-growing populations on the planet, and its people are eating well. Indian cuisine has even become popular around the globe. Regardless of prior predictions falling short, scientists continued to voice concerns about the food supply for decades despite continuously improving conditions.

By the 1970s, a new ice age had been predicted, and the President of the United States announced that the world would run out of oil by 2010. If those predictions weren't bad enough, maybe being attacked by nuclear weapons while you were at school would do the trick.

In the 1980s, the alignment of the planets was predicted to cause a massive earthquake which would cause worldwide damage, but even if you survived that, the hole in the ozone layer and acid rain would kill you off.

Approaching the year 2000, a global programming glitch was anticipated to cause worldwide system failures when computers were expected to have trouble processing the year '00. In 1999, over a dozen other end-of-the-world predictions raised concerns. It was the end of a millennium after all. Later, in 2012, the completion of the Mayan calendar led many to believe the world would end that year.

A 2020 YouGov survey found that 29% of Americans believe an apocalyptic event will happen during their lifetime. We are psychologically complex beings, and for many of us, believing the world will end can oddly offer a sense of comfort, from knowing the date we are going to die, to the relief from responsibility, to a feeling of togetherness as everyone goes through the disaster together. Because we are so predisposed to give pending disasters our attention, the media will always be there to pander to our needs.

Fidelity Investments recently found that 45% of Gen Z and Millennials say they don't see the point in saving for retirement. They cited things like global warming or the coronavirus pandemic as reasons. Respondents say they think they should wait until things get back to "normal" first. But what is normal? Throughout history, just about every decade argued its case for why the world was about to end. Now that we've survived the COVID pandemic as a society, what will be the next event to end the world? Perhaps this decade will be punctuated by the fear of a takeover by artificial intelligence. I suspect we will survive the same as we have endured every world-ending catastrophe to date. The disasters that await us are beyond anything we can imagine, but history has so far shown that the solutions will be too.

POLITICS

Americans had elected a Hollywood celebrity as president based on promises to cut taxes and boost the U.S. economy. There were concerns about his experience and age and whether he had become senile by the time he was in office. The president was reportedly unwilling to read the important documents given to him. The White House was said to be in chaos. Aids sent a memo to the chief of staff suggesting they consider using the 25th amendment to remove the president from office for lacking the capacity to lead. Oh, he also used an astrologer to consult the stars when making certain presidential decisions and thought his dog was barking at the ghost of Abraham Lincoln in the White House. These are facts of the Ronald Reagan presidency. With political leadership like this, one might think that the economy would grind to a halt and stock markets would crash, but during the Reagan presidency, the Dow Jones index rose 147.3%.

Two decades later, Barack Obama won election running on a decidedly anti-business platform, yet the Dow Jones index rose 148.3% during his tenure. Each president was different in every way possible, from political beliefs to personality and age, yet both presided over two of the most robust stock market runs in presidential history. The presidents in office during the two best-performing periods, while decades apart, came under the leadership of Calvin Coolidge and Bill Clinton, both from opposite political parties. History tells us there's no predictable link between stock market performance and the political party in charge.

TIMING IS NOTHING

Who can predict the future when it comes to investing? Well, politics don't seem to make much of a difference, and scientists haven't been able to predict the future yet, so where does that leave you and me? It's simple. We cannot predict the future, and shouldn't try.

In the previous chapter, I offered two predictions. In all likelihood, they'll both be wrong; time will tell by what degree. Imagine going back in time, without knowledge of stock market history and guessing based on events the worst possible time to invest. There hasn't been a greater disaster in American history than the U.S. Civil War, resulting in over half a million deaths and the destruction of the country's infrastructure. Without looking at stock market charts from the time, you'd assume investing just prior to the worst disaster in American history would be a horrendous time to invest. Yet, a few hundred dollars invested in major company stocks just before the war broke out would leave you a multi-billionaire today.

You might say, "I don't have 150 years to invest!" That's true, but while investing, it's easy to get bogged down trying to time your investment around the next election, the next war, or the next pending disaster even if history tells a different story.

Take a moment to think of all the chaos and disaster you've

witnessed throughout your lifetime. Now, take a moment to look up the average value of the S&P 500 on the day you were born. Compare it to today. How has the stock market performed through all the chaos you've witnessed during your lifetime?

If we create a hypothetical set of investors who have $1,000 to invest in the stock market each year, let's see how they would fare with different approaches over a twenty-year period (using data from 2001-2020 in this example). The first investor, Mr. Perfect, achieves a miracle and invests his money annually on the precise day when the market reaches its lowest point of the year. Mrs. Quick, the second investor, invests her money on the first possible day each year without regard to market levels. Then, finally, Mr. Awful has terrible luck and invests his money at the peak of the market every single year for twenty years. How do you think they did? Naturally, Mr. Perfect had the best results, accumulating $75,696. Mrs. Quick, who simply invested her money on the first day of the year, ended up with $67,736, but even Mr. Awful did well, growing his investment to $60,586. By utilizing a crystal ball and picking the perfect moment to invest his money each year, Mr. Perfect only accomplished an improvement to his annual return of less than 1% over Mrs. Quick, who used no timing strategy at all. Mr. Awful, who had the worst timing, had annual returns that were only about 1% worse compared to Mrs. Quick.

A fourth investor, who decided to spread his investment over twelve equal monthly amounts, would have seen results just a hair below Mrs. Quick. Assuming you do not have a crystal ball, when would you invest?

History has shown that investments perform best not by focusing on timing the market, but by focusing on your time in the market. Ignore all the noise. You may be thinking about saving yourself from the next 20% market downturn by timing your investment just right, but what if it's at the cost of the next 200% upswing? The sooner you invest, the more time you'll have in the market, and the better your returns will be over time. The best time to invest is now.

WHO WANTS TO BE A MILLIONAIRE?

The late Regis Philbin was the first game show host to ask the question, "Who wants to be a millionaire?" The famous trivia game show of the same name was the first game show to offer contestants a chance to win a life-changing, one-million-dollar grand prize. The show originally aired in 1999, a time when a million dollars meant you were set for life, but, depending on your age, becoming a millionaire isn't simply a game show fantasy, it's a necessity. For most people born in the 1980s, it will take a million dollars just to scrape by in retirement. Anyone born in the 1990s or later should focus on becoming a multi-millionaire for a comfortable future. The numbers may be daunting, but if you're feeling intimidated, don't get discouraged!

If we break things down to the most basic level, it's apparent there are only three ways to become a millionaire:

- Earn it with a high paying job or successful business

- Get lucky and win the lottery or inherit a fortune

- Invest

Of the three, which do you think is the most likely to work for you? After all, you can only work so hard and so long. If you're like me, you've probably learned by this point in life that hoping to get lucky doesn't work.

I like to think of money as a loyal employee. Our money will do anything we ask it to without question. Money will wash your car, paint your house, fly you to Hawaii, and cook you dinner any time you ask it to. Money can even go out and recruit new employees for you, and those employees will be just as loyal as the originals. Those new recruits can then recruit even more employees until eventually you have so many working for you, there'll be no limit to what you can have them do.

When you invest your money, you're telling your dollars to go out and recruit more dollars to come work for you and the beauty is that they'll do it for you night and day, whether you're awake, asleep, sick, or on vacation. What an opportunity to change your life. But it won't happen on its own. You must be the one who tells your money what to do.

One of my favorite personal development coaches, Jim Rohn, used to say, "If someone hands you a million dollars, best you become a millionaire, or you won't get to keep the money." The only way a person can become a millionaire and stay a millionaire is by developing a millionaire mindset. Generally, people believe a millionaire lives an audacious life, wearing luxurious clothes and driving fast cars, but studies over the decades consistently find millionaires are regular, hard-working people who likely live in an average neighborhood and work a regular job. The difference is that they've been intentional about paying off debt and steadily investing money over time. Ramsey Solutions recently conducted a study of over 10,000 millionaires. Some of the interesting facts uncovered by the study follow:

- 94% of millionaires live on less than they earn vs. 55% of the general population
- Most graduated from public universities or state schools, while 8% went to prestigious schools
- The top five careers for millionaires include engineer, accountant, teacher, management and attorney
- 93% of millionaires use coupons when making purchases
- The typical millionaire spends $200 or less per month on eating out.
- 79% received no inheritance
- 97% believe they control their own destiny
- 85% use a written list when grocery shopping

One particularly fascinating note about this study is that the findings and statistics are remarkably similar to the makeup of millionaires researched by Dr. Thomas J. Stanely and Dr. William D. Danko over twenty-five years ago for their book, *The Millionaire Next Door*. It would seem that the characteristics and traits of typical millionaires have remained consistent over time. This is good news because it means that anyone who is not yet a millionaire can become one by emulating what others have done in the past and adopting the traits that got them there. To put the findings of millionaire studies short, avoid a flashy lifestyle and remain diligently intentional with how you use your money over a significant period of time.

THE RULE OF 72

The Pythagorean theorem, the theory of relativity, and Schrodinger's equation all involve formulas conjured up by people far more intelligent than me. They are now taught in high schools, regardless of whether we'd ever have a practical opportunity to use them again. Yet, a not so famous formula, which has been around for hundreds of years, may have a significant impact on your life and future wellbeing but isn't taught in schools. This simple formula is known as the Rule of 72.

The Rule of 72 gives us a shortcut to calculating how fast (or slow) we can double our money depending on our investment return. Simply take the number 72 and divide it by your rate of return. The result is the number of years it will take for your money to double.

Based on this rule, at a 3% rate of return, your money would double every 24 years. At a 1% rate, like in a bank account, you'd wait 72 years before your money doubled. Take a look at the chart in Figure 9.1 illustrating the growth of a one-time $10,000 investment at different investment returns.

	Years	3%	6%	12%
Using the Rule of 72	0	$10,000	$10,000	$10,000
	6			$20,000
	12		$20,000	$40,000
How many years will it	18			$80,000
take your investment	24	$20,000	$40,000	$160,000
to double? Divide the	30			$320,000
number 72 by your	36		$80,000	$640,000
expected rate of return	42			$1,280,000
to estimate how fast your money will double.	48	$40,000	$160,000	$2,560,000

Based on the Rule of 72, a $10,000 investment would double six more times at a 12% rate of return than at 3%.

Figure 9.1

When thinking of your life, how many doubling periods do you have left? I've always liked to use the Rule of 72 to illustrate the impact that even a relatively small increase to your rate of return can have over time. Many times, I'll have clients who are hesitant about investing in stocks, but sharing the Rule of 72 literally causes their eyes to open wider as they realize what type of lifestyle they could potentially miss out on in the future if they continue their low return strategy.

BEFORE YOU START

Let's take a minute to pause before we start chasing after the highest possible rate of return. Naturally, investing involves different degrees of risk. I'll talk more about risk a bit later in Chapter 11, but it's important that an investor is in a financial position to weather those risks before taking them on. Think of this section as a stripped-down, five-minute, generic financial plan with six basic steps.

Step One: Assess the situation. Are you making ends meet? Are you paying the rent, utilities, and buying groceries without going into debt? Investing can't dig you out of a dire scenario quickly, so if you're under financial duress, now is not the time to start investing. Before investing, take an honest look at your income and expenses. Amazing online tools exist today that can easily help categorize your expenses and automatically give you monthly totals. I don't ask my financial planning clients to create a budget every month, but I often request that they make periodic reviews of their spending over a three-month period to make sure it's in line with what they want to accomplish. If more money is going out than coming in, it's called a recipe for disaster. Before moving to Step Two, review your situation and make the major or minor adjustments needed to ensure you're not running at a financial deficit.

Step Two: Review your insurance. Nobody likes paying for insurance, talking about insurance, or reading about insurance (sorry!), but it's paramount that you have the appropriate coverage based on your situation before you start investing. The goal of investing is to allow that money to grow over time. If your insurance is lacking, you'll be more likely to cash out investments before they've had a chance to grow the moment your life hits a rocky road. Make sure your auto, health, homeowners, life, and all other appropriate insurance is sufficient to prevent a financial disaster in your life when the unexpected happens.

Step Three: Build up a preliminary emergency fund. This is your starter emergency fund, and it's needed before you can move on to Step Four. For many people, this fund is a piece of cake, and they've already got it in place, but for others, this can seem like a mountain to climb. The preliminary emergency fund needs to be in place to prevent you from getting into debt or going deeper if you're already there. This fund doesn't have to be much, but it should be enough to cover significant auto repairs, and at the very least should be enough to cover deductibles on your insurance. For most people, this fund should be $1,000 to $5,000 dollars and kept in a separate bank account.

Step Four: Pay off expensive debt. Does it make any sense for you to pay 29% interest to the credit card companies while you try to beat that rate on investments? Not even investing with Bernie Madoff would have matched those rates. Paying off high interest debt is often the best return on an investment you can find. For the purposes of moving on to Step Five, you should be focused on paying down debt with interest rates of 6% or higher, excluding real estate loans before moving on. The reason for this number is that it's relatively difficult to find a guaranteed rate of return above 5% on your investments, and paying off that debt is like a guaranteed return on your money at the debt's interest rate.

Step Four and a Half: If you've taken a look at your debt and decided that you're sick and tired of owing people money, and you've resolved to never go into debt again, you're ready to knock out Step Four and skip over this paragraph. But, if you're not quite that motivated to pay off your debt and plan to keep credit card debt and car loans for most of your life, consider Step Four and a Half. This step allows you to invest through a 401(k) or similar work-based investment plan only up to the point that the company matches your contributions. Completing Step Four is far and away the best option, but many people don't have the conviction to pay off their debts quickly and can't afford to miss a decade of matched retirement contributions. Which step you decide to take is up to you.

Step Five: Create a full emergency fund. Like your preliminary emergency fund, this fund will help prevent you from going back into debt once you've gotten out. A full emergency fund protects you from major setbacks such as a layoff or major medical condition. Your full emergency fund should cover three to six months of your living expenses. Once this is in place, you're ready for Step Six.

Step Six: Invest. You're now in a strong position to start investing. In the next section, we'll talk about the different options you have for where to invest your money.

WHERE WILL THE MONEY GO?

You're now ready to invest, but how do we get started? Fortunately, getting investments started today is easier than ever, but selecting the right avenue depends on various other factors in your life. The following investment accounts can be opened just as easily as opening a new bank account.

The 401(k)

A 401(k) is a type of investment account tied to a job. The name 401(k) comes from the particular section of the U.S. tax code which authorizes these types of accounts. For most people, a 401(k) will be their first experience with investing, and for most people, a 401(k) will also be their best option.

There are several benefits to a 401(k). Number one, contributions made to the account reduce your taxable income. Depending on your tax bracket, these contributions can provide substantial tax savings. The 401(k) offers one of the highest annual limits for deductible contributions, $23,000 for 2024. Additionally, many employers offer to match a portion of your contributions by adding additional funds to your account on your behalf. An employee match paired with tax savings means a 401(k) contribution makes you money even before you invest.

Once you've contributed to a 401(k), you'll be provided with a fying expenses revolve around attending college such as tuition and books, though recently, the accounts have been authorized to be used for limited student loan payments and k-12 private school. If you wind up not using the funds to pay qualifying education expenses, you'll pay taxes on the investment gains at your normal tax rate, as well as a 10% penalty.

Be mindful when contributing to a college savings plan. As much influence as we have on our kids, there's no guarantee they'll go to college, and the last thing you'll want is to be hit with taxes and penalties just to pull your money out of the plan. Generally, I recommend that people max out their 401(k) and Roth IRA before contributing to a college savings plan. One of the best things we can do for our kids is make sure they'll never have to worry about taking care of us financially.

Annuities

An annuity is an insurance contract that guarantees an income stream over a period of time. The amount of income you receive will be based on how much you invest in the contract and how long you want the benefits to last. Generally, benefits can be paid for either a set number of years, for the rest of your life, or in some cases, carried on after you die. The longer the payments go on, the smaller they will be relative to what you've invested. Annuities are generally used by retirees who have concerns about outliving their assets or feel more comfortable with a steady income stream instead of withdrawing money from a traditional investment account. Investments in an annuity contract grow on a tax-deferred basis, meaning you don't pay taxes on growth year-to-year, but pay taxes when the money is withdrawn. Annuities frequently offer peripheral benefits such as long-term care coverage or a death benefit for additional costs. They commonly provide a guaranteed rate of return and can be invested in a selection of index funds. Annuities are long-term investments and require investors to keep their money in the annuity for a certain number of years or face significant early

number of investment options. Most 401(k) plans offer a selection of mutual funds or index funds, but a few plans also offer the ability to purchase any individual stocks you'd like. You'll have options including money market funds (which provide returns and stability similar to a savings account), bond funds, stock funds, and a selection of target date funds (which automatically adjust your investments as you approach your retirement date).

Of course, a 401(k) does have downsides. Primarily, once you've contributed to a 401(k), you generally can't take the money out until you leave your job. Even once you qualify to take money out, it counts as taxable income, and if that withdrawal happens before you reach age 59 1/2, you'll pay an additional 10% tax penalty (or more depending on your state) unless you meet a specific exemption. In the past, 401(k) plans had a reputation for charging high fees compared to accounts you could open outside of your job, but these concerns have subsided significantly in recent years with the proliferation of index funds and increased awareness by investors which has helped to drive fees down.

Some of the downsides can be mitigated. For example, most plans allow you to borrow against your funds if you need immediate access. Also, most people can expect to have a lower income in retirement, and therefore, a lower tax rate, so despite withdrawals from the account counting as taxable income, it's still beneficial to reduce your taxable income during your high earning years, and deferring it to your low-income retirement years. The easy access, tax benefits, and employer match make a 401(k) the first place to look to invest your money.

Traditional Individual Retirement Account (IRA)

An IRA is an account that you set up with a brokerage outside of your job. A traditional IRA works in a very similar manner to the 401(k). Contributions will count as a tax deduction in the year you make them but count as taxable income when you take withdrawals. You can withdraw funds anytime you'd like, but they'll still be subject to a 10% early withdrawal penalty if you do so before you reach age 59 1/2. You won't get any employer match with an IRA, but you'll typically have a much broader selection of investment options with some providers even offering crypto-currency investments within an IRA. The annual limits on contributions to IRAs are significantly lower than what you can contribute to a 401(k), usually the IRA limit is less than one-third of the 401(k) limit (the limits are adjusted periodically for inflation). Additionally, if your employer offers a 401(k), you may not be able to deduct your contributions to an IRA depending on the amount of your income.

Roth IRA

The Roth IRA is just like a traditional IRA, aside from taxation. When you contribute to a Roth IRA, you don't get a tax deduction, but you also don't have to pay any taxes when you take the money out, even if it grows to a million dollars. For this reason, there's room for just about everyone to fit a Roth IRA into their investment plans. Of course, it will depend on the specifics of your personal situation. If you're in a low tax bracket, it usually makes sense to max out Roth IRA contributions before maxing out a 401(k) because when you're in a low tax bracket, there isn't much benefit to making tax deductible contributions to the 401(k). Someone in a low tax bracket can't typically afford to make the maximum 401(k) contribution anyway.

Roth IRAs have limits on contributions from high earners. High income individuals are generally prohibited from contributing to Roth IRAs, however, a working loophole exists known as a "backdoor Roth." The backdoor Roth is executed by making a non-deductible contribution to a traditional IRA and converting that IRA to a Roth, however, there are a few pitfalls that can occur in this procedure, and I see them happen almost every time someone attempts to do it on their own. Seek advice from a professional *before* you attempt it.

Brokerage Account

A brokerage account is the simplest way to buy investments. It's much like a bank account with the ability to hold stocks and other investments. There are no complicated tax rules surrounding contributions or distributions. You can deposit any amount of money in a brokerage account, and you can withdraw the money anytime. Simply deposit your funds and buy the investments you want. Unlike an IRA or 401(k), taxes are not based on withdrawals from your brokerage account but the buying and selling of investments within it. If you sell an investment for a profit in a brokerage account, you'll need to count that as income on your tax return for the year it was sold. Also, your taxable profits can be offset if you sell any other investments at a loss. Brokerage accounts do offer a tax advantage in many cases. Investments you've held for a year or longer can qualify for a favorable capital gains tax rate. For most Americans, this rate will be 15%, but lower income investors may qualify for a 0% capital gains rate while higher earners may pay 20%, plus a potential 3.8% investment tax. Whichever capital gains rate you qualify for, it will be significantly less than the tax rate on your regular income. Another point on the taxability of brokerage accounts is that you'll pay taxes on any dividends you earn from your investments, even if you choose to have those dividends reinvested. Investments held in a brokerage account can pass to your heirs income tax free, a distinct advantage over a 401(k) or IRA.

College Savings Plans

A few types of college savings plans exist which allow for investing. While these plans are rigid as far as how their funds can be used, the rules surrounding the accounts have been loosened in recent years. Typically, a college savings plan does not give you a tax deduction when you contribute to the account but will allow your investments to grow each year without paying taxes on an annual basis and can eventually be withdrawn tax free if the funds are used for qualified education expenses. Most quali-

withdrawal penalties.

Annuities can be quite complicated and generally come with significantly higher fees than investing in brokerage or retirement accounts. The more you want an annuity to do, the higher the costs will be. You're likely to receive better investment returns in either a brokerage or traditional retirement account after all expenses are considered. An annuity allows you to trade off potentially higher overall returns for a guaranteed income stream.

Accounts other than those listed above exist as well, however most are types of retirement accounts with similarities to 401(k)s and IRAs or may be useful for the self-employed and small business owners. The idea of life insurance as an investment vehicle (cash-value life insurance) has begun to make its rounds again, even becoming a trendy topic on TikTok and Instagram, but I would only recommend using life insurance in this way to very few people. Typically, the reduction in your rate of return due to restrictions and fees far outweighs any benefits you would hope to receive by investing with a life insurance contract. The profile I'd recommend using life insurance as an investment to is as follows: a person who is already a multi-millionaire, who makes the maximum contributions to their 401(k) and Roth IRA every year, has investments in a brokerage account, and may own investment real estate. Basically, someone who has nowhere left to invest their money may want to consider cash-value life insurance as an investment. The best plan involves a mix of 401(k)/Traditional IRA, Roth IRA, and brokerage accounts. The correct mix will depend on your current tax bracket, however, there's no perfect formula to follow. What I've found by working with clients over the years is that flexibility is invaluable, and having your investments in a mix of different accounts grants you the best ability to manage taxation when you're ready to withdraw funds and the flexibility to withdraw them sooner than expected if necessary.

-CHAPTER SUMMARY-

- We often hear the phrase, "timing is everything," but when it comes to investing, remind yourself that timing is practically nothing. The sooner you invest, the better.

- Almost everyone reading this book should be focused on becoming a millionaire by adopting a millionaire mindset.

- The Rule of 72 can help you estimate how long it will take your investments to double based on your rate of return.

- Before investing, put yourself in a solid financial position to avoid unnecessary setbacks.

- Many accounts are available to hold your investments. A mix of traditional retirement accounts, Roth accounts, and brokerage accounts will provide most people with the greatest benefit.

CHAPTER TEN

Trading

*"The market can stay irrational longer than
you can stay solvent."*
– John Maynard Keynes

DURING THE SUMMER OF 2009, Daniel Spivey, a former
options trader, had set in motion a secret construction project laying fiber optic cable from Chicago to New Jersey. The
estimated cost of the project would be $300 million, funding he
didn't have a lot of trouble finding once investors understood
what the project could accomplish. The company he formed to
run the project was given the name Spread Networks, and in
March of 2010, just three months before the work was completed, Spread Networks announced that they'd be offering five-year
leases to as many as two-hundred users for the price of $14 mil-
lion each.

Before embarking on the project, Spivey spent nearly a year
researching its feasibility. The line would need to travel through
various geographical environments, from farmland to granite
mountains. Existing fiber optic lines had typically been laid
along old railroad routes. Spivey's goal was to lay a fiber optic
cable that traveled in the straightest line possible between the
data centers for the Chicago Mercantile Exchange and Nasdaq
Exchange. Spread Networks' new cable trimmed roughly 100
miles off the next shortest fiber optic route and allowed data to

transfer between the locations three milliseconds faster than existing connections.

As a trader, Spivey learned the huge profits that could be made by cashing in on tiny discrepancies in price between futures contracts trading in Chicago and their equity counterparts in New York, a trading strategy known as arbitrage. Computers were programmed to identify these price discrepancies and execute buy and sell transactions in less than the blink of an eye. Arbitrage trade opportunities evaporate quickly, because as the price discrepancies are discovered, traders quickly buy up positions that close the gap. These trades happen so rapidly that Spread Network's extra three milliseconds meant a possibility for traders on its direct line to cash in on millions more than they could have using existing routes.

This book is primarily about investing. Trading involves the buying and selling of various assets with the primary goal of capitalizing on short-term movements in price. While trading involves many of the same assets investors utilize, it is not investing. Still, I'm aware that many people (especially in recent years) who educate themselves about investing are drawn into trading as well. For that reason, I thought it was important to include a short section on the subject. Keep in mind, if you decide to try trading, you'll be competing against high-end technology driven traders who pay millions of dollars to get their trades executed a fraction of a second faster than you.

Earlier in this book, I talked about methods to research and analyze the operations of companies to determine whether the company was worth investing in. That type of research is known as fundamental research, and it has relatively little value when it comes to trading. Most traders look to profit from fluctuations in price over very short periods, commonly buying and selling the same stock multiple times a day. Whether a company has a bright future is of very little concern to a trader. Traders who buy and sell securities several times per day are labeled day traders. Day traders sell off all of their bets by the end of each day. Swing traders, on the other hand, are traders who may look at a slightly longer timeline, holding positions for several days or even weeks before closing out.

Traders tend to primarily rely on technical research, not fundamental research. Technical research focuses on factors related to the security itself, not the performance of the company it represents. For example, how many people are buying the security? How has the price moved recently? Are there trends in positive or negative bets on the security? When it comes to trading, fundamental research can actually be detrimental to a trader's prospects as it may cause them to focus on the wrong areas. For example, knowing that a company is fundamentally strong may cause a trader to anticipate a quick price rebound despite the stock's existing downward trend. Traders need to focus on the demand for the security itself at a given time, not the long-term performance of the company.

KEYS TO TECHNICAL ANALYSIS

Technical analysis helps demonstrate the supply and demand for a given security by examining the price, time, and volume of trading activity. Technical analysis helps give traders hints into what the market as a whole may be thinking and feeling towards a particular security at a given moment. All of this information is compiled into charts that give traders a quick means to reference multiple data points in a single glance.

The major building blocks of trading charts are bars or candlesticks. Bars and candlesticks are very similar to each other and contain several data points displayed in a simple configuration. Each bar or candlestick represents a specific period of time, commonly a day's worth of market trading, but traders can choose to review them for longer or shorter periods, for example, the trading events over the last hour or the last month.

For the period being examined, each tool shows the price at which the security started, the price at which it ended, and the highest and lowest points throughout. Figure 10.1 provides examples for a bar and candlesticks.

Bars and Candlesticks

These tools help traders quickly identify trends in stock price movements by listing the open and closing price for a period as well as the peak and bottom price for that period. The hollow candle shows a postive period, while the solid candle is a losing period.

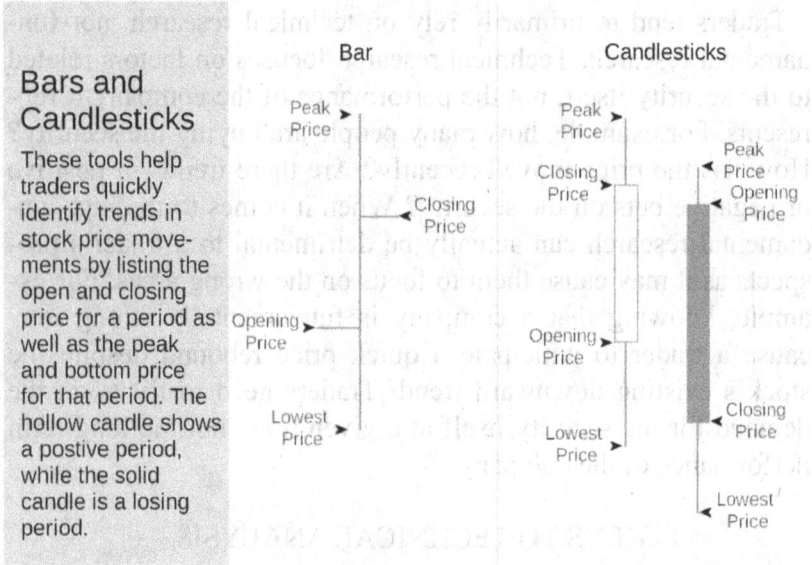

Figure 10.1

A series of bars or candlesticks will be used to build a chart. Traders hope to use these charts to identify patterns that will hopefully indicate a future price move, either up or down. Aside from price, traders should examine trading volume on the security they are researching. Volume helps traders understand how many or how few other people are interested in the security at a given price and time. Many traders rely on their software to automatically notify them of these types of patterns so that the trader may react for his or her benefit.

SPOTTING TRENDS

Traders can use charts to spot trends, and the first place to start is by adding trend lines to their charts. A trend line is just how it sounds, a line drawn on a chart connecting data from bar to bar to help identify a trend. A basic trend line tracks the average price of the security over time. However, creating a trend line which connects each of the high points over the period and a trend line doing the same for low points will help create a visual indicator of how the security is likely to perform. These two trend lines identify a *resistance level* along the highs and a *support level* across the lows. The price of the security is generally expected to remain within the boundaries of the two levels unless something happens to break the trend, like a new earnings report or a general market change. Securities reaching the resistance level may indicate a good selling point and securities touching the support level could mean a good opportunity to buy

Trend Lines

Trend lines can help traders visualize potential future stock price movements. Often, stock prices follow a trend until outside factors cause the trend to break.

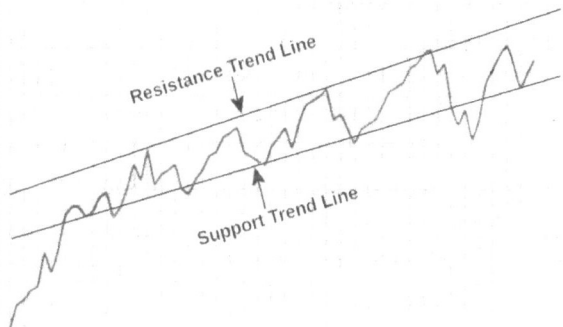

Resistance Trend Line

Support Trend Line

Figure 10.2

MOVING AVERAGES

Several other metrics exist which traders can utilize in addition to reviewing trend lines. Moving averages are another technical analysis tool that can be used to identify trends and potential buy and sell signals. A moving average is simply a line that smooths out price fluctuations over a certain period of time. This can help to identify the overall trend of the market or security, which can help inform traders' actions.

There are many different moving averages that can be used, but traders most frequently use the 50-day moving average, the 100-day moving average, and the 200-day moving average. These moving averages are calculated by taking the average price of a security over the past 50 days, 100 days, or 200 days.

Tracking moving averages can help spot several signals, including:

- **Crossovers:** When a shorter-term moving average crosses above a longer-term moving average, this is often seen as a signal to buy. The shorter-term trend crossing above the longer-term trend indicates that the more recent trend may have been an anomaly or misalignment away from the security's actual trend.
- **Bounces:** When a security's price bounces off of a moving average, this can also be seen as a signal to buy or sell. Bouncing away from the moving average suggests that the price is finding support or resistance at the moving average, which could be a sign that the trend is about to reverse.
- **Breakouts:** When a security's price breaks above a moving average, this can also be seen as a signal to buy. This is because it suggests that the price is breaking out of a trading range and is likely to continue to move higher. The opposite is true for downward breakouts. Of course, false breakouts are common. True breakouts are typically accompanied by higher trading volume and a price that holds outside of the moving average.

RECOGNIZING CHART PATTERNS

Aside from trend line patterns and moving averages, several other chart patterns have been recognized by traders to frequently indicate a potential Bullish (positive) or Bearish (negative) price movement. Here are some of the most common patterns to watch for:

- **Double bottom:** This pattern occurs when the price of a security forms two consecutive troughs at roughly the same price level. The double bottom is considered a bullish pattern because it shows that there is strong support at the bottoms.
- **Cup and handle:** This pattern occurs when the price of a security forms a rounded bottom, followed by a sharp decline, followed by a consolidation period (generally meaning a sideways movement within the trends), followed by a breakout. A cup and handle pattern is considered bullish and typically develops over several weeks or months.
- **Hammer:** The hammer is a bullish candlestick pattern that occurs after a downtrend. The hammer is a single candle with a long lower wick and a small body. The long lower wick indicates that sellers drove the price down during the day, but buyers were able to push the price back up to close near the open.
- **Head and shoulders:** This pattern occurs when the price of a security forms three consecutive peaks, with the middle peak being the highest. The head and shoulders is considered a bearish pattern that tends to occur after a long positive price run.
- **Descending triangle:** This pattern occurs when the price of a security forms a series of lower highs and steady lows, forming a triangle with a level base and downward sloping upper trend line. The descending triangle is considered a bearish pattern because it demonstrates that demand for the security is weakening, especially when paired with diminishing trading volume.
- **Falling wedge:** This pattern occurs when the price of a security forms a series of lower highs and lower lows, with the converging trend lines pointing downward. The falling

wedge is considered a bullish pattern because it suggests the decline is losing momentum and may soon reverse.

- **Flags and pennants:** These patterns are both considered to be continuation patterns, meaning that they suggest that the current trend is likely to continue. Flags form when the price of a security consolidates after a sharp move, while pennants form when the price of a security consolidates in a symmetrical triangle.

Aside from the charts and patterns I've discussed above, traders may use several other indicators and strategies such as ratios, volatility measures, and indexes. Ultimately, traders have to determine whether the price of the security they are researching is going to continue on its current trend or if something indicates the price will diverge.

SUPERCHARGING YOUR BETS BY ADDING RISK

Suppose you've found every indicator and pattern is telling you that a stock is about to skyrocket. Wouldn't it be nice to make the most money possible when it does? There are a few ways to increase the potency of your bet without the need for extra cash, but be warned, your risk goes through the roof, and it can be hard to stomach the losses when you're wrong (and you will be).

Margin

We talked about it before, but margin is a form of leverage that allows investors to buy more securities than they can afford with their own cash. When you trade on margin, you essentially borrow money from your broker to buy securities. The amount of money you can borrow is typically a percentage of the value of the securities you buy, and the loan's interest rate is usually variable.

Margin trading can magnify your profits if the securities you buy increase in value. However, it can also magnify your losses if the securities decrease in value. This is because you are not only responsible for paying back the money you borrowed from your broker, but you are also responsible for paying interest on the loan.

For example, let's say you have $10,000 in your brokerage account and want to buy 100 shares of a stock currently trading at $100 per share. If you buy the stock on margin, you may be able to borrow $5,000 from your broker, which would allow you to buy 150 shares of the stock. If the stock goes up in value, you will make a profit on both the 100 shares you bought with your own money plus the 50 shares you bought on margin. However, if the stock goes down in value, you will lose money on both the 100 shares you bought with your own money and the 50 shares you bought on margin.

If the stock losses are significant enough, you could lose more than your original investment and wind-up owing money to the broker. Also, falling stock prices can cause your margin ratio to exceed the broker's set limit. This would trigger what's known as a margin call. Your broker will ask you to deposit more money to bring your account value to margin loan ratio back in line with their requirements. If you don't deposit the money in time, the broker will automatically sell some or all of your stock.

Options
In trading, an option is a contract that gives the buyer the right, but not the obligation, to either buy or sell an asset at a specified price on or before a specific date. The specified price is known as the strike price while the specified date is known as the expiration date. The price of an option is typically a fraction of the underlying security's price, and the expiration date can be anytime from within a day or as long as multiple years into the future.

There are two types of options, calls and puts. A call option gives the owner the right to buy the underlying security at the strike price at any time before the expiration date. A put option gives the owner the right to sell the underlying security at the strike price by the expiration date. A call option is a bet that the price will rise, while a put option is a bet that the security price will fall.

Imagine Ford stock is trading at $14 per share on June 15th, and you're convinced that before July 15th, Ford stock will reach $15 per share. If you had $1,000 to invest, you could buy about 71 shares at $14 and turn a profit of $71 in a month's time when the share price hits $15. Alternatively, with the same $1,000 investment, you could have purchased 3,000 call options for about 30 cents each. The options would have a strike price of $14 and expiration date of July 15th. If Ford's stock price hits $15 per share by the expiration date, you could sell your options for $1.00 each (or more) allowing you to profit at least $2,100 (Options sold for $1.00 - $0.30 purchase price = $0.70 profit x 3,000 options purchased).

The call option becomes valuable when the share price of the underlying security ($15 in this example) exceeds the option strike price ($14) and other traders will be willing to buy the options from you. In this example, other traders will buy the call options from you for $1 each because they can exercise those options to buy Ford shares for just $14 per share instead of buying Ford shares on the open market for $15.

In addition to the intrinsic value of an option (the value between the option strike price and the share price), options carry what's known as a time value. Time value exists depending on how much time remains before the option's expiration date. It represents potential for additional profits from the present date up until the expiration date. There's no formula to calculate this value; it's simply determined by market price movements of the underlying security and demand. The time value of an option steadily diminishes as the expiration date approaches until no time value remains once the option reaches its expiration date.

Going back to our example of Ford stock reaching $15 per share, if the stock price reached $15 per share by July 1st when the option expiration date wasn't until July 15th, the call options would sell for more than $1 each due to their time value because traders would anticipate that Ford's stock price had the potential to continue climbing past $15 per share before the expiration date. If traders think Ford stock could reach $15.75 before July 15th, they may be willing to buy the $14 call options from you for $1.50, leaving themselves $0.25 room to profit. For this reason, you'll pay a much higher price for options with distant expiration dates.

It's important to understand a few things about trading options. After you've bought an option contract, you're not required to exercise the option. Also, you're not required to hold the option until the expiration date. You can sell off the contract at any time, in fact, most option traders sell off their contracts well before the expiration date. Another point to mention is that the underlying security does not need to reach the strike price for you to make a profit. The value of options contracts is very dependent on price movement trends of the underlying security. If a security price continues moving in a positive direction, call options will gain in value even before reaching the strike price. If a security price continues falling, put options should increase in value. However, if a security price remains steady, both calls and puts tend to lose value due to the decay in their time values.

Most important to discuss is the extreme volatility of options. Every single day there are options contracts which lose 30%, 40%, or 50% of their value. Without caution, you can easily lose 50% of your investment in a few hours of time. If you don't sell your contracts and they expire before reaching the strike price, you'll lose 100% of your investment.

Trading is not for the faint of heart. It can be overwhelmingly emotional which can cause poor decision making. The majority of trading today is done by computers who act fast, fast enough that three milliseconds matter. If you want to compete against computers, you'll need to keep your emotions in check and make trading decisions based on the data and then stick to it. Psychologist Jonathan Haidt introduced a useful analogy explaining our decision-making abilities. He explains that our mind works like a rider on an elephant. The rider, representing analytical and rational decisions, holds the reins and appears to be the leader. But if the elephant, who represents emotional response, and the rider can't agree on a direction at any point in their journey, the elephant will lead the way, unhindered by the rider's input. Are you prepared to wrangle the elephant?

If you're someone who's interested in trading, be sure not to use your nest egg to do it. Studies have found that most traders (90-95%) lose money. Trading can and does make money for a percentage of the people doing it, but be sure you have most of your investment dollars working as investments, not used to bankroll high risk activities. The information I've provided here should serve as a starting point if you're seriously considering trading, but there is a wealth of subjects on the topic that I'm simply not able to cover here. In the final section, I'll be covering the strategies you need to get the most out of your investments.

-CHAPTER SUMMARY-

- Trading, while more popular than ever before, is not investing.

- The keys to successful trading are understanding technical analysis and controlling your emotions.

- Options, like Puts or Calls, can exponentially increase your gains, but they'll do the same for your losses.

- Don't use your life savings for trading activities. Most traders don't profit over the long run.

CHAPTER ELEVEN

Choosing Your Strategy

"It is remarkable how much long-term advantage people like us have gotten by trying to be consistently not stupid, instead of trying to be very intelligent."
– Charlie Munger

YOU MAY HAVE ARRIVED at this point of the book thinking, "Wow, I've read a lot but still don't know exactly how to invest!" The honest truth is that there is no exact science to making investments, despite what other experts may try to sell you. So then, what was the point of reading it all? Philosophy. Successful investing first requires the development of a well-rounded investment philosophy. In my experience over the years, everyone already has an investment philosophy. It may be as basic as, "Investing is something rich people do, but I'm not rich, so it doesn't concern me." Whatever your existing investment philosophy is, my goal through this entire book has been to develop it to the fullest.

Philosophy is most generally defined as the pursuit of wisdom, truth, and knowledge. More romantically, the word philosophy comes from the Greek language, meaning love of wisdom, making a philosopher a lover of wisdom. To develop your personal investment philosophy, it's important to understand not only the technical aspects and language of investing, but to understand what's happened in history, how fraud is perpetrated, the operations of investment professionals and advisors, traditional investment theories, and the emotions that can be experienced as an investor. Only with a broad understanding around all of these topics can an investor form a philosophy that weighs a breadth of ideas and remains appropriate for the individual's circumstance. Let's keep this love affair moving forward and work on refining your philosophy a bit further.

TRADITIONAL STRATEGY

Many strategies and investment theories have been developed through the decades. Let's examine a few so we can add them to your toolbox.

The Efficient Market Hypothesis

The efficient market hypothesis is a widely accepted idea that says financial markets react very swiftly to new information, and through a collective response, the price of a stock almost immediately reflects all of the publicly available information. The hypothesis suggests that because the price immediately reflects all of the available data, an individual investor cannot consistently achieve returns over the long term that exceed market averages, and therefore, fundamental and technical investment research is irrelevant. Based on this hypothesis, investors are best served by selecting index funds that simply mirror the market overall.

Yet, despite this hypothesis being widely accepted and taught for several decades, it's clear that investors like Ray Dalio, who ran Bridgewater Associates, George Soros, of the Quantum Fund, and Warren Buffet, of Berkshire Hathaway have handily beat market averages for their entire careers using fundamental research. The efficient market hypothesis suggests that the current price of a stock reflects its true value. But is that accurate?

If you're an older reader, you may remember Palm Pilots from the late 1990s and early 2000s, but for those who don't, Palm Pilots were personal digital assistants (PDAs) which had become popular tools amongst business men and women at the time. Think of the Palm Pilot as a smartphone that couldn't make phone calls and had a very limited Internet connection. They were mostly used to maintain a contact list, keep schedules, and write memos while out in the field. You'd manually sync those files with a computer when you got back to the office.

3Com owned Palm, and 3Com decided, due to the popularity of the Palm devices, that they would spin off Palm as a separate company. Initially, 3Com offered up 5% of Palm shares to the public with an IPO and retained ownership of 94%. The market value of that 5% was driven up by investors to $53 billion. At the same time, the market value of 3Com, which still owned 94% of Palm and substantial other business assets, was valued at roughly half of Palm at $28 billion. When is 5% worth twice as much as 94%? Not in an efficient market. The Palm portion of the business represented just 13% of 3Com's total sales, and anyone who held shares of 3Com was entitled to 1.5 shares of Palm. If the market is incredibly efficient, how was it possible that shares of Palm could be worth nearly twice the value of 3Com stock which promised to provide each shareholder 1.5 shares of Palm?

Even if 3Com had no other profitable business operations, its share value should have been at least equal to 1.5 times the value of Palm stock. The market had the price of Palm wrong. In just over a year's time, Palm's stock price fell from $95.06 per share to $6.50. The differences between 3Com's stock price and Palm's stock price early on clearly show the market doesn't always reasonably reflect the available information.

In the Summer of 2007, Citigroup, the largest bank in the U.S. at the time, invited stock market analysts to meet their new chief financial officer. While attending this event, analyst Meredith Whitney was shocked when she heard one of the industry's top banking sector analysts remark that he had given up on modeling Citigroup's business because it had become too large and complicated. Whitney realized if top industry analysts weren't doing the work, no one was.

Over the next several weeks, she pored over Citigroup's financial information and determined Citigroup had much higher debts than other banks and was running out of money. They'd need to sell assets, stop paying dividends, and raise additional funds. She released a report detailing her findings, and based on those details, she called for the stock's price to fall roughly 30%. In response to her report, Citigroup's CEO was fired that weekend. The stock price fell 21% over the next month. Citigroup ultimately needed to be rescued with over $400 billion in federal bailouts. Within a year and a half from Whitney's report, Citigroup stock collapsed 97%.

The efficient market hypothesis doesn't seem to hold up to scrutiny. Whitney exclusively relied on publicly available data to determine that Citigroup was in serious financial trouble, yet that information was not reflected in the stock's price until after Whitney's report. The market was not efficient at all in processing the available data, in this case and in many others. The efficient market hypothesis is significantly flawed, and it's certainly possible for individuals to find stocks that are mispriced by the market.

Modern Portfolio Theory

Modern portfolio theory was originally developed by Harry Markowitz in 1952 and has since become a staple with financial planners and investors. Modern portfolio theory explains that there is an optimal investment mix for a desired level of risk. While certain aspects are rather complex, the core of modern portfolio theory is that the performance of various assets may have different levels of correlation, and understanding that correlation can help investors form a more stable portfolio. For example, bond prices often negatively correlate to stock prices, meaning, when stock prices fall, bond prices often rise. So, owning both stocks and bonds could help reduce your level of risk. In modern portfolio theory, risk is essentially defined as market volatility. The more the price of an asset tends to move up and down, the riskier it is considered. In the back of the book, I've included an investor profile questionnaire based on modern portfolio theory, which assesses your tolerance for risk in investing and provides an example portfolio based on your answers.

Modern portfolio theory is extremely popular amongst professional advisors and investment institutions. Utilizing the theory with their customers allows them to provide an investment plan that customers are comfortable with. Investment professionals know that if markets crash and their customers' portfolios are insulated from the full brunt, those clients are less likely to fire their advisor and take their investments elsewhere. But is modern portfolio theory really the best way to allocate your investments?

WHAT IS RISK REALLY?

Of course, with investing comes various risks. Most people would simply say the risk of investing is that, "I might lose my money." Modern portfolio theory suggests that risk can be measured by how frequently an investment's price goes up and down. There are a few clearly defined traditional risks to investments, including:

- *Business Risk* - If you've invested money in a business by buying stocks or corporate bonds, you're dependent on that business staying successful. If the business fails, you'll lose your investment. Business risk includes events like changes in strategy, management overhauls, scandals, lawsuits, and employee strikes to name a few. Business risk is known as an *unsystematic* risk, meaning the risk applies specifically to a particular investment as opposed to the general industry, market, or broader economy.

- *Inflation Risk* - We were fortunate to experience several decades with incredibly moderate inflation, but inflation showed up with a vengeance in 2021. Inflation puts investors at risk when they depend on fixed rates of interest or have significant cash savings. As inflation increases, the value of their fixed income will erode. Inflation can also impede the economy, which in turn impacts other investments.

- *Interest Rate Risk* - Rising interest rates directly impact bond prices. If you own a 10-year bond that pays 3% interest and current interest rates spike to 5%, suddenly, your 3% bond is much less valuable. Yes, you'll still earn 3%, but if you want to sell it and replace it with a new 5% bond, you'll have to sell at a steep discount. Interest rates also impact stock prices on more than one level. Rising interest rates will lower profits for most businesses as they must pay higher rates to borrow money, and lower profits typically translate into lower stock prices. Also, rising interest rates will help investments like government bonds, CDs, and even savings accounts become more attractive to investors, which will entice them to sell off some of their stocks to invest in these other more stable options.

- *Political Risk* - The risk that political changes or instability could alter the value of your investment. New government leaders, military takeovers, or even new legislation can wreak havoc on a particular investment. The longer you plan to hold a particular investment, the more likely political risk becomes a factor.

- *Market Risk* - This is the risk that overall changes in the broader investment market have an impact on your specific investments. If the stock market as a whole crashes, it's more than likely that the specific stocks you hold will be negatively impacted, regardless of whether the individual performance of those companies remains strong.

Limiting Traditional Risk

The risks listed above are not comprehensive and cannot be eliminated. The best one would hope to do is limit their exposure to these particular risks. For the purposes of limiting traditional investment risks, we want to examine the three D's of investing: Diversification, dollar-cost averaging, and discipline.

- *Diversification* - By having your investments spread over several assets, you can reduce the impact of various risks on your entire portfolio. This idea brings us back to modern portfolio theory. Diversification in not only the companies you invest in but the types of investments you have will limit the impact of any particular risk. Investments in government bonds may reduce the impact of a stock market crash on your investments as a whole. Spreading investments globally may reduce your exposure to certain political risks. Investing in different types of industries may limit risks of unforeseen challenges such as material shortages or technological obsolescence.

- *Dollar-Cost Averaging* - Dollar-cost averaging is a strategy that can help minimize the risk of fluctuating market prices. Essentially, this strategy is the act of purchasing a particular investment incrementally over a determined period of time, rather than making a single lump sum investment. For example, instead of investing $4,200 at the start of the year, you may invest $350 per month over the year.

    As the price of your investment fluctuates through the year, the number of shares you purchase will also fluctuate but not the dollar amount of your monthly investment. When prices go down, you acquire more shares. When prices go up, you purchase fewer. See figure 11.1 Over the course of the investment period, this strategy can help lower your average price per share. Now, this works great for volatile prices or if you're investing through a retirement plan where your contributions are on a weekly or monthly basis. However, markets move up over time, and while protecting yourself from market volatility risk feels important, history has shown that if you have a lump sum to invest, you'll get better results by investing as soon as possible, especially if you're investing in a broad market through index funds.

Dollar-Cost Averaging

Would you rather be investor A or investor B? Both invest $500 a month for 6 months.

In a rising market, investor A purchases 212 shares with an ending value of $4,240.

In a fluctuating market, Investor B purchases 629 shares with an ending value of $6,290.

Share Price by Month

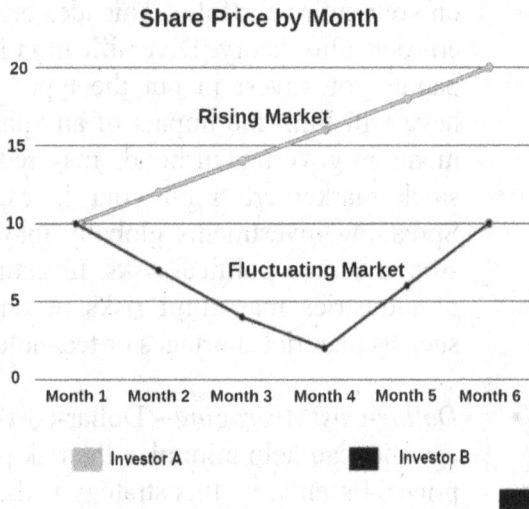

Figure 11.1

- *Discipline* - Paramount to your investing success is discipline. Once you've developed your investing philosophy, you'll need to maintain discipline to stick with it. The elephant of your emotions will try to carry your logical but helpless rider into a panic when things turn south. Will you have the discipline to stick it out? There may be no greater risk to your investments than you.

HOW ABOUT A DIFFERENT PERSPECTIVE?

History cannot predict future performance, but as far as formulating any coherent strategy for investing, we need to understand how stocks have performed in the past. Through the 95 years leading up to 2020, the S&P 500 experienced seventy years of positive growth and twenty-five years with losses. During those positive years, the average investment return was 21.2%, and for negative years, the average loss was -14.2%. So over that 95-year period, we've had significantly more positive years (73% of years were positive) and the gains during positive years have been substantially more than the losses in negative years. On average, the S&P 500 provided a 10.3% annual return on investment over that period.

What does this tell us? Stock market losses happen a lot, and when they do, they tend to dominate financial news cycles. What doesn't get talked about is how overwhelmingly positive stock market performance has been, year over year. In any given year, your odds of a positive return in the stock market were terrific, with an almost three out of four chance of gains. So, what else is this telling us? Stock market losses have historically been temporary, sandwiched between multiple positive years. Nearly 100 years of stock market history have been compellingly positive despite horrific tragedies and crises the entire time. Looking at that history, how could we conclude that the long-term trend of mostly positive years with occasional down years wouldn't continue?

In the last forty years, the value of the S&P 500 has risen from $167.08 to $4,769.83. That's a gain of over 2,700%. Yes, there were seven negative years during that period, including 2008, the second worst year on record at -37%. But, as I said, stock market downs have been temporary, and the long-term upward trends are permanent. The ups and downs of the stock market are the very factors that result in better overall returns. Amateur investors fear the ups and downs, and they wind up being chased out of the market as a result. Because so many investors are afraid of downturns, stocks must provide better returns than alternatives in order to incentivize people to tolerate the volatility. When we see market ups and downs, we should look at those price movements in a positive light, even as a necessity, if we want to realize better overall returns for ourselves.

If stock market downward movements are temporary and long-term gains are permanent, what exactly is risk? As I said before, typically, risk is the idea that an investor will lose their money. And yes, there are different components and variations of specific risks, as discussed earlier in the chapter, but if we believe that markets will eventually produce a positive result over time, we need to look at risk differently. In my view, there are two risks that investors need to watch out for. An investor's biggest risk is himself. Will he finally panic when the market is capitulating? Will he forget that market downturns are temporary and sell at the bottom? Will he then keep his assets sidelined while waiting for the right time to reinvest?

Secondly, investors face the growing risk of outliving their money, even if they retire with a significant nest egg. At a time when few employers are funding pensions, and the government is facing reductions to Social Security benefits, advancements in technology will lead to longer lives in retirement. Most retirees underestimate how long they'll live. According to the CDC, in 2023, U.S. life expectancy was 76.4 years. However, these numbers reflect rising numbers of younger Americans dying. As your life goes on, the older you get, the longer your overall life expectancy will be. For example, a woman who reaches age 60 should statistically expect to live to age 85. If she lives to age 85, she could expect to live to 92. As technology improves, life expectancy will continue to increase rapidly. Those born in 1900 only had a life expectancy of 47, while those born in 1950 would live 68 years on average. Today, it's widely believed that the first person who will live to age 150 has already been born.

Based on those numbers, someone retiring at age 65 needs to plan for at least twenty years of retirement. This could be a challenge using the most accepted investing strategies like modern portfolio theory. Remember, modern portfolio theory says that volatility is risk. To reduce the risk of volatility, it's suggested that investors include a percentage of various bonds in their portfolio. Commonly, a simple 60% stock to 40% bond portfolio is promoted. Generally, as a person approaches retirement age, the typical advice is to increase the bond percentage and reduce the percentage of stock investments.

However, bonds posted an annual return of about 5% over the same 95-year period we talked about in the prior pages, while the S&P 500 provided a 10.3% return. So, diversifying your portfolio with bonds comes at the cost of overall returns. This is the price you must pay to reduce volatility. Yet, if we believe that longevity of life is our most serious risk, and if we are confident that downward trends are temporary while upward trends are permanent, why would we want to reduce our overall returns when we still have at least another twenty years to invest? Remember the Rule of 72. With a 10% rate of return, your money would double every seven years, but with a 5% return it would only double every 14 years. Over a 25-year period, a 10% return wouldn't mean your investment grows to twice what it would be with a 5% return, it would be more than triple the value. I guess if your goal is to have the most money reasonably possible a year or two from now, you'd want to reduce volatility at the cost of long-term results. But if you wanted the best chance of your money sticking around and growing over a twenty to twenty-five-year period, historically speaking, a 100% stock portfolio would have won, hands down.

Despite this history, you would be hard-pressed to find a financial advisor, an investment book, a financial institution, or even an expert blogger who confidently suggests a 100% stock portfolio. The evidence tells us the best way to combat the risk of outliving your money is by investing in stocks and, for even better returns, stocks of smaller companies. Yet, the vast majority of advice is focused on the first major risk to investors: themselves.

The financial industry is all too aware that you will panic. You will sell your stocks at the worst possible time and only invest again once prices have rebounded. See figure 11.2.

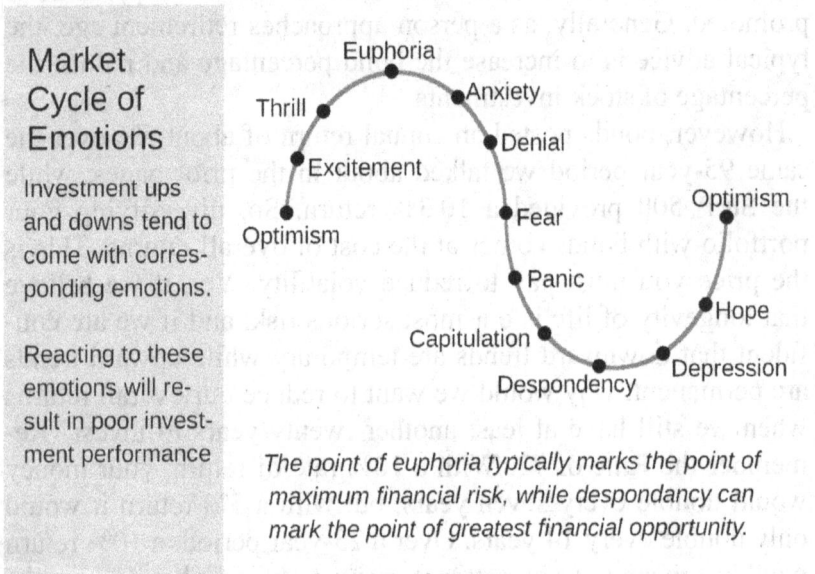

Market Cycle of Emotions

Investment ups and downs tend to come with corresponding emotions.

Reacting to these emotions will result in poor investment performance

The point of euphoria typically marks the point of maximum financial risk, while despondency can mark the point of greatest financial opportunity.

Figure 11.2

This type of strategy would decimate your returns. So, instead of telling you about the best formula for long-term growth, you're advised to protect yourself from your emotions by accepting muted returns for muted volatility. To be fair to traditional strategy, even if your portfolio doesn't get the best return, if its reduced volatility helped stop you from selling stocks or worse, getting out of investing entirely, you'd fare far better than if you weren't investing at all.

A BETTER PERFORMING PORTFOLIO

Traditionally, investment portfolios are put together for a specific investor by reviewing their overall financial situation. Things like income, age, and risk aversion are considered. From these factors, a profile is created to label the investor as conservative, moderate, aggressive, or somewhere in between. Based on where the investor lands, they'll be recommended a portfolio that consists of specified percentages of cash, bonds, and stocks in ratios that align with their profile. Again, these types of portfolios are widely accepted as the best way to invest because they protect you from yourself, even at the cost of lower returns over the years. To an extent, it seems to defy common sense. Advisors will tell you to invest in stocks because they'll give you the best returns, yet they have no conviction behind the recommendation. They want you to get the best return on your investment but only suggest getting in up to your waist when, if something really provides the best return, you should be diving in.

But how can you protect yourself from your own emotions while sacrificing as little return as possible? Remember, your emotions are the elephant, and you are just the rider, so we definitely do not want to dismiss the fact that emotions will strongly influence your actions when investing. The one thing that will help keep your emotions in check will be the level of confidence you have in your financial safety. You'll effectively increase your feeling of security by building a financial wall between yourself and your investments. What it takes to build this wall will vary depending on your situation and how close you are to retirement, but the concept is quite simple. Create a separation between the money that will protect you now and the money that will protect your future. You'll have future money accounts which are invested for the best possible return and today money accounts which are focused on stability. This way, when you see the value of your future money accounts moving up and down, you'll be able to remind yourself that that is what it looks like when money is at work doing the job you want it to do, all the while confident that it's not impacting the money that is protecting you now.

If you're relatively far off from retirement and rely mostly on income from work, most of your financial security comes from your job or business. This creates somewhat of a natural separation between your present financial security and your future security. Most of your investments will be within retirement accounts with built-in restrictions from early withdrawals making it particularly painful to cash out your investments in a panic. At this point, as long as you maintain emergency savings of at least three months (preferably six months) of your living expenses and understand the temporary downs and permanent ups in the market, you'll rarely worry about your future account performance.

Naturally, when you're approaching retirement or have already retired, you'll find yourself much more concerned with the performance of your future security accounts. However, creating a wall of security is a simple step. Assign a portion of your portfolio specifically as a safety net that will cover all your living expenses for a one to two-year period. This portion of your portfolio should be held in a money-market investment or a savings account, but you shouldn't spend any time worrying about how to invest this money. Its one purpose is to keep you feeling secure while you get the best possible return from the investment portion of your portfolio. Five years before your retirement, start ramping up the allocation for this purpose. You'll want a full year of your expenses allocated for this purpose by the time you're two and a half years from retirement. If you feel a greater personal need for safety, increase the money market savings to as much as two years of your expenses by your retirement date, but no more than two years. We want as much of your money invested for long-term growth as possible.

Individual Stocks, Alternative Investments, or Index Funds?
We've covered in detail many different investment types and how to make informed selections, but what's really the best investment to choose?

There is a history of great investors who have routinely beat average market returns over long periods of time by using the evaluation methods you learned earlier, so we know it is possible to do. However, the reality is that the few people who have been able to accomplish this have dedicated their lives to studying investments. Ray Dalio first started investing at age 12. As a child, Warren Buffet hung around his father's stock brokerage offices learning about their work, and by age 11, he had researched and purchased his first stocks. Other greats such as Benjamin Graham, George Soros, and Peter Lynch had all begun seriously investing by age 20. For every one of the great investors who proved they could consistently pick investments that performed better than market averages, there are thousands of investment managers who have been able to beat the market average for as long as a decade, just to drop off to below average for the rest of their careers. And for every investment manager who was able to do that, there are thousands more who beat the market consistently for shorter periods before getting totally wiped out.

Around 2017, Cathie Woods started gaining media attention with the performance of her ARK Innovation fund, which focuses on investments in advancing technology. By that time, the fund had performed with returns around double what the S&P 500 averaged over the previous three years. By early 2021, Cathie Wood's fund generated a six-year return that was over six times the S&P 500 return. It appeared that Cathie Woods knew something that other investors were missing. It was easy to understand why investors became enamored with her fund's accelerating returns. Unfortunately, as fate would have it, the ARK Innovation Fund took a severe beating in the years to follow. Not only taking major losses and falling 79% through 2022 but giving up all of its lead over the S&P 500 and then some. It seems that an individual beating the market's average returns is more of an anomaly than a realistic expectation. *Most* of those who beat the market for a short period eventually take a beating from the market.

People tend to use a strange sort of mental accounting to keep themselves in a state of denial when it comes to money. I live just a few hours from Las Vegas, so it's a pretty popular vacation spot for friends and family as well as many of my clients. I've found that when people recap their trips, no one ever seems to lose money in Las Vegas. Almost everyone comes back to report how much they won or in the worst-case scenarios, that they broke even. How do the casinos keep all those lights on, I wonder? The stories take on an eerily similar tone when people are recapping their ability to pick stock investments. They tend to mentally discount their frequent losses and focus on their rare big wins. In their heads they feel like they're doing great, but the financial ledger would tell a different story.

A 2017 study by Pew Research found that over 71% of men and women believe that for a man to be considered a good husband or partner, he must be able to support a family financially, while only 32% believe that a woman should do the same. So clearly, the expectations for men to be good with money are high. Studies like the above make it clear why so many men tie their self-worth and identity to how much they earn as well as their overall financial standing. Society tells men that money is a major factor in determining their value as a person. As a result, men are naturally more driven to study investing and seek education on other financial topics more intently than women. I haven't done the research on it, but I'd assume men, in general, are much more likely to read this book. A separate study by FINRA found that 57% of men possessed high investing knowledge compared to 36% of women. FINRA and other studies have also found that women have significantly less confidence about investing and are substantially less comfortable making investment decisions.

If you've been paying attention up until this point, FINRA would now consider you to be someone with a high level of investment knowledge. If that's the case, you may be wondering why those prior studies matter. Despite the surveys and research showing women had an investing disadvantage, women have been beating men's investment performance for at least three decades! That's right, women have been the better investors despite lower knowledge and confidence, but how?

Evidence shows that men used their knowledge against themselves. With deeper knowledge and confidence, men more frequently bought and sold stocks. Also, more driven by money, men tend to look at their account balances twice as often as women. When the market crashes, men are almost twice as likely to cash out their accounts. Men are also twice as likely to believe their investment choices perform better than average and are much less likely to work with an advisor.

A Berkeley study in the 1990s found that women outperformed men by nearly 1% per year but be warned, that gap is closing. Women have been steadily becoming more involved with investing through the years. They're investing earlier in their lives, doing more research, and becoming more active. This may be to their detriment. In 2017, Fidelity found that women's advantage over men had fallen to 0.4%, and a later 2022 study by Wells Fargo found that women only had a 0.22% edge. Perhaps as female investors improve their knowledge and increase their confidence, they're beginning to act more like men.

All the research shows that the best path to long-term investment returns is a steady approach with as little meddling by the investor as possible. This type of approach would favor investing in index funds over individual stocks. Investing in individual stocks inherently involves a more active role by the investor, such as monitoring the companies you're invested in as well as their industries and the market in general. Therefore, most investors should focus on building a portfolio of index funds.

Building a Stock Portfolio

Since we already know that an investment mix that focuses on stocks will give us the best return over the long run, building a portfolio becomes relatively simple. An investment portfolio should have a broad mix of stocks with investments in companies of different sizes, industries, and worldwide regions. Fortunately, using stock index funds to obtain this mix makes it easy. Here are four examples of the core investment types you should consider basing your portfolio around and a sample of an index that tracks each specific category:

Large Companies - The S&P 500 comprises the 500 most successful American companies. Companies are added or removed from the S&P 500 index based on a committee decision. The committee considers several factors such as market value, profitability, level of public ownership, and how much of the company is based in America. Presently, companies listed as part of the S&P 500 have a minimum market value of $14.5 billion.

Medium-Sized Companies- The S&P 400 works in a similar manner to the S&P 500, however, it includes companies with values between $5 billion and $14.5 billion.

Small Companies - The S&P 600 index focuses on 600 of the smallest publicly traded companies. Companies in the S&P 600 index, on average, have a market value of less than $2 billion. It's unlikely you've heard of any of the companies in the S&P 600 index.

Small Foreign Companies - The MSCI ACWI ex USA Small index, wow, that's a lot of letters. It stands for the Morgan Stanley Capital International All Country World Index. The "ex USA" version of this index excludes companies from the United States and focuses on small companies in countries worldwide.

Using indexes makes a stock investor's life easy. As successful companies grow, they are added to the index, allowing you to profit from their growth, but if they falter, they'll end up being automatically removed from the index. Over the course of years, indexes like the S&P 500 continuously add new companies and cull poor performers from the mix. While this system won't completely protect you from some companies that end up total losses, it ensures a consistent and automatic review of the companies you're invested in and automatically reduces your investment in those companies as their performance fades.

Although we've seen that the stock market typically has permanent gains with temporary downsides, large, medium, small, and foreign companies, while posting similar long-term returns, typically have peak performances at different points in a cycle. Therefore, spreading your investment over these four different categories can reduce the fluctuation of your investment balances compared to investing in a single index. Now, I know I've already said fluctuation is not necessarily a bad thing, and in fact, it is somewhat necessary if you want to earn higher returns on your investment, but if there is a way to reduce fluctuations within your portfolio without compromising overall return, I think that's something worth having.

Let's set expectations first. By no means am I suggesting that you won't see significant fluctuations by investing in these four types of indexes. It's entirely possible that in a major economic downturn, all four investment types will fall in synchrony. Historically, however, the different categories move up and down at slightly different points in a cycle. For example, when a recession is imminent, stocks in small companies typically fall first as investors move to "safer" large companies. Once the recession takes hold, the stocks of large companies begin to fall as well, but by then, there's a chance that small company stocks have already reached their bottom. The idea is that small stocks will potentially start to rebound while large stocks are still falling. During a poor economic cycle, small stocks may fall 20%, and large stocks may fall 20%, but since each segment tends to move at slightly different times in the cycle, your portfolio as a whole may not experience a full 20% decline. This difference may make it just a bit easier for you to stomach downturns and remain disciplined.

A stock portfolio spread evenly between these four categories will give you significant diversification between U.S. and foreign stocks, small and large companies, and a mix of different industries. Note that even though 75% of the portfolio would be allocated to S&P indexes that track U.S. stocks, the ongoing globalization of the economy means that most major "U.S." companies are, in fact, global companies with significant foreign operations. For this reason, we don't need to add indexes that track large foreign companies. It is useful, however, to add an investment allocation specifically to small foreign companies and companies operating in developing foreign countries that are not part of the S&P indexes to create a diverse global mix of investments. Every couple of years, review the investment mix to ensure that each category holds about 25% of your total investment and make adjustments if the percentages are out of balance (either too high or too low).

At first glance, you may think that merely investing equally in four indexes is too simple. This kind of thinking is a trap that many investors fall into. We're taught that investing should be confusing, risky, scary, complicated, etc. In general, we want there to be a secret hack to investing that most other people haven't figured out; hey, that's the same thought process that brought so many victims to Bernie Madoff's door.

Remember, nothing will have a greater impact on your investment accounts than the amount of time your investments have to grow. In her book, *The Art of Choosing*, Sheena Iyengar discusses a study of shoppers who were presented with a selection of jams to purchase. One display showcased 24 varieties of jam, while the other offered six. More shoppers were drawn to the display with 24 varieties, but far more shoppers bought from the merchant offering just six varieties. I call it analysis paralysis.

While we'd naturally assume that more choice is good, after all, if you couldn't find the perfect jam in a selection of 24, what hope do you have to ever find happiness? The reality is that humans are easily overwhelmed when presented with too many options, and instead of taking the time to make the right choice, we decide not to choose anything at all. This concept has been proven true by investors as well. In studies analyzing 401(k) plans, it was found that plans that offered more investment choices to participants consistently had fewer people willing to invest and had lower investment returns than plans that offered fewer choices. Eligible employees were overwhelmed with choices, and many of them, true to human nature, decided not to make any choice at all. A simple plan, while boring, is a key to long-term success. The fewer choices you have as an investor, the sooner you'll invest, and the longer your investments will have to grow. While Warren Buffet is considered one of the most proficient investors in history, the greatest contributor to his success was time. By starting his investing at only eleven years old and continuing into his 90s, his wealth grew to nearly $150 billion. But had Warren put off investing until age 30 and retired at age 60, even with his investment prowess, he would have struggled to grow his investments to $10 million, and we would have never heard of him.

INCLUDING YOUR PERSONAL TOUCH

For most people, traditional investments in stock index funds with appropriate savings set aside in a money market account is the only investment setup they'll ever need. Pilots have an old adage that flying is hours and hours of boredom punctuated by moments of sheer terror. Successful, long-term investing is similar as long as you remember that staying the course through those moments of terror is what separates you from unsuccessful investors. Still, I acknowledge that you may feel compelled to take a more active role in your investments and active investing can be a lot of fun. For those with such a compulsion, I'd like to offer a suggested plan to help you scratch that itch while protecting you from underperforming the stock market averages over long periods.

Instead of one portfolio of investment funds, you'll want to create a portfolio of portfolios, each containing a specific type of investment based on your interests. Maybe you'll have two underlying portfolios or a dozen; it will all depend on you and which investments draw your interest. You can have portfolios of peer-to-peer lending, precious metals, commodities, cryptocurrency, individual stocks, real estate, or any of the other types of investments we talked about earlier. Regardless of which portfolios you want to build, you'll want to keep the lion's share of your investments in an index fund portfolio.

Let's say, for example, you decide on three portfolios, an index fund portfolio, a cryptocurrency portfolio, and an individual stock portfolio. Realistically, 70-90% of your investments should be in index funds, even in this scenario. Beyond that, you'll want to allocate the remainder of your investments however you'd like across your other portfolios. So, to continue our example, say you have 70% of your investments in the index fund portfolio and you decide to spread the rest out evenly: 15% in cryptocurrencies and 15% in individual stocks. In each portfolio, make the best investment selections you are capable of.

The trick to making sure you minimize the risk of your investment portfolio doing worse than the market on average: you can only rebalance your investment portfolios on a one-way street. Here's what I mean: over time, you want your portfolio to stay relatively close to the initial setup of 70% index funds, 15% crypto, and 15% individual stocks except if index funds beat your other portfolios. If one of the categories performs better than another, its percentage will climb higher. Once every couple of years, if crypto or your individual stocks have grown to represent more than 15% of your portfolio, you'll want to transfer the additional percentage to your index fund portfolio to rebalance the mix back down to 15%. But, if crypto or individual stocks fall below 15%, do not transfer funds from your index fund portfolio back to crypto or stocks to bring those portfolios back up to 15%.

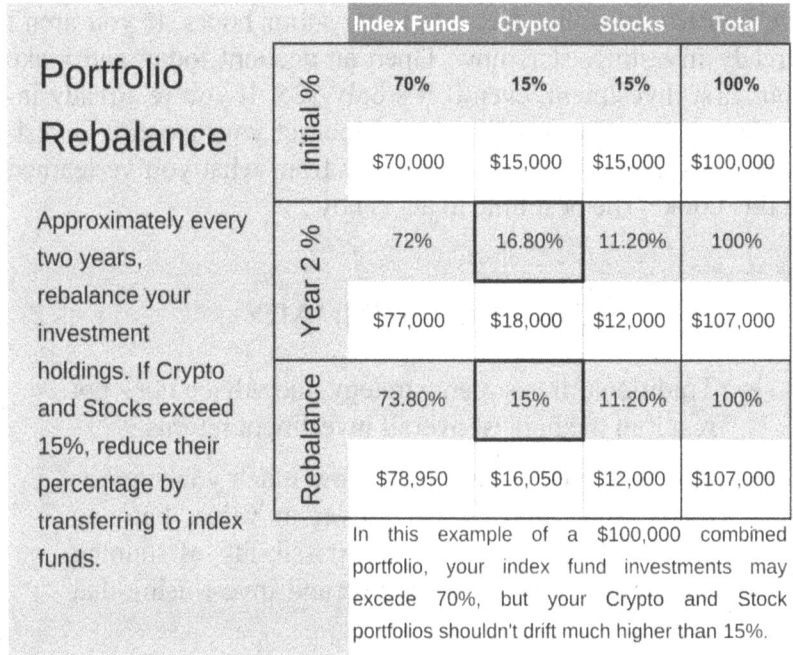

		Index Funds	Crypto	Stocks	Total
Portfolio Rebalance	Initial %	70%	15%	15%	100%
		$70,000	$15,000	$15,000	$100,000
Approximately every two years, rebalance your investment holdings. If Crypto and Stocks exceed 15%, reduce their percentage by transferring to index funds.	Year 2 %	72%	16.80%	11.20%	100%
		$77,000	$18,000	$12,000	$107,000
	Rebalance	73.80%	15%	11.20%	100%
		$78,950	$16,050	$12,000	$107,000

In this example of a $100,000 combined portfolio, your index fund investments may excede 70%, but your Crypto and Stock portfolios shouldn't drift much higher than 15%.

Figure 11.3

Here's why this concept works: if you are successful with your alternative portfolios and they perform better than index funds, the entire group of portfolios grows and maintains its percentage allocations. Now, as discussed, the odds that any individual will select investments that consistently outperform the market are stacked against you. So, if your alternate portfolios perform worse than the index funds, they'll wither and die. If the percentage allocated to the alternate portfolios consistently shrinks, it will allow the index fund portfolio to take over and relieve you from active investment duty. The only way your other portfolios can survive is if they truly perform better than index funds, and if they don't, they're not worth keeping.

You now have the knowledge to confidently invest but knowledge is of no value if you do not put it to use. I strongly encourage you to act within the next twenty-four hours. If you aren't already investing, start now. Open an account today and make your first investment, even if it's only $25. If you're already investing, log into your account and look at your existing investment selections. What can you apply from what you've learned in this book? The best time to act is now.

-CHAPTER SUMMARY-

- Traditional investment strategy and advice does not result in the highest overall investment returns.

- Risk is typically defined as how much your investment might move up or down in value, but you should re-define risk as the possibility of running out of money in your lifetime and invest using that mindset

- Over 100 years of history have shown that stocks have provided the best investment returns over long periods of time. If we want the best returns, and we know stocks have historically provided the best returns, we should be committed to stocks.

- It's difficult, almost impossible, to beat the stock market's average return over long periods of time.

CLOSING

"If you do not change direction, you may end up
where you are heading."
– Lau Tzu

Some years ago, an ambitious preacher came to town, eager to make an impact. He toured his new church on the edge of town, expecting a great crowd. The preacher spent a week preparing and rehearsing the greatest sermon he could conceive. Finally, the first night of service comes, and he walks inside the chapel and finds it empty. He thought, *Something must be wrong.* He waited until seven o'clock, but no one showed up. Waited until seven-fifteen, nothing. Finally, at seven-thirty, one lone cowboy rode up on his horse, tied up his horse outside, and came and sat down on the front bench closest to the preacher's platform. The preacher thought, *Well, I guess I better go down and talk to him.* The preacher says to the cowboy, "Look, I'm sorry about this cowboy, but we were supposed to have a big crowd here tonight, and you're the only one who's shown up. I'm really not sure what to do." The cowboy looks at the preacher and responds, "Well, I'm not a preacher, I'm just a simple cowboy and don't know much about these things, so I can't tell you what to do. But I do know this; if I went out to feed my cattle and only one showed up, I'd at least feed him."

The preacher was feeling inspired that the cowboy still wanted him to go on, so he jumped up on the platform and started on his sermon. He started preaching as if he had a full house and really got into it. Pretty soon, he had gone on for forty-five minutes, then an hour, and eventually, after an hour and thirty minutes, he wound it down. Then the preacher stepped back down feeling he'd just given one of the best sermons of his career and walked over to the cowboy and asked, "So what did you think of my sermon? How was it?" The cowboy thought a moment and said, "Well, I'm just a cowboy, not a preacher so I don't know much about these things, but if I went down to feed my cattle and only one showed up, I'd feed him, but I sure wouldn't dump the whole load of hay on him!"

I'm glad you made it this far, and I hope you're not feeling like I dumped the whole load on you. We've covered an extensive set of topics around investing with the specific goal of developing a solid investment philosophy.

At the beginning of the book, we assessed what has happened in the past that has caused so many people to fear investing. You learned how fraud and how Bernie Madoff's Ponzi scheme impacted the investing philosophy of not only his victims but effectively anyone who heard the story in the news. To address these fears, we talked about the specific types of fraud that are common today and how to identify them, as well as understanding some of the protections provided to investors by the government. While not everyone will choose to use a financial advisor, statistics show that most people can benefit from professional advice. That's why we discussed the different types of advisors, how they're paid, and how to pick one that may be right for you.

You also learned about many potential investment types, along with their pros and cons and how to make informed decisions when choosing an investment. I shared with you various bubbles and crashes throughout history and why you are best off not worrying about that next inevitable crash. Finally, we discussed specific strategies for investing, including various choices for the type of account to hold your investments in and why some of the most common investment advice will result in lower overall returns.

As I noted in the opening of this book, the broad selection of topics I covered was specifically chosen based on thousands of personal interactions with customers over the last decade. The questions and concerns voiced by the people I've met consistently fell into similar themes. I knew the people I talked to represented only a tiny fraction of the public who had the same fears and doubts regarding investing. I am excited knowing that you're now equipped to invest more confidently than ever. With that being said, I know you may have questions about topics we covered in this book or perhaps some topics that weren't covered. My website, www.christophermunchhof.com, offers articles on numerous topics including investing, paying off debt, and taxes. You're invited to submit questions directly to me through my website or I invite you to reach out to me through email at chris@christophermunchhof.com. I hope you agree that this book was worth far more than your original investment. If you found this book to be valuable, please leave a review online. I can't thank you enough for buying this book and sticking with me until the end. Thank you!

I want to leave you with one more story. By the 1950s, decades had already passed with men pursuing the goal of running a mile in less than four minutes. Many believed that the feat was impossible to achieve. It was in 1954 that Roger Bannister completed a mile in 3 minutes, 59.4 seconds, becoming the first human to break the barrier. While the goal had been pursued for many years, once it was accomplished by Bannister in 1954, people suddenly *knew* it was possible. It took only six weeks after Bannister broke through the barrier for his record to be broken by someone else. A year later, three men broke the barrier in a single race. Today, the sub-four-minute mile has been achieved thousands of times. This is a testament to the power of human belief above all else. Consider that the winning horses running the Kentucky Derby have all finished within a few seconds of the two-minute mark in every race for the past 100 years. The nutrition, training, and science around horse racing has advanced tremendously over the last century, but the time it takes a winning horse to complete the race has only improved by two to three seconds over all that time. The horse does not have the ability to understand records or that they can be broken. They have no reason to. This is what makes humans so unique. We can see what has been done before, learn from it, and change our beliefs about what is possible.

Part of investing is giving you the chance to accomplish something that you may have never seen as possible before. Investing gives you a path to freedom and a path to pursuing your dreams. The most important step in investing is starting. This book should only be a piece of your broader education. The greatest investment you can continue to make is in yourself, physically, emotionally and intellectually. What you believe is possible will determine how amazing your life can be. I wish you the best.

APPENDIX

Appendix

Questions to Ask Advisors

When working with financial professionals, it's important to give them a full interrogation. Besides the information you'll gain from the answers to these questions, you'll learn a great deal about the advisor's willingness to be transparent and address your concerns. These are questions the SEC recommends you ask an investment advisor or investment product salesperson.

Questions About Products

• Is this investment product registered with the SEC or my state securities agency?

• Does this investment match my investment goals? Why is this investment suitable for me?

• How will this investment make money (dividends? interest? capital gains?)? What could cause this investment to increase or decrease in value (for example, changes in interest rates, real estate values, or market share)?

• What are the total fees to purchase, maintain, and sell this investment? Are there ways that I can reduce or avoid some of the fees that I'll pay, such as purchasing the investment directly? After all the fees are paid, how much does this investment have to increase in value before I break even?

• How liquid is this investment? How easy would it be to sell if I needed my money right away?

• What are the specific risks associated with this investment? What is the maximum I could lose (for example, what will be the effect of changing interest rates, economic recession, high competition, or stock market ups and downs)?

• How long has the company been in business? Is its management experienced? Has management been successful in the past? Have they ever made money for investors before?

• Is the company making money? How are they doing compared to their competitors?

• Where can I get more information about this investment? Can I get the latest reports filed by the company with the SEC: a prospectus or offering circular, or the latest annual report and financial statements?

Questions For People Who Sell Investments

• Are you registered with our state securities regulator? Have you ever been disciplined by the SEC, a state regulator, or other organization (such as FINRA) or one of the stock exchanges?

• How long has your firm been in business? How many arbitration awards have been filed against your firm? Have you personally been involved in any arbitration cases? What happened?

• What training and experience do you have? How long have you been in the business? What other firms have you been registered with? What is the status of those firms today?

• What is your investment philosophy?

• Describe your typical client. Can you provide me with some names and telephone numbers of your long-term clients?

• How do you get paid? By commission? By the amount of assets you manage? By another method?

• Do I have any choices on how to pay you? Should I pay you by the transaction or a flat fee regardless of how many transactions I have?

• Do you make more if I buy this stock, bond, mutual fund, or ETF rather than another? If you weren't making extra money, would your recommendation be the same?

• Are you participating in a sales contest? Is this purchase really in my best interest?

• You've told me what it costs me to buy this stock, bond, mutual al
fund, or ETF; how much will I receive if I sell it today?

• Where do you send my order to be executed? Can we get a better price if we send it to another market?

• If your broker changes firms, ask: Did they pay you to change firms? Do you get anything for bringing me along?

Questions About the Progress of Your Investments
• How frequently do I get statements? Do I understand what the statements tell me?

• Is the return on my investment meeting my expectations and goals? Is this investment performing as I was led to believe?

• How much money will I get back if I sell my investment today?

• How much am I paying in commission or fees?

• Have my goals changed? If so, are my investments still suitable?

• What criteria will I use to decide when to sell?

How to Handle Problems

Act promptly! By law, you only have a limited time to take legal action. Follow these steps to solve your problem:

1. Talk to your investment professional and explain the problem. Where is the fault? Were communications clear? What did the investment professional tell you?

2. If your investment professional can't resolve your problem, then talk to the investment professional's supervisor (which, for brokers, is often the firm's branch manager).

3. If the problem is still not resolved, write to the compliance department at the firm's main office. Explain your problem clearly, and how you want it resolved. Ask the compliance office to respond to you within 30 days.

4. If you're still not satisfied, file a complaint online with the SEC or send your complaint by mail to:

> Securities and Exchange Commission
> Office of Investor Education and Advocacy
> 100 F Street, N.E.
> Washington, D.C. 20549-0213

Cryptocurrency Glossary

51% Attack: The term given to a malicious attack on a blockchain network achieved by taking control of 51% (over half) of the mining nodes.

Address: An address is an alphanumeric identifier providing a virtual location to where cryptocurrency transactions can be sent. They are intended to be single use and only refer to the destination of a transaction, not where it came from.

Airdrop: The free distribution of a specific cryptocurrency to a targeted group as a means of promoting its adoption or increasing its visibility.

Altcoin: Any cryptocurrency besides Bitcoin.

Astroturfing: The practice of hyping a product or service such as an ICO without disclosing personal interest. Commonly done by celebrities or social media influencers.

Bitcoin (BTC): The first and best-known cryptocurrency.

Buying the dip: Utilizing a recent downward movement of an asset as a buying opportunity under the assumption the price will eventually recover.

Blockchain: A distributed digital ledger of cryptographically-signed transactions that are grouped into blocks. Each block is cryptographically linked to the previous one (making it tamper evident) after validation and undergoing a consensus decision. As new blocks are added, older blocks become more difficult to modify (creating tamper resistance). New blocks are replicated across copies of the ledger within the network, and any conflicts are resolved automatically using established rules.

Coin: A term used to identify a specific cryptocurrency.

Cold wallet: A physical storage device such as a flash drive or hard drive used to store cryptocurrency offline.

Cryptography: The science of information hiding and verification. It includes the protocols, algorithms and methodologies to securely and consistently prevent unauthorized access to sensitive information and enable verifiability of the information. The main goals include confidentiality, integrity authentication and source authentication.

dApp: Short for decentralized application, a dApp is an app that isn't controlled by a central authority. Most social media platforms are examples of centralized apps, where users rely on them as a middleman to send and receive messages. A dApp utilizes a blockchain, so users can send and receive data directly without the middleman.

DeFi: Short for decentralized finance. Instead of individuals needing to rely on centralized entities like major banks, decentralized finance allows people to execute financial transactions directly with the person they want to transact with.

DAO: Stands for decentralized autonomous organization. It is a type of organizational structure that uses blockchain technology to manage an entity without a central authority. DAOs are also sometimes called decentralized autonomous corporations (DACs)

Distributed ledger: Traditionally, an institution like a bank holds and controls the records of all its customers' transactions. A distributed ledger uses a network of computers known as nodes to verify and store the transactions. No single node has controlling authority over the ledger.

Fiat currency: Any currency declared by a government to be legal tender. The U.S. dollar is a fiat currency.

FOMO: Fear of missing out. This term is typically used in relation to investors who eagerly invest into rallying assets after the assets have already experienced significant gains.

Fork: A cryptocurrency fork occurs when there is a divergence in the blockchain, leading to the creation of two separate paths. This happens when the community or developers of a cryptocurrency make changes to the blockchain's protocol or underlying software.

Gas: Ethereum network transactions require a fee for processing paid with Ethereum. This fee is referred to as gas. Gas is required to compensate validators and to help limit network attacks.

Hash: a digital fingerprint for data. It takes any input (like a file or a piece of text) and creates a fixed-length string of characters that looks random. Even if you change just one tiny bit of the input, the resulting hash will be completely different. This makes crypto hashes useful for verifying data integrity and security, ensuring that data hasn't been tampered with

Hot wallet: A means to store your cryptocurrencies online typically through a crypto exchange or other third party. Hot wallets can be accessed with passwords and can be a target for hackers. However, if a user loses their password, the hot wallet administrator may be able to help assist the owner in recovering access to their account.

ICO: Like an corporate IPO(initial public offering) an ICO (initial coin offering) describes the event when investors are given the opportunity to invest in a project for the first time.

Ledger: A record of transactions which may include parties involved, dates, times, and amounts.

Mining: Miners use powerful computers to solve complex mathematical problems, which confirms the transactions and secures the network. As a reward for their work, miners earn new cryptocurrency coins and transaction fees. This process ensures the integrity and consistency of the blockchain.

Meme coin: An altcoin based on social media hype or jokes. Meme coins are linked to extreme volatility with little or no fundamental explanation for their price movements.

Node: A computer linked to a blockchain network. Each node carries a copy of the blockchain and helps validate transactions on the network.

Metaverse: Online virtual worlds that stand alone or are interconnected. These virtual worlds provide users with an immersive experience by utilizing virtual or augmented reality technologies.

NFT: A digital certificate of ownership that represents a digital or physical asset. An NFT has a unique code that allows it to be identified as something that can be digitally owned. Think of NFTs as digital ownership of something like art work, sports memorabilia, photos, etc.

On-chain: A transaction that occurs on a blockchain, reflected on a distributed, public ledger.

On-ledger currency: A cryptocurrency that utilizes blockchain technology

P2P: Short for peer-to-peer. When related to the crypto environment P2P describes transactions directly between two parties without the need for a third-party intermediary.

Private key: A lengthy "password" that should be known only by the crypto owner. It is used to authorize transactions involving the owner's crypto assets.

Public key: This key is publicly available. You share your public key to receive cryptocurrency transactions. Your public and private keys work together to complete crypto transactions.

Proof of work: This is a system used by many blockchains to prove that miners have done computational work to solve the complex computational puzzles necessary to add a block to the blockchain.

Proof of stake: Similar to proof of work, this is a system which gives validators the opportunity to mine blocks for validation based on how much of the token the validator has staked. Proof of stake transactions validate faster than proof of work networks.

Satoshi: The smallest denomination of Bitcoin (BTC).

Smart contract: A set of rules defined in code automatically executed on a blockchain once specific conditions are met.

Seed (Seed Phrase): A random series of automatically generated words used to access your crypto wallet.

Staking: Depositing a specific amount of cryptocurrency with a provider or protocol under specific conditions and in return for specific rights or rewards.

Terahash: The rate at which a computer or network can guess one trillion hashes per second when mining for cryptocurrency.

Validator: Someone who pays for the chance to validate transactions and earn crypto in proof of stake protocols.

Wallet: A digital storage device or location for keeping crypto assets secure. Wallets can be online (see hot wallet) or offline (see cold wallet).

Whale: Investors with enough cryptocurrency to make large enough transactions to manipulate the market.

Whitepaper: A technical document released alongside new crypto projects that explains how the system works.

Investor Profile Questionnaire

The following questionnaire is a sample of an interview most professional investment advisors or investment institutions will give you to help determine the type of investment portfolio that would be a good match for you. The questionnaire assesses two primary areas, your time horizon and your risk tolerance.

For each topic, circle the number that best corresponds to your scenario.

Section 1: Time Horizon

1. I plan to start using funds from my investments in:

Less than 3 years	1
3-5 years	3
6-10 years	7
11 years or more	10

2. Once I begin using the funds from my investments, I expect to use up the entire investment in:

Less than 2 years	0
2-5 years	1
6-10 years	4
11 years or more	8

Your Total Time Horizon Score:_____

Section 2: Risk Assessment

3. When it comes to investing, I would describe my-self as:

Very inexperienced	0
Somewhat experienced	2
Experienced	4
Very experienced	6

4. When I am investing, I am:

Most concerned about losing money	0
Equally concerned about my investments losing or gaining value	4
Mostly concerned about my investments growing	8

5. Circle the investment type that you currently own or have owned in the past with the highest score:

Money market funds or savings accounts	0
Bonds or bond funds	3

Stocks or stock funds	6
International investments	8

6. Consider the following scenario:
Imagine in the past 90 days, the stock market has fallen 20% of its value. Additionally, a stock you own has lost 20% of its value during the same time. What would you do?

Sell all of my shares	0
Sell some shares	2
Take no action	5
Buy additional shares	8

7. In general, I prefer an investment with little to no ups and downs and am willing to accept lower returns from these types of investments:

Strongly disagree	8
Disagree	4
Agree	2
Strongly Agree	0

Your Total Risk Score:_____

Take the totals from each section of this questionnaire and locate their corresponding numbers on the next page.

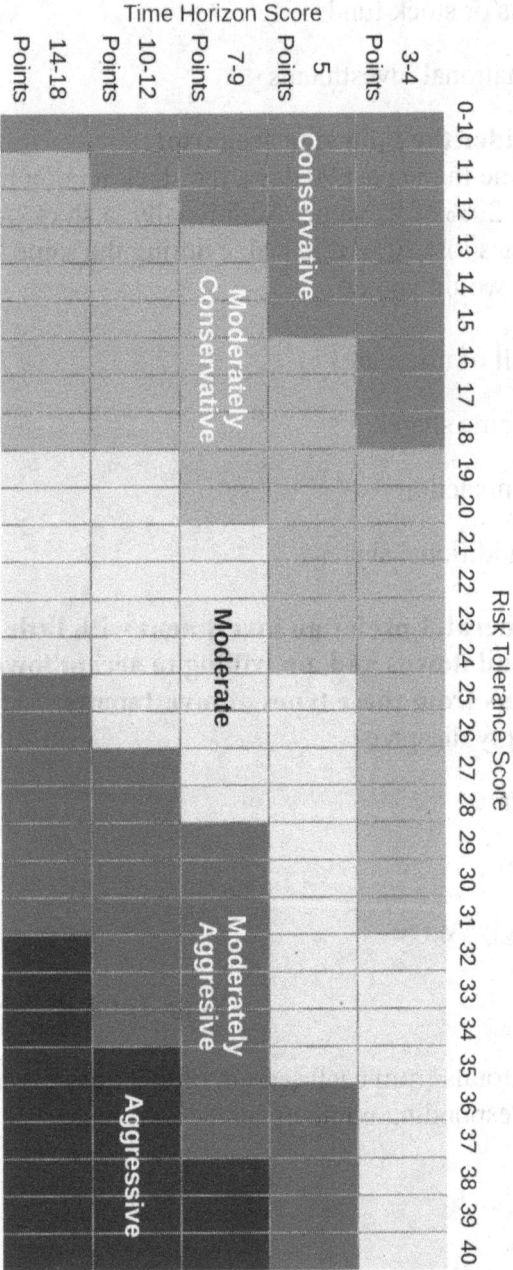

Time Horizon Score

Risk Tolerance Score

	0-10 11 12 13 14 15 16 17 18 19 20 21 22 23 24 25 26 27 28 29 30 31 32 33 34 35 36 37 38 39 40
3-4 Points	Conservative
5 Points	
7-9 Points	Moderately Conservative
10-12 Points	Moderate
14-18 Points	Moderately Aggressive — Aggressive

The point at which your Time Horizon and your Risk Tolerance scores cross each other will indicate what type of investor personality you have. Investment professionals will use your personality type to recommend a mix of investments. I'll provide examples of what those recommendations would look like next.

Based on your answers to the questionnaire, you've determined that you'd be a conservative, moderately conservative, moderate, moderately aggressive, or aggressive investor. Here are some examples of the type of investment allocation professional advisors would recommend based on your profile.

Conservative
- 15% Large Company Stocks
- 5% International Stocks
- 50% Bond Investments
- 30% Cash Investments (savings or money markets)

Moderately Conservative
- 25% Large Company Stocks
- 5% Small Company Stocks
- 10% International Stocks
- 50% Bond Investments
- 10% Cash Investments

Moderate
- 35% Large Company Stocks
- 10% Small Company Stocks
- 15% International Stocks
- 35% Bond Investments
- 5% Cash Investments

Moderately Aggressive
- 45% Large Company Stocks
- 15% Small Company Stocks
- 20% International Stocks
- 15% Bond Investments
- 5% Cash Investments

Aggressive
- 50% Large Company Stocks
- 20% Small Company Stocks
- 25% International Stocks
- 5% Cash Investments

If you finished reading this book before completing the investor profile questionnaire, you'd know that a 100% stock portfolio is the investment allocation that has historically generated the best returns. Yet, professional advisors and institutions would only offer that recommendation to investors who are considered "Aggressive." Where did you end up on the scale? Would typical advisors have recommended that you invest in bonds, reducing your long-term returns?

Acknowledgments

The way pieces and people can fall into your life and change its entire trajectory is truly amazing. I am fortunate to have many people in my life who have made this book possible.

First and foremost, all of the clients who have asked me the tough questions over the years. Those customers who weren't willing to just take my advice, but needed to know *why* they should follow my suggestions. These conversations not only taught me how to clarify my strategies, but inspired me to write this book.

Next, I'd like to thank the magnificent John and Mercy Murphy. Many years ago, at the precise moment I was preparing to give up on a career in financial planning because the path seemed too difficult, I met John who encouraged me to start working at his firm. Along with his wife Mercy, they showed me how to get licensed and how to get my first client. They constantly told me how much they believed in me and my future. Even if they were lying, it gave me the motivation to dramatically change the direction of my life. There is simply no chance I'd have written a book let alone multiple books without having met them.

References

In the process of compiling this book I utilized countless resources. The most substantial portions of this book were written using the information I've learned over the course of many years. However, I've added specific examples and stories to help illustrate the lessons. Here, I've compiled references related to those topics which I used while writing this book.

Chapter 1
Giannetti and Wang (2016) find that federal securities enforcement actions against fraudulent firms lead to reduced stock market participation of households in the fraudulent firm's state

Umit G Gurun, Noah Stoffman, Scott E Yonker (2017) Trust in financial markets was biggest victim of Madoff case

Henriques, Diana. (2011) *The Wizard of Lies: Bernie Madoff and the Death of Trust* , St. Martin's Griffin

Chapter 2
https://nypost.com/2018/04/28/he-promised-people-paradise-and-sent-them-to-their-deaths/

Sinclair, David (2004) [2003]. *The Land That Never Was: Sir Gregor MacGregor and the Most Audacious Fraud in History*. Boston, Massachusetts: Da Capo Press

Strangeways, Thomas (1822). *Sketch of the Mosquito Shore, Including the Territory of Poyais, etc.* Edinburgh: William Blackwood

Couple Charged for Operating Multimillion-Dollar Pyramid Scheme
https://www.justice.gov/opa/pr/couple-charged-operating-multimillion-dollar-pyramid-scheme

https://coinweek.com/bullion-direct-another-bullion-biz-bankrupt-vault-virtually-empty/

SEC Charges Atlanta Investment Adviser with Fraudulent Securities Offering and Misappropriating Investor Funds and Obtains Temporary Restraining Order
https://www.sec.gov/litigation/litreleases/lr-24963

Georgia investment adviser on the run for years ordered to pay $12M
https://www.fox5atlanta.com/news/gwinnett-county-chris-burns-wanted-lawsuit-payment

Friedman, Milton (2002), *Capitalism and Freedom: Fortieth Anniversary Edition (40th Anniversary Edition)* University of Chicago Press
bomb

Chapter 3

The Neuroscience of Everybody's Favorite Topic | Scientific American
https://www.scientificamerican.com/article/the-neuroscience-of-everybody-favorite-topic-themselves/

Carnegie, Dale (2001) *Dale Carnegie's Lifetime Plan for Success: How to Win Friends & Influence People : How to Stop Worrying & Start Living*

Hopkins, Tom (2005) *How to Master the Art of Selling,* Business Plus; Rev Upd edition

Chapter 4

http://www.finra.org/investors/professional-designations

https://www.investor.gov/

Chapter 5

Must Reads: The crowd-sourced, social media swarm that is betting Tesla will crash and burn
https://www.latimes.com/business/autos/la-fi-hy-tesla-short-sellers-musk-20190408-story.html

https://www.npr.org/2016/10/10/497087643/the-analyst-who-gambled-and-took-on-trump)(https://www.nytimes.com/1991/07/18/business/chapter-11-for-taj-mahal.html)

Pumping and Dumping
https://content.time.com/time/specials/packages/article/0,28804,1907771_190 7778_1907820,00.html

Chapter 6
Keller, Gary (2005), *The Millionaire Real Estate Investor*, McGraw Hill

https://reventureconsulting.com/how-hgtv-and-alan-greenspan-created-a-perpetual-housing-bubble/

https://www.housingwire.com/articles/investors-are-buying-up-single-family-homes-across-the-us/

https://scvhistory.com/scvhistory/lw2045.htm

https://scvhistory.com/scvhistory/lw2575a.htm

https://scvhistory.com/scvhistory/signal/coins/worden-coinage1005.htm

First Discovery of Gold in California
https://cdnc.ucr.edu/?a=d&d=SFC18950908.2.137&e=-------en--20--1--txt-txIN--------1

https://scvhistory.com/scvhistory/sw3001.htm

https://www.history.com/topics/westward-expansion/gold-rush-of-1849

Price of Bread
https://www.johndclare.net/Weimar_hyperinflation.htm

Paper money used as kindling or toys
https://alphahistory.com/weimarrepublic/1923-hyperinflation/

Venezuela Inflation
https://www.cnbc.com/2019/08/02/venezuela-inflation-at-10-million-percent-its-time-for-shock-therapy.html

Chapter 7

John McAffee Genitals
https://www.the-sun.com/news/3150322/john-mcafee-pledged-eat-manhood/

Bitcoin Processing Times
https://www.blockchain-council.org/cryptocurrency/top-cryptocurrencies-
with-their-high-transaction-
speeds/#:~:text=If%20we%20talk%20about%20the,of%207%20transactions
%20per%20second.

Visa Processing Times
https://dk.review.visa.com/dam/VCOM/global/about-visa/documents/visa-
fact-sheet-july-2019.pdf

Worthless ICO
https://irishtechnews.ie/10biggestcryptoscams/

P2P Default Rate
https://www.p2pfinancenews.co.uk/2020/07/28/what-can-banks-learn-from-
p2ps-about-default-
manage-
ment/#:~:text=Unlike%20big%20banks%2C%20P2P%20lending,at%20aroun
d%20two%20per%20cent.

Bombas Growth
https://insidergrowth.com/bombas-net-worth/

Robinhood

Pyle, Howard (1883) *The Merry Adventures of Robin Hood of Great Renown
in Nottinghamshire*

Robinhood Fine/Trading More Expensive
https://www.sec.gov/news/press-release/2020-321

Alex Kearn Suicide
https://www.cnbc.com/2020/06/18/young-trader-dies-by-suicide-after-
thinking-he-racked-up-big-losses-on-robinhood.html

Alex Kearn Lawsuit
https://www.acrodocz.com/wp-content/uploads/2021/02/WRONGFUL-
DEATH-COMPLAINT-AGAINST-ROBINHOOD.pdf

Alex Kearn Suicide Note
https://twitter.com/BillBrewsterTBB/status/1273292130769932288

Beanie Babies
http://www.fundinguniverse.com/company-histories/ty-inc-history/

http://www.aboutbeanies.com/original9.shtml

https://nypost.com/2015/02/22/how-the-beanie-baby-craze-was-concocted-then-crashed/

Chapter 8
Tulipmania
https://www.uv.mx/personal/clelanda/files/2013/02/Garber-2000-Famous-first-bubbles.pdf

Tulip mania: The flowers that cost more than houses (bbc.com)
https://www.bbc.com/culture/article/20160419-tulip-mania-the-flowers-that-cost-more-than-houses

Crisis Chronicles: Tulip Mania, 1633-37 – Liberty Street Economics (newyorkfed.org)
https://libertystreeteconomics.newyorkfed.org/2013/09/crisis-chronicles-tulip-mania-1633-37/

South Sea Bubble
https://thetchblog.com/2020/07/13/the-south-sea-bubble-in-writing/

https://libertystreeteconomics.newyorkfed.org/2013/11/crisis-chronicles-the-south-sea-bubble-of-1720repackaging-debt-and-the-current-reach-for-yield/

https://blog.nationalarchives.gov.uk/the-south-sea-bubble-of-1720/

https://history.barnard.edu/sites/default/files/inline-files/GiaCuratola_LadyoftheSouthSea_2007.pdf

Mississippi Bubble
https://mshistorynow.mdah.ms.gov/issue/john-law-and-the-mississippi-bubble-1718-1720

https://www.stewartinvestors.com/content/dam/stewartinvestors/pdf/global/StAPLFTPMississippi0920FINAL.pdf

John Law - The First Financial Engineer - A History of Paper Money and The Mississippi Bubble
https://www.youtube.com/watch?v=H5uKPUPQSyQ&t=2s

Railway Mania
https://mpra.ub.uni-muenchen.de/21820/1/MPRA_paper_21820.pdf

https://www.focus-economics.com/blog/railway-mania-the-largest-speculative-bubble-you-never-heard-of

https://www.bancamarch.es/recursos/doc/bancamarch/20160107/2016/inform e-mensual-septiembre-2016-historia-en.pdf

The Great Depression
https://www.nber.org/digest/jan05/economics-world-war-I

1929 Stock Market Crash and the Great Depression - Documentary
https://www.youtube.com/watch?v=qlSxPouPCIM

https://www.nber.org/digest-202011/wwi-liberty-bonds-and-culture-investing

https://www.federalreservehistory.org/essays/liberty-bonds

https://www.federalreservehistory.org/essays/stock-market-crash-of-1929

https://www-tc.pbs.org/wgbh/americanexperience/media/pdf/transcript/Crash_of_1929_tra nscript.pdf

1987 Crash
https://www.latimes.com/archives/la-xpm-1987-10-20-fi-14582-story.html

Japan
https://www.investorschronicle.co.uk/education/2021/07/27/how-the-sun-set-on-japan-s-asset-bubble/

Price of land
https://hbr.org/1990/05/power-from-the-ground-up-japans-land-bubble

How 1980s Japan Became History's Wildest Party
https://www.youtube.com/watch?v=E3rtq7EdXwI

https://www.investing.com/analysis/this-is-what-a-bubble-looks-like:-japan-1989-edition-200197309

Dot Com
https://www.theatlantic.com/technology/archive/2017/04/a-search-for-the-zombie-websites-of-1995/523848/

https://www.hpe.com/us/en/insights/articles/how-search-worked-before-google-1703.html

Dot Com Bubble Wall Street Documentary
https://www.youtube.com/watch?v=V5iE-4JsUms&t=3211s

https://ideas.ted.com/an-eye-opening-look-at-the-dot-com-bubble-of-2000-and-how-it-shapes-our-lives-today/

Cracking the enigma of asset bubbles with narratives
https://journals.sagepub.com/doi/10.1177/1476127016629880

https://internationalbanker.com/history-of-financial-crises/the-dotcom-bubble-burst-2000/

https://www.nasdaq.com/articles/is-the-tech-bubble-about-to-burst-again-2020-09-04bhoo

Housing Crash
Bush contribution to 2008 housing bubble
https://www.nytimes.com/2008/12/21/business/worldbusiness/21iht-admin.4.18853088.html

Flippers Cause Crash
https://finance.yahoo.com/news/house-flippers-triggered-us-housing-175705459.html

Home ownership boom and bust
https://surface.syr.edu/cgi/viewcontent.cgi?article=1106&context=ecn

Homeownership
https://ipropertymanagement.com/research/homeownership-rate-by-year

High credit score defaults.

https://mitsloan.mit.edu/ideas-made-to-matter/rethinking-how-housing-crisis-happened

How it Happend- The 2008 financial crisis
https://www.youtube.com/watch?v=GPOv72Awo68

Warren Buffet on the 2008 Crisis
https://www.youtube.com/watch?v=MQcPC31KRqA

New Housing Market
Pandemic Housing Surge
https://www.dallasfed.org/research/economics/2021/1228.aspx#:~:text=Instead%2C%20the%20combination%20of%20lower,evictions%20pushed%20up%20house%20prices.

Housing Affordability
https://www.wsj.com/articles/housing-affordability-index-drops-to-lowest-level-since-2006-11657288800

Chapter 9
Ehrlich, Paul R. (1968) *The Population Bomb*, Ballantine Books

https://today.yougov.com/society/articles/28484-apocalypse-climate-change-pandemic-coronavirus

https://cdn.ramseysolutions.net/media/company/pr/everyday-millionaires-research/national-study-of-millionaire-new.pdf

Stanley, Thomas; Danko, William D (1996) *The Millionaire Next Door: The Surprising Secrets of America's Wealthy*, Longstreet Press

Chapter 10
Lewis, Michael (2015) *Flash Boys: A Wall Street Revolt,* W. Norton & Company

Traders lost money
https://markets.businessinsider.com/news/stocks/if-you-re-day-trading-you-will-probably-lose-money-here-s-why-1030667770

Chapter 11
Iyengar, Sheena (2011) *The Art of Choosing,* Twelve

Whitney, Meredith (2023) *Mastering the Markets*, MasterClass

https://www.cnet.com/culture/3com-spins-off-palm-computing/

Women Investing
https://www.fool.com/research/women-in-investing-research/

FidelityInvestmentsWomen&InvestingStudy2021.pdf
https://www.fidelity.com/bin-
public/060_www_fidelity_com/documents/about-
fidelity/FidelityInvestmentsWomen&InvestingStudy2021.pdf

95-year returns
https://awealthofcommonsense.com/2023/01/stock-bond-cash-returns-over-
the-past-95-years/

Men Seen as Providers
https://www.pewresearch.org/short-reads/2017/09/20/americans-see-men-as-
the-financial-providers-even-as-womens-contributions-grow/

Index

www.ingramcontent.com/pod-product-compliance
Lightning Source LLC
Chambersburg PA
CBHW011158220326
41597CB00026BA/4665